D1520955

Hanging Together

Difference and disagreement can be valuable, yet they can also spiral out of control and damage liberal democracy. Advancing a metaphor of citizenship that the author terms "role-based constitutional fellowship," this book offers a solution to this challenge. Cheng argues that a series of "divisions of labour" among citizens, differently situated, can help cultivate the foundational trust required to harness the benefits of disagreement and difference while preventing them from "overheating" and, in turn, from leaving liberal democracy vulnerable to the growing influence of autocratic political forces. The book recognizes, however, that it is not always appropriate to attempt to cultivate trust, and acknowledges the important role that some forms of confrontation might play in identifying and rectifying undue social hierarchies, such as racial-ethnic hierarchies. *Hanging Together* thereby works to pave a middle way between deliberative and realist conceptions of democracy.

ERIC W. CHENG is Assistant Professor of Political Theory at the School of Political Science and Economics, Waseda University.

Hanging Together

Role-Based Constitutional Fellowship and the Challenge of Difference and Disagreement

ERIC W. CHENG
Waseda University

CAMBRIDGE
UNIVERSITY PRESS

CAMBRIDGE
UNIVERSITY PRESS

University Printing House, Cambridge CB2 8BS, United Kingdom

One Liberty Plaza, 20th Floor, New York, NY 10006, USA

477 Williamstown Road, Port Melbourne, VIC 3207, Australia

314–321, 3rd Floor, Plot 3, Splendor Forum, Jasola District Centre, New Delhi – 110025, India

103 Penang Road, #05–06/07, Visioncrest Commercial, Singapore 238467

Cambridge University Press is part of the University of Cambridge.

It furthers the University's mission by disseminating knowledge in the pursuit of education, learning, and research at the highest international levels of excellence.

www.cambridge.org
Information on this title: www.cambridge.org/9781009179287
DOI: 10.1017/9781009179294

First published 2022

A catalogue record for this publication is available from the British Library.

ISBN 978-1-009-17928-7 Hardback

Contents

Acknowledgments

This book is the product of several years' worth of conversations. I am grateful to everyone who helped me develop the ideas and arguments presented in this book, as well as to everyone who has supported me more broadly.

This book grew out of the doctoral dissertation I wrote at Duke University. Duke was an ideal place for me to begin developing this project, and I believe that the diversity of perspectives I consider in this book reflects the diversity of approaches to political theory (and its adjacent fields) that exists at Duke. I would like to thank my dissertation committee members: Michael Gillespie, Ruth Grant, Ian MacMullen, and my chair, Thomas Spragens Jr. Each of them offered valuable feedback, particularly when I was working to lay the foundations of the project, and it was during one of Ruth's classes that I began to develop an interest in political friendship. I would especially like to thank Ian and Tom for reading so many versions of my chapters, and Michael for suggesting the title of this book, *Hanging Together*.

I would also like to thank other faculty members, fellow graduate students, and staff members at Duke: Fonda Anthony, Jed Atkins, Samuel Bagg, Kyle Beardsley, Nolan Bennett, Scott Bennett, Pablo Beramendi, Gent Carrabregu, Colin Devine, Nora Hanigan, Mike Hawley, Kathy Ivanov, Chris Kennedy, Shaun King, Alexander Kirshner, Jack Knight, Antong Liu, Abdeslam Maghraoui, Elliot Mamet, Charles Nathan, Wayne Norman, Alexandra Oprea, Geneviève Rousselière, Richard Salsman, Brian Spisiak, Isak Tranvik, and Somia Youssef, as well as the Department of Political Science, the Graduate School, the Kenan Institute for Ethics for generously awarding me a Graduate Fellowship, and the Political Theory Workshop. I would especially like to thank Antong and Isak, my cohort-mates, for spending five years "in the trenches" with me, and Alex O. for being a trusted reader of all things rough. I would also like to thank Emily Davis and Lawrence Schätzle, my former students and now friends, as well as Susan Dunn, Ted Federle, David Heid, Wayne Lail, and

Daniel Seyfried in the music department and all my friends in the "OpShop" community (now the "D.O.T." community).

I revised my dissertation into a professional monograph at the University of Toronto, where I was a Faculty of Arts and Science / Max Planck Institute for Religious and Ethnic Diversity Postdoctoral Fellow. The University of Toronto was a wonderful place for me to develop my independent voice – indeed, the core concept of "role-based constitutional fellowship." I would like to thank two members of the University of Toronto community in particular. First, I would like to thank Andrew Sabl, my faculty advisor. Andy carefully read through the entire manuscript and generously provided me with sound professional advice on a regular basis, including guidance on the book-review process. Second, I would like to thank Ayelet Schachar, the organizer of my fellowship. Although the coronavirus pandemic regrettably frustrated our plans to have me spend a summer at the Max Planck Institute in Göttingen, I deeply appreciate her faith and interest in my research. I would not have been able to complete my manuscript in nearly as timely a fashion as I did had Ayelet not provided me with this opportunity.

In addition, I would like to thank other faculty members, fellow postdocs, and graduate students at the University of Toronto and in Ontario more broadly: Ronald Beiner, Zachariah Black, Leah Bradshaw, Joseph Carens, Rachael Desborough, Daniel Ferris, John Grant, Rob Goodman, James Ingram, Rebecca Kingston, Margaret Kohn, Chi Kwok, Patti Lenard, Mary Johanna Macdonald, Stefan Macleod, Emily Nacol, Steve Newman, Clifford Orwin, Schulyer Playford, Torrey Shanks, Igor Shoikhedbrod, Caitlin Tom, Zhichao Tong, Matthew Walton, Melissa Williams, and Erfan Xia, and other participants of the Political Theory Research Workshop. I would also like to thank my University of Toronto students, with whom I had the pleasure of sharing and exploring many of the themes discussed in this book.

During my time at the University of Toronto, I was fortunate to hold a day-long book manuscript workshop. This conference provided a critical boost to the quality of my book. Due to the coronavirus pandemic, this workshop was held online. While I am generally skeptical about the merits of online conversations relative to face-to-face conversations, I am glad to say that the workshop discussions were stimulating. The online format also allowed me to be more ambitious from a geographical standpoint in terms of whom I asked to serve as discussants. I would like to thank Benjamin Bardou, Joe Carens, Robin Celikates, Çigdem Çidam, Joseph Reisert, and Jennifer Rubenstein for discussing my manuscript. All of them read significant portions of the manuscript – sometimes, all of it – and provided me with invaluable, detailed feedback. I would also like to thank Matt Walton for initially suggesting to me the idea of a manuscript workshop.

I presented portions of this book at the annual conferences of the American Political Science Association, the Association of Political Theory, the Midwest Political Science Association, the Northeast Political Science Association, and the Western Political Science Association. I also presented a chapter at the Georgia State University Political Science Research Conference. I am grateful to all the scholars whom I encountered in these venues – discussants, chairs, fellow panelists, and interested audience members. They include Stephanie Ahrens, Lisa Beard, Yuna Blajer de la Garza, Quinlan Bowman, Billy Christmas, Nick Cowen, Paige Digeser, Kevin Elliott, Mario Feit, Jill Frank, Taylor Green, Vicki Hsueh, Jeremy Keats, Jimmy Lim, Paul Ludwig, Stephen Macedo, Jin Gon Park, Armando Perez-Gea, Briana McGinnis, Benjamin Nienass, Wendy Sarvasy, Naomi Scheinerman, Molly Scudder, Anthony Spanakos, Nadia Urbinati, Greg Wolcott, and Baldwin Wong. The Duke Department of Political Science and the Institute for Humane Studies reimbursed me for some of the expenses associated with travelling to these conferences; I am grateful for their support.

At the time of writing, I began an appointment at the School of Political Science and Economics, Waseda University. I would like to thank the university for this opportunity, especially Hun Chung, Kazutaka Inamura, Takeshi Kawanabe, Takahiro Koga, Yuji Matsuzawa, Junichi Saito, Atsushi Tago, Naoyuki Umemori, and Masashi Yazawa. I had the pleasure of sharing the central claims of this book with faculty and students during a book talk.

I would like to thank my editor at Cambridge University Press, Robert Dreesen, for his enthusiastic interest and support since I initially submitted the book manuscript for consideration. I would also like to thank my two anonymous reviewers for their exceptional comments. Responding to their suggestions helped improve my argument significantly and complete the transformation of the dissertation into a professional monograph. In addition, Chapter 3 is partly based on my article, "Aristotelean Realism: Political Friendship and the Problem of Stability," which was previously published in the *Review of Politics* 81(4) (2019). The material that appears there is reprinted with permission here.

While I formally developed this book as a doctoral student and a postdoctoral fellow, I have been thinking about many of the issues that I explore here since my time as an undergraduate at Georgetown University. I would like to thank my mentors, instructors, and interlocutors at Georgetown, especially Frederick Binkholder, William Blattner (whose "Text Seminar" taught me to "live with the texts" and disciplined my writing), Matthew Caulfield, Anthony DelDonna, Gerald Mara, David Miller at the Center for Clinical Bioethics, Nancy Sherman, Karen Stohr, and Linda Wetzel. (I will return to Anthony and Gerry later.) I would also like to thank my instructors, classmates, and friends at University College London, where I earned a master's degree in Legal and Political Theory. In particular, I would like to thank Anna Clart, Bruce Easop, John Filling, Victoria Lukyanova, Emily McTernan, and Marat Sultanov.

Moving beyond the academy, I would like to thank those who played important roles in my development as a human being and who have supported me in a more personal capacity. I appreciate the love and support that I received during my ten years at Crescent School in Toronto. I would like to thank my teachers, especially my favourites: Sandra Boyes, Sonya Gosse, Aggie Maksimowska, Doug Smith, and Fabienne Trippini. I would also like to thank Carol Johnson and Heather Perry, my writing mentors outside of Crescent.

I would like to thank Anthony DelDonna and Gerald Mara once again. A scholar of Neapolitan music, Anthony has supported me steadfastly ever since I first walked into his classroom for "Opera History" during my freshman year. It has been a pleasure to develop a close friendship with him and his family, Tina and Alessandra. Likewise, Gerry has been a close mentor and interlocutor ever since I first cold-emailed him to ask if he might be able to supervise my Senior Honours Thesis in Philosophy – my first foray into the debate between deliberative democracy and democratic agonism. (Indeed, this book can be understood to be a more mature intervention into that debate.) It is my honour to have been Gerry's last undergraduate student prior to his retirement as dean of the graduate school.

I would like to express my deep gratitude to Dr. James Brierley, Dr. Hamid Mojab, Dr. Lorne Rotstein, Dr. Richard Tsang, and their teams. They provided me with excellent care and shepherded me through some considerable health challenges.

Last but not least, I would like to thank my closest friends and my family. I would like to thank Anna Jolly (my big sister) and Devi Sahny (my sister). I met both of them during my senior year at Georgetown. Needless to say, in the absence of such serendipity, my life would be much impoverished. Among family friends, I would like to thank Angela Chou, Andrea Chun, Cynthia Ho, Jean Lau, and my godmother, Mayble Zay. Among my extended family, I would like to especially thank my grandparents; my aunt, Judy Cheng ("Sai Goo Ma"); my grandaunt, Susan Loh ("Look Goo Po"); my uncle, Gregory Chan ("Cao Fu"); my first-cousin-once-removed, Gunther Loh; and the Sieks: my cousins, Audrey and Victor, and my aunt and uncle, Eunice ("Ee Ma") and Tijep ("Ee Jeung"). Finally, I would like to thank my brother, Nicholas, and my parents, Veronica and Tony. Their love is something that I probably do not acknowledge enough, but something that I never doubt. I won the lottery of birth.

I

Introduction

Difference, Disagreement, and Civic Aggression

This book investigates how citizens who have differences and disagreements ought to relate to one another in a liberal democracy. Specifically, this book advances a metaphor of citizenship that I call "role-based constitutional fellowship." Role-based constitutional fellowship, I argue, is a desirable way for citizens to relate to one another in conditions of modern pluralism, where multiple races, ethnicities, religions, and economic statuses exist ("difference") and where citizens adhere to and pursue competing political interests, creeds, and objectives ("disagreement"). Under role-based constitutional fellowship, citizens share a sense that they are united in a common aim and that they are largely committed to doing what is necessary to pursue that aim – that they are *fellows*. I describe this sense of fellowship as *constitutional* and *role-based*. It is constitutional because that common aim consists of the preservation (and improvement) of liberal democracy, a certain constitutional regime. And it is role-based because citizens do not observe the same set of practices of citizenship, but rather behave in different ways, (1) according to which spheres of activity they find themselves in and (2) according to what normative roles they each occupy within those spheres. My central claim is that the more citizens share in role-based constitutional fellowship, the more a liberal democracy can harness the benefits of difference and disagreement and avoid unduly squashing difference and disagreement, yet also sidestep the potential perils of difference and disagreement.

Now, I understand liberal democracy to be the political regime type that takes the rule of law, individual liberties, the freedom of the press, the independence of the judiciary, the freedom and fairness of elections, and the legitimacy of political disagreement ("the ideal of political pluralism") seriously.[1] A liberal democracy is not necessarily a polity where no wrongs or evils exist. For example, relations of dominance might persist, with some social groups and demographics enjoying privileges that are denied to others. Indeed, those dominant groups might even enjoy those privileges at the expense of others, and the basic structure and institutions of society and of liberal democracy itself might help perpetuate those imbalances. Likewise, a liberal democracy might not be "fully legitimate" simply by virtue of having secured those core definitional essentials. For example, "deliberative democrats" insist that liberal democracy can only be fully legitimate if citizens work through their disagreements in manners that satisfy additional normative standards of rational deliberation, and do not merely compete with one another.[2] Meanwhile, left-leaning thinkers maintain that a liberal democracy can only be considered just if relations of dominance are redressed,[3] or if the state secures certain substantive distributive outcomes[4] – say, through social democracy.

Still, we can say this: a polity is liberal democratic when it has largely secured those core definitional essentials and can claim to have a meaningful degree of legitimacy as a result – when it does largely protect the individual from undue interference and empowers him or her with a say in collective decision-making processes. A polity is liberal democratic when plausible arguments can be made on its behalf – that it secures important normative goods and is thus not irredeemable, even if some injustices do persist, and even if it does not yet meet more expansive procedural and substantive standards of legitimacy.[5]

This book explores the rather equivocal attitude contemporary liberal democracy maintains toward difference and disagreement. Specifically, I consider how liberal democracy can harness the benefits of difference and disagreement and avoid unduly squashing difference and disagreement, yet also sidestep the potential perils of difference and disagreement.

---

[1] This definition tracks mainstream definitions of liberal democracy. E.g., Yascha Mounk, *The People vs. Democracy: Why Your Freedom Is in Danger & How to Save It* (Cambridge, MA: Harvard University Press, 2018); Steven Levitsky and Daniel Ziblatt, *How Democracies Die* (New York: Crown Publishing, 2018).

[2] Amy Gutmann and Dennis Thompson, *Why Deliberative Democracy* (Princeton: Princeton University Press, 2004). As we shall see, democratic realists disagree with this expansive notion of liberal democratic legitimacy, insisting that a liberal democracy is legitimate insofar as it can realize the ideal of political pluralism or prevent great evils like cruelty.

[3] Iris Marion Young, *Justice and the Politics of Difference* (Princeton: Princeton University Press, 2011).

[4] John Rawls, *A Theory of Justice: Revised Edition* (Cambridge, MA: Harvard University Press, 1999).

[5] As we shall see, however, I deem it vital to find ways to redress persistent injustices within the liberal democratic framework. Not only is it important to redress injustices for the sake of redressing injustices; it is important to do so for the sake of preserving liberal democracy.

THE BENEFITS OF DIFFERENCE AND DISAGREEMENT

Why is difference and disagreement valuable for liberal democracy? Why is it important to try to harness the benefits of difference and disagreement? Here are just three preliminary reasons.

First, beyond embodying the ideal of political pluralism, disagreement – political competition – can help hold powerful political actors to account. They cannot take their positions for granted, and they cannot abuse power wantonly, when others threaten to replace them. Indeed, competition can inspire competitors to great legislative heights. William Gladstone and Benjamin Disraeli detested each other, yet their rivalry produced a tremendous joint record – the expansion of the franchise, the decriminalization of trade unions and peaceful picketing, major improvements to public sanitation, the introduction of the secret ballot, and the establishment of universal education for children aged 5–12.

Likewise, competitive elections can inspire political participation. According to some theorists, it is vital that elections perform this function, for only so can citizens feel like they are not being excluded by formal political actors. When electoral competition feels like *kabuki*, citizens might gravitate toward more extreme political movements and parties in order to express their frustrated demands and passions, even if those movements and parties threaten or disavow liberal democracy. Indeed, these theorists attribute the rise of xenophobic, far right political forces in advanced liberal democracies today to the inability of electoral systems during the "neoliberal" era to present meaningful choices to the general electorate. The differences between the center-left and -right were akin to the differences between Coca Cola and Pepsi.[6]

Second, even though a liberal democracy does not necessarily have to be characterized by racial, ethnic, religious, and cultural difference – *diversity* – in order to be a liberal democracy, there is good reason to believe that an *openness* to encounters of difference is valuable for liberal democracy. This is because the more hostile citizens are to difference, the more they will either employ autocratic tools and strategies to enforce homogeneity or tolerate the inferior treatment of "outsiders" and "others." For example, in the United States, widespread white supremacist attitudes led the state to sanction the slavery of African Americans and practice segregation, and fear of Asians prompted the establishment of Japanese internment camps during World War II. In several European countries, Islamophobia has resulted in laws that place unique burdens on Muslims.[7] Likewise, given the historic influence of the Catholic Church, Ireland has long struggled to achieve gender equality and to

---

[6] Iñigo Errejón and Chantal Mouffe, *Podemos: In the Name of the People* (London: Lawrence & Wishart, 2016), 98–99.

[7] Engy Abdelkader, "A Comparative Analysis of European Islamophobia: France, UK, Germany, Netherlands, and Sweden," *Journal of Islamic and Near Eastern Law* 16(1) (2017): 29–63.

accommodate the rights of sexual minorities.[8] Japan too has never been as homogeneous as many Japanese believe it to be. Around one million residents today are Korean descendants who were brought to Japan as forced labourers in the early twentieth century. These ethnic Koreans are denied Japanese citizenship and are often shut out of mainstream Japanese society.[9] Accordingly, foreigners are routinely rejected from government employment for "looking foreign," and schools may refuse foreign children if those schools deem it "too difficult" to teach those children.[10] By allowing these practices to persist, liberal democracies compromise the degree to which they live up to their own fundamental commitments. The more and longer they employ such practices, the less plausibly they can claim to even be liberal democracies.[11] Put differently, even if liberal democracy does not necessarily imply diversity, an openness to difference expresses liberal democratic values.

Third, when difference is structured hierarchically, the underprivileged and the oppressed can practice a disruptive brand of politics of difference: they can interrupt the fluidity of social relations in a bid to redress those hierarchies. For example, many attribute the successes of the Civil Rights Movement to various forms of resistance – from the sit-ins, marches, and deliberate lawbreaking of Martin Luther King Jr.'s nonviolent civil disobedience movement to the more uncompromising threats of revolution, exemplified by Malcolm X's early activism. Similar disruptions helped the women's suffrage movement win the right to vote in the 1920s, just as general strikes and the formation of unions helped workers win concessions from management – safety standards, the eight-hour workday, and the barring of child labour. So, more than ensure that dominant groups abstain from wielding autocratic tools and strategies to enforce homogeneity or hierarchy, a politics that embraces (or at least accepts) difference can help rectify injustices and, in the long run, perhaps counterintuitively, render liberal democracy itself more secure.

... AND THE POTENTIAL PERILS

We have good reason, however, to believe that it is also necessary to be wary of the potential perils of difference and disagreement. When the expression of difference and disagreement overheats, difference and disagreement become forms of *civic aggression*. Political actors and citizens come to interpret their

---

[8] Tom Inglis, "A Snapshot of How Ireland Has Changed," *The Irish Times*, June 17, 2016, www.irishtimes.com/culture/books/a-snapshot-of-how-ireland-has-changed-1.2687369.

[9] "Contemporary Japan: Japanese Society – Ethnic Minorities," Asian Topics: An Online Resource for Asian History and Culture, http://afe.easia.columbia.edu/at/contemp_japan/cjp_society_02.html.

[10] "Joint Civil Society Report on Racial Discrimination in Japan," Japan NGO Network for the Elimination of Racial Discrimination, August 2018, https://tbinternet.ohchr.org/Treaties/CERD/Shared%20Documents/JPN/INT_CERD_NGO_JPN_31918_E.pdf.

[11] Today, Hungary and Poland exemplify this sort of liberal democratic backsliding.

differences and disagreements not as *mere* differences and disagreements but as reasons to understand politics and their social relations in terms of warfare. As Michael Ignatieff explains,

An adversary has to be defeated, while an enemy must be destroyed. You cannot compromise with enemies. With adversaries compromise is possible ... Democracy depends on persuasion, on the idea that you might be able to win over an adversary today and turn him or her into an ally tomorrow ... One of democracy's crucial functions ... [is] to keep adversaries from becoming enemies ... [when we] have the politics of enemies ... politics is modelled as war itself ... [and is no longer] alternative to it [war].[12]

In such conditions, even if political actors and citizens are committed to liberal democracy, they will feel increasingly compelled to employ "take no prisoners" strategies and tactics to realize their objectives. That is, even if they would prefer to not undermine liberal democratic norms and institutions, they will feel pressured to do so, lest others benefit from appealing to those strategies and tactics.

For example, following the Cold War, American politics became more and more polarized, and bipartisanship, rare. The Republicans in particular were willing to play hardball. Congressional Republicans, led by Newt Gingrich, subjected Bill and Hillary Clinton to a steady stream of investigations that largely failed to confirm that the Clintons were guilty of their alleged crimes.[13] Congressional Republicans also explicitly obstructed the Obama Administration's legislative agenda as much as possible, subjecting Barack Obama to several (futile) investigations into whether the tragic security failures at US government facilities in Benghazi were evidence of nefarious motives.[14] Both parties began to "gerrymander" districts wherever they could in order to give themselves unfair electoral advantages, and both embraced negative campaigning.[15]

Similarly, although the Civil Rights Movement succeeded in moving the center of gravity of American social attitudes and intuitions away from white

---

[12] Michael Ignatieff, *Fire and Ashes: Success and Failure in Politics* (Cambridge, MA: Harvard University Press, 2013), 150–152.

[13] Sometimes, these investigations uncovered behaviour that could be described as ethically ambiguous. Nonetheless, that behaviour was typically unrelated to the stated purposes of those investigations. See David A. Graham, "From Whitewater to Benghazi: A Clinton-Scandal Primer," *The Atlantic*, November 6, 2016, www.theatlantic.com/politics/archive/2016/11/tracking-the-clinton-controversies-from-whitewater-to-benghazi/396182/. The questionable nature of these investigations also does not detract from the accusations leveled at Bill Clinton during the MeToo Movement.

[14] Jonathan Capehart, "Republicans Had It in for Obama before Day 1," *The Washington Post*, August 10, 2012, www.washingtonpost.com/blogs/post-partisan/post/republicans-had-it-in-for-obama-before-day-1/2012/08/10/0c96c7c8-e31f-11e1-ae7f-d2a13e249eb2_blog.html.

[15] Even Obama, who ran on "Hope and Change" in the 2008 General Election, conducted a decidedly negative, personal campaign against Mitt Romney in the 2012 General Election.

supremacy, racial inequalities and inequities have persisted. "Mainstream" whites largely no longer assert their dominance as aggressively as mainstream whites often did during the Civil Rights Movement, and many mainstream whites today do earnestly support liberal democracy. Yet even if they might oppose the most blatant forms of racism (e.g., hate crimes), many of them remain complacent with subtler forms of systemic racism – education and health inequities, discriminatory drug laws, de facto segregationist housing and residential policies, and implicit biases among the police, not to mention instances of outright brutality. This intransigence has led many minorities (Blacks in particular) to grow impatient with the rate of progress in race relations and to become pessimistic about the possibility of reconciliation with whites. Indeed, in 2020, mass protests against police brutality and systemic racial injustices erupted following the murder of George Floyd, with some of these protests turning into riots.

Certainly, from a purely normative standpoint, the "aggression" of the underprivileged and the oppressed should not be conflated with or considered morally equivalent to the aggression and even the complacency of the privileged and the dominant. Aggression in the name of justice is not the same as aggression in the name of injustice; the two should not be considered two sides of the same coin or in any way symmetrical. Still, we can say that there is a practical or *strategic* danger that such aggression on the part of the underprivileged and the oppressed can inspire the privileged and the dominant to assert their power more boldly – to become increasingly aggressive, rather than "merely" complacent, in order to fend off perceived threats.[16] (Of course, the privileged and the dominant often do not require such "provocation" to assert their power. The assassination of Martin Luther King Jr. demonstrates that sometimes the mere threat of losing privilege can prompt the privileged and the dominant to assert their power murderously.)

Indeed, partly in response to these perceived threats of "lawlessness," but also in response to anxieties over long-term demographic shifts that this book shall explore, more and more "complacent" whites have, ironically, grown comfortable sharing in a political coalition with white supremacists who are far from "merely" complacent. That is, more and more whites who earnestly

---

[16] What this means is that even if the rectification of injustices requires aggressive disruption, the preservation of liberal democratic norms and institutions demands that steps be taken to ensure that the general effort to rectify injustices does not consist wholly (or even mostly) of such aggressive disruptions. There is a need to balance or somehow combine the demands of liberal democracy and the pursuit of greater justice. In other words, claims of injustice should be taken seriously in their own right, but we should also take those claims seriously for their implications on the challenge of difference and disagreement and on the survival of liberal democracy. In this book, I focus on articulating ways to: (a) provide those who do have claims of unjust treatment with avenues to express their concerns and (b) promote a sense that their fellow citizens largely do take their claims seriously, *even if* those fellow citizens might ultimately disagree about whether those claims are sound or not.

support liberal democracy and oppose clear instances of racism, despite being complacent with subtler forms of racism, are moving into political alignment with *enemies* of liberal democracy. Some of these enemies of liberal democracy advocate for ethnocracy, "a nominally democratic regime in which the dominance of one [racial-]ethnic group is structurally determined."[17] Others, frequently called "Identitarians," go even further by advocating for "the remigration and deportation of non-whites or non-Europeans."[18]

What this example indicates is that conditions of civic aggression are dangerous for liberal democracy not simply because committed liberal democrats will feel compelled to damage liberal democracy in an effort to stay alive or to pursue their own goals; these conditions are also dangerous because they make it easier for those who seek to destroy liberal democracy to exploit the deep divides which exist between liberal democrats. Indicatively, concurrent with the political alignment between complacent whites and white supremacists, mainstream Republican politicians have moved beyond their prior obstructionism; they have now formed an alliance with autocratic political forces who threaten to jail their political opponents, deem the press "the enemy of the people," and welcome the help of hostile foreign agents to win elections. Despite the fact that many Republicans privately resent this autocratic takeover of the Party,[19] they nonetheless deem this arrangement worthwhile as a means to advance their partisan objectives – tax cuts, deregulation, and a conservative civil service and judiciary. An enemy of my enemy is my friend, even if that "friend" is an enemy of liberal democracy.

The expression of difference and disagreement, in short, can be valuable for liberal democracy. Political disagreement can ensure accountability, inspire political participation, and prevent more extreme forms of political contestation. Similarly, an openness to difference helps ensure that the social majority does not wield autocratic tools and strategies to enforce its dominance, and civic disruption can help the underprivileged and the oppressed combat injustice. However, when either competition or civic disruption overheats, civic aggression emerges. Viewing one another as enemies, political actors and citizens at large alike who are committed to liberal democracy become more tempted or feel compelled to employ take no prisoners strategies and tactics to realize their objectives. While some of these appeals to civic aggression (specifically, by the underprivileged and the oppressed to combat injustice) can be

---

[17] Cas Mudde, *The Far Right Today* (Medford: Polity Press, 2019), 115.

[18] Cynthia Miller-Idriss, *Hate in the Homeland: The New Global Far Right* (Princeton: Princeton University Press, 2020), 5.

[19] Anna Luehrmann, Juraj Medzihorsky, Garry Hinde, and Staffan I. Lindberg, "New Global Data on Political Parties: V-Party," V-Dem Institute, October 26, 2020, www.v-dem.net/media/filer_public/b6/55/b6553f85-5c5d-45ec-be63-a48a2abe3f62/briefing_paper_9.pdf finds that the Republican Party now has more in common with the Polish, Hungarian, and Turkish far right than with its traditional Western European and British Commonwealth conservative sister parties.

justified, these actions can nonetheless corrode liberal democratic institutions and norms, and the increasing enmity between committed liberal democrats can – ironically – make some of them more inclined to team up with enemies of liberal democracy for the purposes of winning.

Therefore, the question we have in front of us is this: how can the expression of difference and disagreement be structured so that it facilitates healthy contestation and the rectification of injustices, rather than (1) fuel no-holds-barred conflict and (2) leave the polity vulnerable to the growing influence of liberal democracy's enemies?[20]

FELLOWSHIP AND NEGATIVE IDEALISM

This book acknowledges that some citizens will likely always be hostile to liberal democracy. Nonetheless, this book argues that in order for liberal democracy to harness the benefits of difference and disagreement and avoid unduly squashing difference and disagreement, yet also sidestep the potential the perils of difference and disagreement, citizens should be encouraged to share in a sort of fellowship. By fellowship, I refer to the sense that citizens are united in a common aim – in this case, the preservation of a certain constitutional regime.

Now, some readers of Aristotle might remark that the sorts of bonds of citizenship I promote in this book might better be described as bonds of *civic* or *political friendship*. Indeed, as we shall see, famously noting that friendship is that which holds cities together, Aristotle uses the term political friendship or *philia* to describe the relations shared by citizens in "correct" regime types; these bonds are oriented toward the common advantage and political justice (variously defined), not the private enrichment of rulers and their favoured factional groups. On Aristotle's account, citizens who are political friends might be differently situated in society. For example, they might be members of different economic groups. Yet they nonetheless have certain political virtues that allow them to do what is required to sustain the regime and ensure that it remains "correct" (or, if it is a "deviant regime," that it is not excessively deviant). Moreover, they sense that their fellow citizens largely share this commitment.

---

[20] Put differently, this book aims to contribute to the general effort to help prevent established liberal democracies from backsliding and to stop liberal democracies that have begun to backslide from continuing to backslide. According to mainstream research organizations like Freedom House and the Economist Intelligence Unit, figuring among those liberal democracies that have begun to backslide are Greece, Italy, Belgium, and most disconcertingly, given its status as "Leader of the Free World," the United States. See Sarah Repucci, "A Leaderless Struggle for Democracy," Freedom House, 2020, https://freedomhouse.org/report/freedom-world/2020/leaderless-struggle-democracy; "Democracy Index 2019," The Economist Intelligence Unit, 2019, www.eiu.com/topic/democracy-index.

Still, given the contemporary meaning of the word "friendship," describing my theory as promoting a sort of friendship might tempt my readers into making understandable but ultimately inaccurate assumptions about the nature and objectives of my theory. After all, we today understand friendship to be a private phenomenon, voluntarily shared among people who have affection for one another; politics is a public phenomenon defined by contestation, if not outright hostility. Indeed, we often maintain friendships by *avoiding* talk of politics. Similarly, we today tend to understand friendship as involving intimacy; most citizens in contemporary societies are strangers. So, the notion of political friendship might tempt readers into assuming that my project is an exercise in nostalgia or utopian fantasy – a yearning for a sort of "folk society" where everyone knows everyone else well, where everyone participates in unanimous decision making directly, and where conflicts are "ignored in the warmth of friendship."[21] Accordingly, even though I do see my vision as following in the lineage of political friendship, I describe my vision as one of fellowship so as to avoid such unnecessary confusion.

As we have seen, I describe this sense of fellowship as "constitutional" because it is oriented toward the preservation (and, as we shall see, improvement) of liberal democracy. That is, this book aspires to cultivate a sense of unity among citizens who have differences and disagreements, but does not envision the primary object of that unity to be the realization of the "perfect" society. So, constitutional fellowship can be described as a sort of *negative ideal*. It is an ideal because it is a target – a North Star – toward which we ought to aspire: it describes how citizens *ought* to relate to one another. As a response to the potential perils of difference and disagreement, constitutional fellowship does not simply take citizens' present social relations as givens and prescribe mere institutional tweaks to channel any antagonistic relations which might exist. At the same time, however, that ideal is negative in that it does not constitute perfection; certainly, it is not an account of the "well-ordered society" of "strict compliance" where "[e]veryone is presumed to act justly and to do his part in upholding just institutions."[22] Rather, this ideal is intended to help prevent certain social or political evils – or, when those evils have arisen, to make a bad situation less bad. That is, the primary purpose of this ideal is to *defend* liberal democracy and, perhaps, to improve liberal democracy slowly – not to pursue liberal democracy's best form, whatever that form might be.

In some ways, this negative idealistic approach to the challenge of difference and disagreement can be seen as emerging out of one of the primary fault lines in contemporary democratic theory – that between discursive and realist approaches to the question of difference and disagreement. The first, represented in this book by John Rawls's "political liberalism" and Jürgen

---

[21] Jane Mansbridge, "The Limits of Friendship" in *Jane Mansbridge: Participation, Deliberation, Legitimate Coercion*, ed. Melissa S. Williams (New York: Routledge, 2019), 15–36.
[22] Rawls, *A Theory of Justice*, 5.

Habermas's "discursive democracy," maintains that the resources of rationally informed philosophical discourse can be mobilized to manage difference and disagreement. Important differences exist between Rawls and Habermas's theories, and these theories do accommodate seemingly non-discursive elements like civil disobedience. However, Rawls and Habermas share a core claim that the development (and continuous revision) of a rational consensus among citizens on how to move forward together can help liberal democracy not only avoid the potential perils of difference and disagreement but also become more fully legitimate.

The second, forcefully articulated by "democratic realists" like William Connolly and Chantal Mouffe, maintains that discursive approaches to the management of difference and disagreement are bound to be counterproductive. At best, discursive approaches will serve to hide undue hierarchies and injustices, thereby perpetuating hegemonic social discourses. At worse, discursive approaches will suppress citizens' differences and disagreements, leading to an illusory sense of unity or harmony that will only erupt later on in the form of even greater aggression. Accordingly, rather than seek to manage difference and disagreement rationally, the realist perspective places its faith in institutionalized competition and contestation. So long as liberal democratic institutions are designed smartly, contestation – indeed, power politics – can prevent marginalized voices from being silenced, rectify injustices, and render liberal democracy more inclusive and, perhaps counterintuitively, more secure.

Constitutional fellowship responds to what I see as the weaknesses of both of these perspectives. The democratic realist perspective rightfully notes that it is important for citizens' differences and disagreements to be expressed, and that the rectification of undue social hierarchies often demands that the underprivileged, the oppressed, and their allies have the space required to engage in civic disruption – sometimes, aggressive disruption. However, as I will demonstrate, this perspective underestimates the important role that a basic sense of unity must play in preventing those exertions of power from spiralling out of control, straining the liberal democratic framework, and leaving the polity vulnerable to the growing influence of liberal democracy's enemies. While well-designed institutions can do some work in preventing such scenarios, this perspective also overestimates the ability of such institutions to channel civic aggression – indeed, to not corrode in the face of such aggression.

Meanwhile, the more discursive perspective is right to insist that citizens be encouraged to share a sense of unity. However, as I will argue, this perspective aims too high. It focuses on helping liberal democracies meet more vigorous standards of legitimacy – "stability for the right reasons" (Rawls) or more fully deliberative forms of democratic decision making (Habermas). Yet it overestimates the degree to which citizens are indeed committed or attached to liberal democracy – the degree to which a "liberal public culture" is secure – and, by extension, the degree to which basic liberal democratic institutions are secure. So, this perspective does not provide convincing accounts of how to pursue the more basic goal of securing liberal democracy – of how citizens can become the sorts of people who will do what it takes to attain and sustain liberal democracy, of how they can continue being those sorts of people, and of how they can become those people again, should they lose faith in liberal democracy.

We can therefore understand constitutional fellowship to be an account of how citizens can come to share a sense of unity, without smothering their differences and disagreements, for the purposes of better securing the basic liberal democratic regime type. As we shall see, under constitutional fellowship, this sense of unity assumes the form of a *culture of trust* where citizens believe that most of their fellow citizens probably "value the continuation of their relationship"[23] *and* are committed to support social and political arrangements that can allow them to continue that relationship: liberal democracy.

DIVISIONS OF LABOUR

What does it take for constitutional fellowship to emerge? What does it mean more specifically for citizens to be constitutional fellows? This book theorizes a "role-based" account of constitutional fellowship. Under this account, citizens do not cultivate a sense of fellowship by engaging in the same set of practices. Rather, citizens first recognize (or act in manners that are consistent with the recognition) that trust assumes different complexions in different contexts, and that different approaches are required to overcome the different barriers to trust which exist in these different contexts. Second, under role-based constitutional fellowship, citizens observe a series of divisions of labour to overcome these barriers. So, under role-based constitutional fellowship, citizens might seem to behave in contradictory manners. However, by fulfilling different normative roles, citizens can work toward overcoming those barriers and contribute to the development of a political culture that is increasingly defined by fellowship.

Accordingly, I argue that such a culture can emerge when citizens observe a series of divisions of labour to cultivate trust within and between different spheres of activity: (1) trust within the formal political sphere (especially among competitors); (2) trust within the general citizenry; and (3) trust between these two spheres of activity.

First, when trust exists within the formal political sphere, political competitors can treat one another as adversaries to be defeated, rather than as enemies to be destroyed. The main barrier to trust here is what I call the "institutionalized enmity problem," the tendency for political competition to become modelled on warfare and for competitors to indeed treat one another as enemies. I argue that to overcome this problem, a division of labour among political actors who are committed to liberal democracy is needed between "principled pragmatists" and "principled purists." Principled pragmatists who are willing

---

[23] Russell Hardin, *Trust and Trustworthiness* (New York: Russell Sage Foundation, 2002), 1.

to compromise can help cultivate a sense of reciprocity, while principled purists who more stubbornly refuse to compromise out of a sense of justice can help keep pragmatists honest and compel pragmatists to compromise for the sake of the public good, rather than their own private interests.

Second, when trust exists within the general citizenry, citizens at large treat one another in manners befitting their equal citizenship, despite their differences. The tricky part of this sort of trust, I demonstrate, is that in the liberal democratic context, citizens who trust one another do not merely "respect difference"; they believe that their fellow citizens do not wish to have unequal privileges of citizenship as a result of their differences, and that their fellow citizens do wish to redress undue social hierarchies. So, the main barrier to trust here is the "social domination problem," the tendency for undue social hierarchies to become sources of antagonism.

I note that some – whom I call "proud oppressors" and "harder complicit oppressors" – will likely undermine efforts to overcome this problem. After all, these citizens either relish such hierarchies or feel threatened by efforts to redress those hierarchies. Still, I argue that the social domination problem can be overcome through a division of labour among the underprivileged, the oppressed, and their allies (who are members of privileged and dominant groups) between the practices of *shouting back* and *talking*. The *threat* of violence or disorder implied by the aggressively disruptive practices of shouting back (including, in extreme cases, vandalism and rioting) can help ensure that those hierarchies do not go unnoticed. Meanwhile the more reconciliatory practices of talking – namely (1) transparent discussions in special forums on the nature of injustices and (2) the more general observance (and revision) of the social conventions of good manners – can mitigate backlash. Talking can help dissuade what I call "unwitting, well-intentioned oppressors" and "softer complicit oppressors" from joining efforts to perpetuate those injustices, rather than supporting efforts to rectify those injustices.

Third, when trust exists between the formal political sphere and the general citizenry, citizens at large believe that political actors largely do try to further the public good. So, the main barrier to trust here is the "representative cynicism problem," the tendency for citizens at large to believe that political actors are largely in it for themselves, individually and as a class. A healthy skepticism toward those with formal political power, of course, is to be encouraged and lies at the root of liberal democracy. However, excessive distrust, I maintain, can leave citizens vulnerable to the influence of "honest" and "sincere" political actors who in fact threaten the rule of law, individual rights, and the freedom and fairness of elections.

I argue that in order to cultivate trust here, political actors (who are committed to liberal democracy) can refrain from excessively demonizing their opponents, explain why they perform compromises (but only after the fact and with careful framing), and avoid encouraging citizens to develop fantastical understandings of politics and unrealistic expectations by which to judge political actors. Meanwhile, although I note that it is the responsibility of political actors to gain the trust of citizens at large, I submit that citizens can prepare themselves to return good faith efforts by political actors to win their trust. Notably, citizens can think about how they sometimes act hypocritically in their various endeavours as well – for instance, in business, in the job market, or even at school. Citizens will more likely do this preparatory work and adopt a less cynical posture toward politics if political actors act in the manners I outline.

AIMING HIGH TO AIM LOW, FLEXIBILITY, AND SELF-INITIATION

I will refrain from going into too much detail about this vision at this moment. However, it is worth highlighting three additional features of role-based constitutional fellowship.

First, even though I have characterized role-based constitutional fellowship as a negative ideal whose primary goal is to prevent the corrosion of liberal democracy, fellowship nonetheless addresses issues that one might not, at first glance, associate with the pursuit of that negative ideal. Namely, role-based constitutional fellowship provides a path through which citizens can identify and rectify undue social hierarchies.

In some ways, as a negative ideal, role-based constitutional fellowship resembles brands of "negative liberal realism." These theories hold that the primary objective of liberal democratic politics should be to avoid certain evils rather than to achieve certain goods.[24] For example, Judith Shklar famously argues that liberal democracy's primary contribution is that it helps to prevent the greatest of evils: cruelty.[25] On this basis, she urges us to not fret as much as we often do over lesser evils, such as hypocrisy and snobbery, and to think twice before discarding liberal democracy, however flawed it might be. Certainly, even though negative liberal realism seems to "aim low," it is nonetheless demanding. As Andrew Sabl notes, "Few remember Shklar's warnings that *truly* putting cruelty first would involve profound personal costs ... a profound political dilemma: while avoiding cruelty requires avoiding politics, attacking existing cruelty and injustices requires engaging in politics."[26] Still, following the general thrust of negative liberal realism, we can say that if the

[24] Matt Sleat, "Liberal Realism: A Liberal Response to the Realist Critique," *The Review of Politics* 73(3) (2011): 477.
[25] Judith Shklar, *Ordinary Vices* (Cambridge, MA: The Belknap Press of Harvard University Press, 1984).
[26] Andrew Sabl, "Judith Shklar, *Ordinary Vices*" in *The Oxford Handbook of Classics in Contemporary Political Theory*, ed. Jacob Levy (Oxford: Oxford University Press, 2019), www.oxfordhandbooks.com/view/10.1093/oxfordhb/9780198717133.001.0001/oxfordhb-9780198717133-e-5 (accessed November 1, 2020).

negative idealism of constitutional fellowship were strictly analogous, then constitutional fellowship would advise that we focus on shoring up liberal democracy, and that we view the rectification of undue hierarchies as a nice bonus.

Yet constitutional fellowship does not take this path. Instead, it addresses those undue hierarchies head-on. Far from papering over undue hierarchies, constitutional fellowship provides a way to redress those hierarchies gradually – that is, in a manner that helps to preserve liberal democracy. At the very least, constitutional fellowship provides a path for the underprivileged and the oppressed in particular to feel that their fellow citizens take the persistence of undue hierarchies seriously, even if those fellow citizens disagree about which hierarchies are indeed unjust. Certainly, I maintain that constitutional fellowship must be ambitious in this manner because those undue hierarchies sit uncomfortably with the equality of standing which underlies contemporary liberal democracy. However, I will also show that constitutional fellowship must be ambitious in this manner because the persistence of those hierarchies jeopardizes its viability. If those hierarchies persist, then people's faith in liberal democracy will waver, and the underprivileged, the oppressed, and their allies might (understandably) deem aggression to be the only viable response to the aggression of the privileged and the dominant. This judgment reflects a theme that will recur throughout this book: even if our goals might be moderate or even conservative (*preserving* liberal democracy), we might nonetheless be compelled to be ambitious. In order to achieve "low" goals, we might have to aim "high."

Second, role-based constitutional fellowship recognizes that different contexts require different courses of action. For example, as I have noted, I will argue that in order to redress the institutionalized enmity problem, some political actors (principled pragmatists) must be willing to compromise in order to cultivate a sense of reciprocity. Yet I will also demonstrate that once some mainstream liberal democratic political forces have forged enduring alliances with autocratic political forces, it is necessary to pursue a different track. Rather than seek reconciliation, it is necessary for liberal democrats who stand outside of those alliances – the *defender*s of liberal democracy – to instead embrace contestation and strive to discern the most effective strategies and tactics to defeat their opponents. That is, the defenders of liberal democracy must aim to fracture those alliances and show that remaining in those alliances is politically costly. So, constitutional fellowship is not a one-size-fits-all vision of liberal democratic citizenship.

Third, as a sort of ideal, albeit a negative one, role-based constitutional fellowship does not describe how formal political actors and citizens at large alike presently relate to one another. So, in a sense, this book can be described as a guide to help political theorists and other observers of politics evaluate political and social practice. However, I do intend for role-based constitutional fellowship to ultimately be a source of motivation – something that citizens can see embodied in practice. In fact, I maintain that fellowship does contain elements that can facilitate its own initiation. Specifically, while the various roles I describe can be understood as component parts of a pluralistic whole (fellowship), performing those roles does not necessarily require that citizens "buy into" the entire apparatus; citizens can fulfill their respective normative roles without realizing it, at least initially. For example, members of oppressed groups and unwitting, well-intentioned oppressors who find themselves in the same economic associations (e.g., businesses) might be moved to cultivate a degree of reciprocity for the sake of pursuing common economic goals. Similarly, pragmatists in the formal political sphere might strike compromises, even if they do not yet share a sense of fellowship, when they believe that they can each benefit politically from those compromises. So, even though it is more likely that citizens will perform their various roles when they already share in role-based constitutional fellowship, its initiation does *not* demand that citizens *already* view themselves as constitutional fellows.

OUTLINE OF THE BOOK

Chapter 2 opens our discussion by examining discursive and realist approaches to the question of difference and disagreement in liberal democracy. As we have seen, the former seeks to outline the discursive conditions under which citizens who have differences and disagreements can attain and sustain a rational consensus on how to move forward together, whereas the latter maintains that liberal democracy should instead place its faith in institutionalized competition and contestation. By noting both perspectives' shortcomings and insights, I demonstrate the need for an approach that encourages citizens to share a sense of unity, but that abstains from suppressing citizens' differences and disagreements – and that pursues that sense of unity for the sake of securing the liberal democratic regime type, not for the sake of satisfying higher standards of discursive legitimacy.

In Chapter 3, I begin to lay the foundations of role-based constitutional fellowship by considering Aristotle's notion of political friendship as presented in the *Nicomachean Ethics* and the *Politics*. Now, this might seem like a surprising place to start. After all, Aristotle wrote over 2,000 years ago. However, I maintain that Aristotle's discussion has particular salience, for political friendship aspires for a sort of unity that is oriented toward the preservation of the political regime. In Aristotle's language, political friendship is a sort of "utility" or "advantage" friendship that is rooted in a shared commitment among citizens who might belong to different factions to further the common advantage of the polity – including the political regime of the polity, providing that that regime is either "correct" or not excessively "deviant." Through my critical engagement with Aristotle, I determine that we ought to strive toward a more abstract culture of trust where citizens *probably* value the continuation of their relationship, despite their differences and disagreements, and are committed to support social and political arrangements that can allow them to continue that relationship – liberal democracy. This culture of trust must not stymie the expression of difference and disagreement, and it must not stymie debates over the meaning of political (in)equality and (in)justice.

I also note, however, that this culture of trust seems to have a problem of initiation: how can a culture of trust that seems *premised* on a shared commitment to liberal democracy get off the ground and running in the first place if many people are not yet committed to liberal democracy? Accordingly, I conclude that either (1) citizens must first develop a non-liberal democratic culture of trust *before* they can be encouraged to view liberal democracy and social inclusion to be expressions of that trust further down the line or (2) citizens must be able to contribute to that culture of trust without realizing it, at least initially. In reaching these conclusions, I pave the way for the remaining discussions of this book. Liberal nationalism pursues the first approach, while role-based constitutional fellowship pursues the second.

In Chapter 4, I consider one broad approach that aims to promote an inclusive, liberal democratic culture of trust by leveraging citizens' shared civic-national identity or membership. As proponents of "liberal nationalism" argue, when citizens feel an emotional connection to a pre-political national community, they can develop "bounded solidarity" – "a set of *attitudes* and *motivations* ... of mutual acceptance, cooperation, and mutual support in times of need."[27] I argue that this broad perspective should not be dismissed wholesale, for it can help citizens who have differences and disagreements feel some degree of unity and propel them to care about one another's fates. In particular, by seeking to unite liberal democracy with the non-political resources of the nation, liberal nationalism offers a path through which a broad commitment to liberal democracy can be initiated, maintained, and restored. (I show that constitutional patriotism – which also aspires toward bounded solidarity but abstains from engaging with the nation – is only viable in special contexts, such as in post–World War II Germany).

I also argue, however, that even if citizens do share in liberal nationalism, it is necessary to move toward role-based constitutional fellowship. First, liberal nationalism typically does not contain adequate safeguards against the perpetuation of xenophobic and autocratic notions of national identity. I trace this danger to the failure of liberal nationalists to "prioritize" liberal democracy over the nation. Second, liberal nationalism aims to manage difference and disagreement by providing citizens with cultural resources to enhance their ability to *tough it out* when their differences and disagreements threaten to overheat. I show that in the absence of something like role-based constitutional

---

[27] Keith Banting and Will Kymlicka, "Introduction" in *The Strains of Commitment: The Political Sources of Solidarity in Diverse Societies*, ed. Keith Banting and Will Kymlicka (Oxford: Oxford University Press, 2017), 3–6.

fellowship to help citizens actually *work through* their differences and disagreements, liberal nationalism can, counterintuitively, aggravate the tensions which might have emerged from citizens' differences and disagreements.

In Chapters 5–8, I outline the details of role-based constitutional fellowship. Chapter 5 lays the foundation for this discussion by describing what trust looks like in the formal political sphere, in the general citizenry, and between the formal political sphere and the general citizenry. I identify the principal barriers to the production of trust in each of these three contexts: the institutionalized enmity problem, the social domination problem, and the representative cynicism problem, respectively.

Chapter 6 argues that a division of labour among political actors who are committed to liberal democracy between principled purists and principled pragmatists is needed to redress the institutionalized enmity problem. This approach emerges out of my critical engagement with two alternative perspectives: one which urges a politics of sincerity, and one which insists upon the persistence of hypocrisy in politics and encourages political actors to practice a politics of salutary hypocrisy. In addition, I note that there are times when trust-building is not appropriate: if autocratic political forces take over mainstream political parties, then the defenders of liberal democracy must embrace contestation. Still, the purpose of such contestation should be to make "former" liberal democrats who have entered into "unholy alliances" with autocratic forces for one reason or another think twice – to disincentivize participation in those alliances. Accordingly, I argue that should unholy alliances be defeated, liberal democrats ought to – cautiously – entice former liberal democrats back into the liberal democratic fold.

Chapter 7 argues that a division of labour among the underprivileged, the oppressed, and their allies between the practices of shouting back and talking is needed to redress the social domination problem. This approach emerges out of my critical engagement with Danielle Allen's notion of equitable self-interest. Allen is right, I maintain, to insist upon the need to cultivate trust between the underprivileged and the oppressed on the one hand and the privileged and the dominant on the other hand. Yet I show that the primary vehicle of that trust production should be the practice and revision of the social conventions of good manners; transparent discourse about justice and injustice can only play a supporting role. I also show that the practices of talking can only develop trust *all the while* rectifying undue social hierarchies if they take place alongside the more aggressively disruptive activities of shouting back.

As part of this discussion, I elaborate on the role that the "allies" of the underprivileged and the oppressed should play. In addition to putting their bodies between the oppressed and the dominant when brutal attacks are imminent (e.g., during instances of police brutality), allies should strive to play a mediating role by *listening well*. By listening well to the underprivileged and the oppressed, allies can afford the underprivileged and the oppressed a degree of recognition in contexts where that recognition is all too rare. Similarly, by listening to unwitting oppressors and softer complicit oppressors, allies can provide a softer touch and assure unwitting oppressors and softer complicit oppressors that they (oppressors) are not merely being condemned as bad people. In these manners, allies can persuade the underprivileged and the oppressed to keep faith that progress within the liberal democratic framework is possible and dissuade unwitting oppressors and softer complicit oppressors from moving into political alignment with what I call "proud oppressors" and "harder complicit oppressors."

Chapter 8 articulates practices that liberal democratic political actors can employ to gain the trust of citizens at large. This discussion further develops insights that emerge in earlier chapters. In particular, taking up the discussion of salutary hypocrisy in Chapter 6, I argue that even though formal politics is defined by the persistence of hypocrisy, people generally distrust hypocrisy; the formal political sphere is distinctive but *not* autonomous. So, liberal democratic political actors must keep this general moral intuition in mind when forming political judgments. They must either limit the degree to which they practice salutary hypocrisy – thereby constricting the degree to which trust can emerge among themselves (political actors) – or justify their apparent hypocrisy in the appropriate manners. I outline guidelines for how they can go about doing so.

In Chapter 9, I identify political institutions and associational structures that can either alleviate the burdens placed on role-based constitutional fellowship or make the realization of fellowship more likely. As part of this discussion, I note that some political institutional frameworks – notably, Westminster systems – seem relatively effective at channelling competition and alleviating the need for fellowship. Accordingly, I urge those systems to resist the push for greater proportional representation. I acknowledge, however, that future reforms will likely trend toward proportional representation; such reforms make the need for fellowship all the more urgent. In addition, I cast doubt on the ability of voluntary associations in civil society to foster a sense of fellowship among citizens at large. By virtue of being easy to exit, these associations tend to be homogeneous – forums where people can *escape* difference and disagreement. Accordingly, I deem the integrated workplace more conducive to the cultivation of fellowship.

Following these concrete recommendations, this book concludes by taking a step back to reassess how role-based constitutional fellowship fits within the broader infrastructure of liberal democracy. I suggest that this investigation into the question of difference and disagreement in liberal democracy logically suggests further inquiries (1) into how non-citizens ought to stand in relation to citizens and (2) into how the enemies of liberal democracy ought to be treated.

2

Aiming Too High, Aiming Too Low

The Limits of Discourse and Contestation

One of the primary fault lines in democratic theory lies between discursive and realist approaches to the question of difference and disagreement. Discursive approaches maintain that the resources of philosophical discourse can be mobilized to develop a rational consensus on how to move forward together. These approaches claim that rational consensus can counteract the possibility of civic aggression, expand the boundaries of social inclusion, and help liberal democracy become more fully legitimate. In opposition, realist approaches argue that efforts to foster consensus and a sense of unity are inevitably counterproductive. They claim that institutionalized contestation is more conducive to the promotion of social inclusion and (perhaps counterintuitively) to the diffusion of antagonism.

In what follows, I show that even though both broad perspectives provide important insights, it is necessary to move beyond them. First, probing John Rawls's political liberalism and Jürgen Habermas's discursive democracy, I show that discursive approaches aim too high. They rightfully insist upon the need for citizens to share in a sense of unity, but overestimate the degree to which a "liberal public culture" is secure. Accordingly, I show that these approaches do not provide convincing accounts of how citizens can *become* the sorts of steadfast liberal democrats who will do what it takes to attain and sustain liberal democracy, how citizens can *continue* being these sorts of people, and how they can become those sorts of people *again*, should they lose faith in liberal democracy.

Second, exploring the notion of "organized disunity," William Connolly and Thomas McCarthy's "soft agonism," and Chantal Mouffe's "hard agonism," I demonstrate that democratic realist approaches do not adequately acknowledge the need to curate a sense of basic unity. Even though these approaches rightly note that exertions of power are often required to rectify injustices and that it is dangerous to squash difference and disagreement, insofar as these approaches value liberal democracy, they underestimate the important role basic unity must play in helping citizens feel that they are in it together for the long run and preventing those exertions of power from spiralling out of control. I also demonstrate that democratic realism overestimates the ability of well-designed institutions to withstand – let alone channel – civic aggression.

Through these critical discussions, I conclude that in order for a liberal democracy to harness the benefits of difference and disagreement and avoid unduly squashing difference and disagreement, yet also sidestep the potential pitfalls of difference and disagreement, citizens should be encouraged to share a sense of unity. However, this sense of unity should not be attained through the suppression of difference and disagreement, and it should be oriented toward the promotion and preservation of basic liberal democracy. In subsequent chapters, by developing my notion of role-based constitutional fellowship, I shall describe what such a sense of unity ought to look like and how such unity can emerge.

JOHN RAWLS'S POLITICAL LIBERALISM

Rawls's primary goal is to deepen a "constitutional consensus," which he believes advanced liberal democracies have largely attained, into an "overlapping consensus" through rational discourse. A constitutional consensus consists of a shared agreement on the basic rights, liberties, and rules of political contestation required to "moderat[e] political rivalry." Citizens support those liberal democratic basics for a myriad of reasons. Some citizens might deem them conducive to their private interests, while others might accept them out of custom.[1]

It is necessary, according to Rawls, to move beyond a constitutional consensus. First, under a constitutional consensus, citizens do not share a conception of how principles like freedom and equality *fit together* and should be interpreted. Second, this consensus only concerns those procedures and institutions that moderate how hard citizens and political actors compete; it does not concern the primary political, social, and economic institutions of society – the "basic structure." Therefore, the constitutional consensus cannot adequately ensure that there are "guarantees [of] liberty of thought generally ... legislation assuring freedom of association [and] freedom of movement ... [and] measures assur[ing] that the basic needs of all citizens are met so that they can take part in political and social life," for "conflict will arise about these."[2]

Accordingly, Rawls deems it necessary to pursue an overlapping consensus. A *political conception of justice*, the overlapping consensus is a *thin*,

---

[1] John Rawls, *Political Liberalism: Expanded Edition* (New York: Columbia University Press, 2005), 158–161. [Hereafter Rawls, *PL*.]

[2] Rawls, *PL*, 166.

free-standing, moral conception that reflects the fundamental intuitions shared by the liberal democratic mainstream. The overlapping consensus is deeper than a constitutional consensus because, under the overlapping consensus, citizens share a conception of how principles like liberty and equality fit together, as well as an understanding of how those principles manifest themselves in the constitution and the economy.

The overlapping consensus thereby realizes "stability for the right reasons." First, it provides citizens with a common point of reference to judge whether the basic structure is just. This does not mean that citizens must agree on a single political conception of justice. However, so long as an "enduring majority" of citizens do adhere to "some member" of a "family of reasonable liberal political conceptions of justice,"[3] citizens can judge whether political and social institutions are just by reference to a common, "publically recognized point of view."[4]

Second, the overlapping consensus enforces a *priority of right*, offering "unreasonable" citizens whose comprehensive doctrines transgress the boundaries of that common point of reference no credence. The overlapping consensus excludes those citizens who fail to provide "public reasons" for their support of the overlapping consensus,[5] as well as those who find the political conception of justice incompatible with their comprehensive doctrines. So, the overlapping consensus excludes religious fundamentalists who cannot reconcile their religious beliefs with freedom, equality, and tolerance, just as the overlapping consensus excludes male supremacists who deny women's right to vote.[6]

I have worries about both sorts of consensus. I am also skeptical about whether the constitutional consensus can propel citizens to pursue an overlapping consensus.

On the Constitutional Consensus

Rawls maintains that the constitutional consensus generates preliminary trust. This trust consists of the mutual recognition that citizens are committed to liberal democracy. Citizens who are committed to liberal democracy develop "the cooperative virtues of life: the virtue of reasonableness and a sense of fairness, a spirit of compromise and a readiness to meet others halfway ..."[7] That is, when citizens believe that institutions and procedures are just, citizens

---

[3] Specifically, citizens must adhere to understandings of the political conception of justice that conform to the following three conditions: (1) they must specify certain liberal democratic rights, liberties, and opportunities; (2) they must prioritize these freedoms; and (3) they must guarantee all citizens "adequate all-purpose means" to make intelligent and effective use of their liberties and opportunities (Rawls, *PL*, xlvi).

[4] Rawls, *PL*, 9.

[5] Rawls, *PL*, 224–225. These "public reasons" conform to certain epistemic constraints: common sense; the scientific method; plain truth; and the norms of reciprocity, liberty, and equality.

[6] Rawls, *PL*, 447.   [7] Rawls, *PL*, 163.

do what is necessary to sustain those institutions and procedures. As citizens observe others doing the same with "evident intention," they become even more willing. This preliminary trust is vital: without it, the journey toward an overlapping consensus cannot begin.

An immediate worry concerns the fact that the trust generated here is grounded in "nationally anonymous" principles.[8] Why should citizens remain loyal to their nation state's political institutions and to their fellow citizens *in particular*? Why should they not feel loyal to the political institutions that best embody those principles, wherever they might be found?

This charge is warranted insofar as there is "a logical gap between a cognitive belief in universal values and a felt solidarity with a bounded 'we.'"[9] However, as we have seen, citizens under Rawls's scheme do not develop an attachment to liberal democratic principles of justice in the abstract. Rather, citizens develop an attachment to those principles because those principles are embodied in *concrete* institutions and procedures: citizens come "to appreciate the good those principles accomplish both for themselves and for those they care for, as well as for society at large."[10] In addition, citizens come to trust one another because they observe one another doing what it takes to sustain those principles and institutions. So, on this score, Rawls's argument stands.

Yet there is good reason to believe that the constitutional consensus' narrow conceptual underpinnings – namely its foundations in citizens' *preliminary acceptance* of liberal democracy – hamper its own initiation, as well as its ability to "stage a comeback" should citizens turn their backs on liberal democracy. By Rawls's own account, a constitutional consensus develops out of a modus vivendi. In a modus vivendi, citizens reluctantly agree to be governed by liberal democratic principles. They would prefer that their respective comprehensive doctrines be fully implemented but are exhausted by the fighting that has ensued. With time, however, these citizens come to appreciate the benefits of liberal democracy and affirm liberal democracy on its merits. A constitutional consensus is therefore viable when autocratic alternatives have proven disastrous or when warring factions have reached a stalemate.

What if, however, autocratic political arrangements succeed in winning the affirmation of citizens? What if the polity is split between adherents and opponents of liberal democracy, as is frequently the case in emerging democracies (e.g., Eastern Europe)? What if a specific comprehensive doctrine, interest, or identity gains supremacy – for instance, a racial-ethnic majority that holds

---

[8] Christian Joppke, "The Retreat of Multiculturalism in the Liberal State: Theory and Policy," *British Journal of Sociology* 55(2) (2004): 253.

[9] Keith Banting and Will Kymlicka, "Introduction" in *The Strains of Commitment: The Political Sources of Solidarity in Diverse Societies*, ed. Keith Banting and Will Kymlicka (Oxford: Oxford University Press, 2017), 16.

[10] Rawls, *PL*, 160.

hostile attitudes toward minorities? This indicates that the Rawlsian project will have difficulties getting off the ground and running – of *initiating* – wherever liberal democratic principles are contested. More than that: the Rawlsian project will have difficulties staging a *comeback*, should citizens turn their backs on liberal democracy. This is increasingly a problem in even established liberal democracies, where more and more citizens judge liberal democracy to be incapable of solving problems or even to be the root of those problems.

It can be argued that Rawls's strategy should not be faulted for being historically contingent. After all, Rawls draws upon the historical experiences that led to liberalism's emergence – the Wars of Religion in the sixteenth and seventeenth centuries. The issue, however, is that Rawls's political liberalism cannot provide an account of how autocratic political arrangements can *evolve* in a liberal democratic direction. It can only say that history will shock or exhaust people into accepting the need for liberal democratic principles.[11]

On the Transition from a Constitutional Consensus to an Overlapping Consensus

It is also unclear whether a constitutional consensus that has emerged can sustain itself and propel citizens toward an overlapping consensus. Now, Rawls is right to expect that trust will emerge when committed liberal democrats observe one another performing the activities required to maintain basic liberal democracy. This is not unlike how members of a team might develop a sense of trust when they see one another behaving as team members should.[12]

It does not follow, however, that citizens will be moved to deepen the constitutional consensus into an overlapping consensus. Rawls maintains that citizens will pursue an overlapping consensus once they come to recognize the constitutional consensus' deficiencies. One of these deficiencies concerns *breadth*. A constitutional consensus is "too narrow ... [and] unless a democratic people is sufficiently unified and cohesive, it will not enact the legislation necessary to cover the remaining constitutional essentials and basic matters of justice, and conflict will arise out of these."[13] Yet why would citizens want to pursue a deeper sort of consensus *as a result* of the *deficiencies* of the thinner consensus? Why would citizens not instead become more polarized? Have US liberals and conservatives, for instance, not developed animosity as a result of

---

[11] During my discussion of liberal nationalism, I will suggest that a liberal democratic culture of trust can more successfully overcome these difficulties if it is supported by non-political resources, such as a national culture and history.

[12] Rawls's argument that this process encourages the development of the "cooperative virtues of political life" resembles Aristotle's theory, that citizens become political friends when they recognize one as politically virtuous and as committed to the common advantage. We shall consider Aristotle's theory in Chapter 3.

[13] Rawls, *PL*, 166.

their persistent disagreements over how to interpret the Constitution?[14] Indeed, it is more likely that citizens will become disgruntled at the constitutional consensus' apparent inability to resolve disagreements. Conservatives and liberals today distrust each other to such an extent that the former has allied with the far right for the purposes of taking ideological control of the legal system. The two sides have not been moved by their disagreements to further deepen any "consensus" they might have had.

The issue with Rawls's argument that an overlapping consensus will follow from a constitutional consensus is thus twofold. First, Rawls's argument assumes that the preliminary sense of trust generated by the move from a modus vivendi to a constitutional consensus will be secure enough to withstand citizens' outstanding disagreements. Yet surely, that trust will erode if citizens lack the proper techniques to *manage* or *negotiate* those disagreements – to ensure that those disagreements do not paralyze liberal democratic institutions. Such techniques do not emerge out of the preliminary sense of trust or, even, out of the mere *spirit* of compromise; one can wish to compromise but lack the ability to do so. For instance, surveys indicate that Americans tend to support compromise in principle while opposing *specific* compromises.[15]

Second, Rawls's argument assumes that those who are committed to the constitutional consensus will move toward an overlapping consensus as they deepen their basic attachment to liberal democracy, develop the virtues of reasonableness and the spirit of compromise, and seek to persuade others to adopt their preferred understandings of the political conception of justice. Yet in order for this to be the case, citizens cannot merely be committed to a constitutional consensus; they must also (1) be committed to the more general *ideal* of consensus and (2) recognize the value of making the constitutional consensus more substantial. Just as we cannot assume that a person who treats a particular person with respect necessarily has the more general disposition to treat people with respect, we cannot assume that the commitment to a *particular* consensus necessarily indicates a commitment to the more general ideal of consensus.

In short, we have reason to doubt the ability of a constitutional consensus to sustain itself, as well as its ability to encourage citizens to seek an even more substantial consensus. Rawls presumes in quasi-Hegelian fashion that politics will largely "stay put" once it has reached a certain stage of progress. Yet it does not follow from the fact that people have reached a certain level of "consciousness" that the only way forward is "up"; they can also go back "down." Rawls underestimates the possibility of *regression* – that "near-just

---

[14] This does not preclude the possibility that those constitutional disagreements might also, in turn, be symptomatic of the animosity between US liberals and conservatives.

[15] Amy Gutmann and Dennis Thompson, *The Spirit of Compromise: Why Governing Demands It and Campaigning Undermines It* (Princeton: Princeton University Press, 2012), 25–27.

societies" can become less just, rather than more nearly just, and that liberal public cultures can turn illiberal.

On the Overlapping Consensus

Given the constitutional consensus' difficulties, it seems that we would be better off trying to discern how liberal democracy can secure "the basics," rather than how liberal democracy can attain higher standards of legitimacy by means of an overlapping consensus. Yet it is unclear whether it is worth pursuing the overlapping consensus in the first place. This is because the overlapping consensus would likely suppress citizens' differences and disagreements.

Rawls maintains that, under the Ideal of Public Reason, citizens can enhance their ability to reach a shared understanding of the political conception of justice by observing a distinction between "private" and "public" justifications. By not referencing their particular comprehensive doctrines in public discourse, citizens are empowered with a "common currency of discussion"[16] that allows them to sidestep metaphysical disputes. They can focus on interpreting freedom and equality together and not get sidetracked by disputes over whose religion is true.

Yet is it not just as likely that this distinction will *undermine* the development of such a shared understanding? The issue is that this distinction can undermine the capacity of citizens to discern *why* their fellow citizens understand the political conception of justice in the manners that they do. For instance, the distinction makes it harder to understand why a Catholic might endorse democratic socialism, and a Calvinist, libertarianism. The reason for this is simple: to abstain from referencing one's comprehensive doctrine or particular interests is to *hide* the background influences that inform how one understands the political conception of justice. By Rawls's own admission, "different social and economic interests may be assumed to support different liberal conceptions. The differences between conceptions express, in part, a conflict between these interests."[17] So, the distinction might make it harder for the Catholic to understand how the Calvinist's adherence to the doctrine of predestination informs the Calvinist's libertarianism, just as the distinction might make it harder for the Calvinist to understand how the Catholic's adherence to the doctrine of good works informs the Catholic's socialism.

This mutual ignorance makes it harder for citizens to recognize that they each adhere to some member of a family of reasonable conceptions of justice. Unable to access one another's background influences, citizens will find it easier to judge one another as guilty of faulty reasoning or, worse still, of opposing liberal democracy. The Catholic socialist might conclude that the Calvinist libertarian does not take equality seriously, while the Calvinist libertarian might conclude that the Catholic socialist does not take freedom seriously.

---

[16] Rawls, *PL*, 165. [17] Rawls, *PL*, 167.

This is no trifle matter, for the distinction is supposed to regulate how citizens "engage in political advocacy in the public forum ... [and even] how citizens are to vote in elections when constitutional essentials and matters of basic justice are at stake"[18] – in other words, when it is perhaps *most vital* that citizens understand where they each come from.

Now, Rawls does maintain that in such circumstances, citizens may appeal to their comprehensive doctrines to demonstrate that their comprehensive doctrines do conform to the political conception of justice. A Christian can explain how his or her faith conforms to the political conception of justice. Yet by virtue of referencing their comprehensive doctrines, citizens risk losing access to that common currency of discussion unless those references are fleeting and sparse ... and those references can only be fleeting and short if citizens already largely agree. The more they disagree, the more they must resort to this exception to the rule.

The Rawlsian might object that the "private sphere" can actually help alleviate these difficulties. Even though citizens usually should not reference their particular comprehensive doctrines and interests when discussing the political conception of justice in public, they may reference those comprehensive doctrines and interests when discussing the political conception of justice in private – not just in the home and among friends but also in non-political associations like churches and universities.[19]

The ability of the private sphere to perform this function, however, is strictly limited. First, associations can only play this role if the range of different understandings of the political conception of justice present in these associations approximates the range of perspectives that exists in the citizenry at large. That is, one can only gain a sense of where adherents of other understandings of the political conception of justice "come from" when they are actually represented in one's associations. If those perspectives are absent from one's associations – as they often are, given the tendency of voluntary associations to be characterized by various forms of homogeneity[20] – then one cannot develop a better sense of those perspectives there.

---

[18] Rawls, *PL*, 215.   [19] Rawls, *PL*, 215.

[20] Brad Christerson and Michael Emerson, "The Costs of Diversity in Religious Organizations: An In-Depth Case Study," *Sociology of Religion* 64(2) (2003): 163–181; Kevin D. Dougherty, "How Monochromatic Is Church Membership? Racial-Ethnic Diversity in Religious Community," *Sociology of Religion* 64(1) (2003): 65–85; Jason Kaufmann, *For the Common Good? American Civic Life in the Golden Age of Fraternity* (Oxford: Oxford University Press, 2002); Miller McPhearson and Lynn Smith-Lovin, "Women and Weak Ties: Differences by Sex in the Size of Voluntary Organizations," *Journal of Sociology* 87(4) (1982): 883–904; Miller McPhearson and Lynn Smith-Lovin, "Sex Segregation in Voluntary Associations," *American Sociological Review* 51(1) (1986): 61–79; Miller McPhearson, Lyn Smith-Lovin, and James M. Cook, "Birds of a Feather: Homophily in Social Networks," *Annual Review of Sociology* 27 (2001): 415–444; Thomas Rotolo, "A Time to Join, a Time to Quit: The Influence of Life Cycle Transitions on Voluntary Association Membership," *Social Forces* 78(3) (2000): 1133–1161; Michael A. Stoll, "Race, Neighborhood Poverty, and Participation in Voluntary Associations," *Sociological Forum* 16(3) (2001): 529–557.

Second, even if the range of understandings of the political conception of justice present in those associations *do* accurately reflect the range of perspectives that exist in the citizenry at large, it is unclear whether those associations are realistic forums to discuss the political conception of justice. As Mark Warren notes, "voluntary social associations" like clubs and churches that are easy to exit tend to be internally homogeneous because their survival depends on the *absence* of disagreement. Not only do dissenters often find it easier simply to leave; "Every utterance in purely social situations tends to communicate cognitive content as well as numerous signals and reassurances that reproduce the social relation. For this reason, disagreements on the cognitive level are more likely to spill over into the reproduction of social relations."[21] So, the more diverse a non-political association is, the *less likely* that association can serve as a forum where citizens discuss politics without disbanding. As an example, in amateur sports clubs, white athletes certainly ought to listen to Black athletes' concerns over racial injustice. Yet in many contexts, there is a practical risk that such efforts by Black athletes to express their concerns will motivate some of their white teammates to simply quit[22] (or force their Black teammates out).[23]

In short, we have good reason to believe that Rawls's pursuit of an overlapping consensus to regulate difference and disagreement "aims too high," somewhat at the expense of securing the humbler goal of safeguarding basic liberal democracy. What if, however, an alternative take on discursive democratic politics can succeed where Rawls's vision falters?

JÜRGEN HABERMAS'S DISCURSIVE DEMOCRACY

Habermas proposes an alternative discursive approach that claims to be more inclusive. Underlying his vision is the conviction that "the procedures and communicative presuppositions of democratic opinion- and will-formation

---

[21] Mark Warren, *Democracy and Association* (Princeton: Princeton University Press, 2001), 112.

[22] Some whites might quit out of hostility, but others might do so for less nefarious reasons. Some researchers find that white liberals who care about racial injustice often (ironically) abstain from such conversations in order to preemptively avoid the possibility that they might say or do anything that might be taken as racist. See *The Cambridge Handbook of the Psychology of Prejudice*, ed. Chris G. Sibley and Fiona Kate Barlow (Cambridge: Cambridge University Press, 2016), 267–294.

[23] There might be times when transparent discussions are more plausible. During the mass 2020 protests against anti-black racism, a substantial amount of transparent discourse about racial injustice took place. However, there is evidence indicating that white Americans' support for the Black Lives Matter movement has since waned, suggesting that such transparent discussions are often difficult to sustain, save (as we shall see in Chapter 7) in some "special forums." See Michael Tesler, "Support For Black Lives Matter Surged during Protests, but Is Waning among White Americans," *FiveThirtyEight*, August 19, 2020, https://fivethirtyeight.com/fea tures/support-for-black-lives-matter-surged-during-protests-but-is-waning-among-white-ameri cans/.

function [are] the most important sluices for the discursive rationalization of the decisions of a government and an administration bound by law and statute."[24] According to Habermas, citizens should engage in *informal* deliberation over how they ought to address "problems affecting society as a whole."[25] The provisional results of those discussions should then be formally institutionalized through elections and legislation.

Habermas argues that citizens should engage in informal deliberation in civil society:

> Civil society is composed of those more or less spontaneously emergent associations, organizations, and movements that, attuned to how societal problems resonate in the private life spheres, distill and transmit such reactions in amplified form to the public sphere. The core of civil society comprises a network of associations that institutionalizes problem-solving discourses on questions of general interest ... [There,] citizens ... seek acceptable interpretations for their social interactions and experiences and ... want to have an influence on institutionalized opinion- and will-formation.[26]

Although deliberations here are spontaneous, civil society works best when it is regulated by the ideals of "communicative action." Under these ideals, all participants have an equal chance to initiate speech acts, to question, and to open debate; all have the right to question what topics are discussed; and all have the right to question the very rules of discourse and the ways those rules are enacted.[27] The more civil society embodies these procedural ideals, the more citizens can shape one another's opinions and wills – that is, the reasons for why they support certain things, and what they would like to achieve together – in manners befitting their equal citizenship. More than that, citizens can deliberate *with full access to their comprehensive doctrines and identities*, without observing any "gag rules" that "depend on received distinctions between private and public spheres":[28] "There is no *prima facie* rule limiting the agenda or the conversation, nor the identity of the participants, as long as each excluded person or group can justifiably show that they are relevantly affected by the proposed norms under question."[29]

As a result, citizens can arrive at (and constantly revise) a shared impartial viewpoint on how to act politically. This viewpoint does not represent some thick Rousseauian ethical consensus or comprehensive doctrine that all citizens are forced to share. Rather, this viewpoint incorporates the input of a plurality

---

[24] Jürgen Habermas, "Three Normative Models of Democracy" in *The Inclusion of the Other: Studies in Political Theory*, ed. Ciaran Cronin and Pablo De Greiff (Cambridge, MA: The MIT Press, 2000), 249–250.

[25] Habermas, "Three Normative Models," 249.

[26] Jürgen Habermas, *Between Facts and Norms*, trans. William Rehg (Cambridge, MA: The MIT Press, 1996), 367. [Hereafter Habermas, *BFN*.]

[27] Seyla Benhabib, "Toward a Deliberative Model of Democratic Democracy" in *Democracy and Difference*, ed. Seyla Benhabib (Princeton: Princeton University Press, 1996), 31.

[28] Habermas, *BFN*, 309.   [29] Benhabib, "Toward a Deliberative Model," 31.

of "forms of life, subcultures, and worldviews" and does not "implicitly prejudice the agenda in favor of an inherited background of settled traditions." The formation of this viewpoint thereby promotes "social integration" across difference.[30]

This deliberation, however, is informal; its (provisional) results are not binding in the way that laws are binding. So, these results must be institutionalized through the formal decision-making processes of the political sphere like elections and legislation: "Informal opinion-formation result in institutionalized election decisions [i.e., communicative power] and legislative decrees through which communicatively generated power is transformed into administratively utilizable power." The solidarity citizens share is, as a result, "developed through widely expanded autonomous public spheres as well as through legally institutionalized procedures of democratic deliberation and decision making."[31] When citizens believe that they had a hand in shaping the law together, they are more inclined to abide by it.

The success of Habermas's brand of discursive democracy hinges upon whether civil society can indeed operate as a "third sphere" of society that is autonomous from the market and the state.[32] That is, civil society must be protected from the pressures of the market and from the administrative power of the state (e.g., the military industrial complex) so that it (civil society) can be regulated by the ideals of communicative action to the greatest extent possible.[33] Only so can citizens who have access to their comprehensive doctrines and identities engage in frank and safe conversations as equals without fear that they will be punished for expressing their initial opinions, and only so can these conversations actually inform formal decision making. If civil society is not protected in this manner, then the political sphere will become "colonized"[34] by the state and the market, and many citizens will feel that the law does not reflect their input. These citizens will then have less reason (besides the threat of coercion) to abide by the law, and they will not share in solidarity.

Habermas's discursive democracy is attractive on multiple fronts. First, it promises frank, fair, and respectful deliberation across difference *without* preemptively excluding anyone. Second, by allowing participants in civil society to reference their comprehensive doctrines and identities, discursive democracy provides the space necessary for citizens to express the *sources* of many of their differences and disagreements – to demonstrate "where they each come from." Therefore, Habermas's discursive democracy appears, at first glance, to sidestep some of the problems that emerge from Rawls's distinction between private and

---

[30] Habermas, *BFN*, 209, 368.   [31] Habermas, "Three Normative Models," 249.

[32] Note that, for Habermas, the political sphere consists of formal deliberative bodies (e.g., legislatures), whereas the state consists of bureaucratic and administrative power.

[33] Habermas, "Three Normative Models," 249.

[34] Jürgen Habermas, *The Theory of Communicative Action, Vol. One: Reason and the Rationalization of Society* (Boston: Beacon Press, 1984), 73–74.

public justification. Still, I worry that Habermas's vision does not contain adequate resources to ensure that civil society can be as inclusive as he intends, to prevent the state and the market from dominating civil society, and to make sure that civil societal deliberations inform formal decision making.

We can begin to see why this is the case by noting what it would take to ensure that civil society is inclusive. Habermas notes that his vision of civil society demands that the state guarantee basic negative rights: freedom of assembly and speech, freedom to form voluntary associations, freedom of the press, freedom of political actors to interact with civil society (to remain sensitive to public opinion), and the right to privacy. However, he recognizes that civil society itself must also be "energetic" and capable of "reproduc[ing] and stabiliz[ing] itself from its own resources."[35] Most obviously, in order for civil society to reproduce itself, it must actually comprise private (non-economic) associations – and ones that are oriented toward collective reflections on the shared impartial viewpoint, not just toward the enjoyment of shared interests (e.g., clubs). More fundamentally, citizens must be capable of actually supporting civil society. Rather than merely pursue their private economic interests without regard to how their behaviour affects the health of civil society, citizens must, by and large, "know they are involved in the *common* enterprise of reconstituting and maintaining structures of the public sphere as they contest opinions and strive for influence ... they directly influence the political system, but at the same time they are also reflexively concerned with revitalizing and enlarging civil society and the public sphere."[36] Accordingly, given that civil society can only fulfill its legitimizing function if it is shaped by a wide plurality of viewpoints and identities, citizens must also be concerned with supporting broad inclusion.

What this means is that the psychological demands of supporting a civil society that is capable of reproducing itself are in fact more rigorous than the demands of supporting Rawls's overlapping consensus. As we have seen, the overlapping consensus demands that people set aside the metaphysical particulars of their comprehensive doctrines for the sake of constructive discourse. Habermas criticizes such "gag rules" for inevitably reflecting received intuitions about the boundaries between public and private, and of being unduly hegemonic.

Given that Habermas intends for civil societal deliberations to generate a shared *impartial* viewpoint on how to act politically, however, citizens must not merely be committed to inclusion; they must also be capable of setting aside their biases when evaluating alternative positions, despite the fact that they might still maintain those biases – *and* despite the fact that they might know, given the absence of gag rules, that their fellow citizens maintain such biases as well. After all, as realists eagerly note, people have a range of irrational and

[35] Habermas, *BFN*, 369.   [36] Habermas, *BFN*, 369–370.

non-rational motivations that are not easily wished away: for instance, subconscious insecurities, passion, anger, hatred, the desire to dominate, and the urge to destroy.[37] Therefore, so long as these psychological features persist, in order for civil society to fulfill its legitimizing function, citizens must be able to set aside these distorting influences when evaluating alternative positions. Yet doing so can prove difficult. Those who deny minorities or gays equal respect or recognition will likely find it difficult to respect the human dignity of minorities or gays in the context of civil societal deliberations. Likewise, minorities and gays might not so easily set aside the anger or hurt they feel toward those whose behaviour continuously offends. So, whereas Rawls's gag rules risk unwittingly privileging hegemonic perspectives and identities, Habermas's rejection of these rules risks fuelling animosities that can make it more difficult to afford one another impartial consideration.

This challenge goes to suggest that Habermas's vision of civil society presumes broad reasonableness. In order to secure an inclusive environment where people feel comfortable discussing matters of general concern openly and with explicit reference to their comprehensive doctrines and identities, either people must have a certain *reasonable psychology* – kindness, openness, and intellectual curiosity – to consider arguments and statements with neither prejudice nor emotional involvement, despite their comprehensive doctrines and identities; or their comprehensive doctrines and identities must predispose them to such fair-mindedness. Put differently, Habermas's vision might eschew gag rules, but it seems to depend on the fact that citizens are already reasonable. There is no need for gag rules when there is no need to gag.

In the absence of such widespread reasonableness, two worrying scenarios emerge. First, some citizens – likely, the marginalized, or those who fall outside the mainstream of "settled tradition" – risk being excluded from informal deliberations. So, even if those deliberations inform formal political decisions, these citizens will not feel that the law reflects their input, and they will not share in any social integration that emerges from those deliberations. Second, informal deliberations might simply shut down because the privileged and the marginalized alike do not feel comfortable engaging with such a wide range of difference directly. Civil society will then collapse, in which case the political sphere will be easily colonized by the dictates of the state and the pressures of the market. As in the first scenario, the marginalized – in fact, anyone who feels left out or left behind by the militarized capitalist order that would follow – will feel that the law does not reflect their input, and social integration will not emerge.

Habermas recognizes these dangers. He proposes a path to promote inclusion and to reassert the salience of civil society in contexts where citizens are not

---

[37] William Galston, "Realism in Political Theory," *European Journal of Political Theory* 9(4) (2010): 385–411.

reasonable. Specifically, he maintains that civil disobedience can help reassert civil society in times when the "political centre" ignores civil society and when the state and the market threaten to colonize the political sphere. Pointing to anti-nuclear, ecological, and anti-poverty movements, among others, Habermas stipulates that civil society groups can reclaim their own relevance by instigating crises in the name of the constitutional order's foundational principles. By engaging in "sensational actions, mass protests, and incessant campaigning,"[38] these groups might seem to violate the very norms that promise to yield a shared impartial viewpoint amidst conditions of pluralism. Nonetheless, given that steep hierarchies of power do exist, it is through such expressive – indeed, *emotive* – acts[39] that these groups can expose how laws do not live up to the constitutional principles of the democratic community, and win approval of "the gallery." In the face of such pressure, the political center must pay attention to civil society and marginalized voices, not just big money, the state, and hegemonic social groups. Civil disobedience, in short, can help prevent the political sphere from becoming detached from civil society and ensure that political decisions reflect the input of a broad range of citizens. So, even if the interactions that follow result in compromise ("some combination of fairness and workability")[40] rather than in an impartial viewpoint, the law becomes more legitimate. Since more citizens feel that the law incorporates their input, social integration becomes possible once again.[41]

Habermas's accommodation of civil disobedience is welcome because it recognizes that even if social integration is the objective, contestation is required to promote inclusion and reduce social hierarchies. This is an insight that democratic realists emphasize and that I will incorporate into my account of role-based constitutional fellowship. So, Habermas's discussion here reveals that discursive democracy has a realistic edge that its critics often overlook.

Still, my worry here is that Habermas's vision does not contain the resources to cultivate the basic unity required to ensure that civil disobedience does not inspire backlash and instigate a spiral of escalating contestation. In order for

---

[38] Habermas, *BFN*, 381.

[39] Stephen K. White and Evan Robert Farr, "'No-Saying' in Habermas," *Political Theory* 40(1) (2012): 46.

[40] White and Farr, "'No-Saying' in Habermas," 42.

[41] Note that White and Farr advance a different understanding of Habermas's goals. According to White and Farr, Habermas is keenly aware not just of the fact that there is a "gap" between positive law and legitimacy but also of the fact that new claims, identities, and settings are constantly emerging and disturbing existing notions of legitimacy. So Habermas's goal is *not* to overcome the gap and realize an impartial viewpoint, but rather to urge us to recognize that contexts constantly change and that people must always encounter sources of dissensus, if the general will is to incorporate everyone's input. Seen in this light, civil disobedience is just as central to Habermas's vision as informal deliberation: civil disobedience is not a way to get rational discussion back on track, but rather a way to ensure that people do encounter dissensus. See White and Farr, "'No-Saying' in Habermas," 40ff.

civil disobedience to function in the manner described earlier, a sense of basic unity must already exist between people who employ civil disobedience (i.e., the marginalized) and people whom those acts of civil disobedience are intended to influence (i.e., the dominant). First, the marginalized must believe that it is indeed worth becoming (alongside the dominant) more equal partners in the effort to shape the law, and that the dominant are not so irredeemably bad that separation is necessary. Second, the dominant must already consider the marginalized equal members of the community to some extent. In the absence of such sentiments, the marginalized would be more inclined to engage in acts of disruption for the sake of divorce, rather than for the sake of pursuing greater inclusion.[42] Likewise, acts of civil disobedience (or disruption) would prompt the dominant to (re-)assert their dominance, rather than to help promote greater inclusion.[43] Indeed, the dominant might become more willing to undermine basic liberal democracy, and drift toward authoritarianism.

By incorporating civil disobedience, Habermas's vision therefore presupposes a more basic sense of unity to hold citizens together when the more robust social integration he aspires toward is lacking or unduly exclusive. Yet does Habermas's vision of democracy contain resources to generate that basic sense of unity? I submit that Habermas's vision does not. Certainly, Habermas acknowledges the historical contingency of his vision, that it is only plausible in conditions where "liberal patterns of political culture" are already established through historical happenstance: "The development of such lifeworld structures can certainly be stimulated, but for the most part they elude legal regulation, administrative control, or political steering. Meaning is a scarce resource that cannot be regenerated or propagated as one likes."[44] However, in the absence of basic unity, it is unclear what can help promote those liberal patterns, besides historical happenstance. More than that, it is unclear whether Habermas's vision of democracy contains resources that can help sustain those patterns during periods of stress – particularly, when the marginalized feel compelled to appeal to civil disobedience or disruption more and more, and when the dominant aim to reassert their dominance. In short, even if Habermas's vision of democracy can potentially *deepen* any basic unity citizens might share into his more robust brand of social integration, Habermas's vision leaves open the question of how that basic unity can arise in the first place. (Note that Habermas does offer a supplementary theory of *constitutional*

---

[42] Following the passages of the 1964 Civil Rights Act and the 1965 Voting Rights Act, which dealt heavy blows to *de jure* segregation, African Americans began gravitating toward more non-conciliatory movements in part because they deemed the white majority (including Northern liberals) uninterested in tackling *de facto* segregation.

[43] Indeed, white supremacists assassinated several civil rights activists, including Martin Luther King Jr.

[44] Habermas, *BFN*, 358–359.

patriotism that provides some answers to this question. In Chapter 4, I cast doubt on constitutional patriotism.)

Given the shortcomings of both Rawls and Habermas's visions, we can say that discursive approaches to difference and disagreement aim too high at the expense of articulating convincing accounts of how to secure basic liberal democracy. Both, in different ways, presume that politics will largely stay put once it has reached a certain stage of progress. Insofar as citizens should be encouraged to feel a sense of unity, we should focus on describing how that sense of unity can be structured so that it can secure basic liberal democracy.

What if securing liberal democracy does not require a sense of unity, let alone consensus? What if it is better to simply allow institutionalized competition and contestation to run their course? Let us now turn our attention to three realist arguments that advance this claim.

DEMOCRATIC REALISM

Realists argue that disagreement is "the essence of politics"[45] and, in explicit opposition to Rawls and Habermas, deny the possibility that citizens can ever reach consensus, even on fundamental issues like the value of liberal democracy. These issues are "[not] philosophical matters that are to be settled in some sense prior to politics,"[46] and we cannot expect anything close to full compliance. "Political theory," William Galston maintains, "must not assume that the motivation or capacity to act in a principled manner is pervasive among all members of a political community."[47]

Accordingly, realists tend to claim that citizens are akin to "strangers who find themselves locked in a very large room together ... moral strangers ... united *only* by the shared circumstances of inhabiting a common political jurisdiction ... [by] happenstance."[48] This does not necessarily mean that realists wish for citizens to never cooperate and to engage in no-holds-barred competition and contestation. However, it does mean that realists tend to encourage citizens to view themselves, at most, as morally responsible fellow travellers, rather than as people who share a lot of substantive goals and commitments. Unsurprisingly, then, realists deem it more vital to discern what sorts of institutions can channel competition and contestation to serve liberal democracy. Indeed, Jacob Levy observes that wealthy democracies have

---

[45] Bernard Williams, *In the Beginning Was the Deed: Realism and Moralism in Political Argument*, ed. Geoffrey Williams (Princeton: Princeton University Press, 2005), 17.
[46] Matt Sleat, "Liberal Realism: A Liberal Response to the Realist Critique," *The Review of Politics* 73(3) (2011): 473.
[47] Galston, "Realism in Political Theory," 395.
[48] Jacob Levy, "Against Fraternity: Democracy without Solidarity" in *The Strains of Commitment: The Political Sources of Solidarity in Diverse Societies*, ed. Keith Banting and Will Kymlicka (Oxford: Oxford University Press, 2017), 108.

become increasingly inclusive *as a result of* – and *not* in spite of – institutional-ized political partisanship:

The expansion of the franchise has routinely been driven by partisan contestation: a winning party enfranchises a pool of voters who it thinks will disproportionately support it: propertyless white males, African-Americans, the working class, women, 18-year-olds, and so on. This has most often been the party aligned with the group's underlying political preferences; it has occasionally been another party that sees the enfranchisement as inevitable and hopes to win political gratitude from the previously excluded. (Think of the lowering of the American voting age to 18 under Richard Nixon.) In either case, the franchise has *not* typically been extended on the basis of the universalistic solidarity among citizens.[49]

In short, we should stop striving "for a unity that is deeper than we should really hope for" and instead settle for "organized disunity."[50]

Realists are right to remind us of the importance of institutions. Indeed, some discursive democrats share this sentiment, arguing that we should focus on *institutional* trust rather than *interpersonal* trust. Citizens who do not judge one another as sometimes motivated or competent to act in one another's interests can nonetheless come to believe that their shared institutions do further their respective interests. Citizens who do not trust one another can trust institutions to fairly adjudicate potential cases of force and fraud, or to provide public goods.[51]

Still, this perspective relies heavily on a certain faith that modern liberal democratic procedures will continue to "regulate disagreement" in a manner conducive to stability, peace, and justice. Unsurprisingly, the notion of organized disunity reminds us of *Federalist 10*, where James Madison argues that addressing the problem of faction requires us to manage the *effects* of faction through smart institutional design – not to eliminate the causes of faction.[52] Yet even if institutions can help organize disunity and bolster trust in the liberal democratic system as a whole, institutional trust and the ability of institutions to play this role depend on interpersonal trust. Indeed, dysfunctional insti-tutions are often symptomatic of a lack of interpersonal trust. As voter sup-pression, the campaign finance crisis, and gerrymandering in the United States indicate, a lack of interpersonal trust frequently leads to a willingness to rig institutions for one's partisan group. This, in turn, makes it more likely that other political actors who would normally abstain from such actions will respond in turn.

Likewise, fixing institutional imbalances usually requires a willingness to compromise and find common ground. In the absence of interpersonal trust, it

---

[49] Levy, "Against Fraternity," 117.   [50] Levy, "Against Fraternity," 116–122.
[51] Mark Warren, "Trust and Democracy" in *The Oxford Handbook of Social and Political Trust*, ed. Eric M. Uslaner (Oxford: Oxford University Press, 2018), 75–94.
[52] Alexander Hamilton, John Jay, and James Madison, *The Federalist*, ed. George W. Carey and James McClellan (Indianapolis: Liberty Fund, 2001), 42–49.

is futile to expect majorities to "do the right thing." For example, even though US Democrats have long complained about Republican gerrymandering, Maryland Democrats retaliated by pulling off one of the most aggressive gerrymanders in US history when presented with the opportunity. Revealingly, despite Madison's argument in favour of institutionalized competition, John Jay remarks in *Federalist* 2 that it is possible to pursue a government of the sort envisioned by Madison precisely because "[p]rovidence has been pleased to give this one connected country, to one united people; a people descended from the same ancestors, speaking the same language, professing the same religion, attached to the same principles of government, very similar in their manners and customs."[53]

We therefore have good preliminary reasons to believe that the realist vision amounts somewhat to a *hope* that competition and contestation, channelled through smartly designed institutions, can continue producing positive results. Let us now probe this insight further by considering two iterations of this general perspective: "soft" and "hard" agonism.

Soft Agonism

Soft agonists like Connolly and McCarthy advocate for a politics of "pluralization."[54] The collective demand for recognition by the oppressed can *pressure* the powerful into developing empathy and revising their identities in an inclusive direction.

At the foundation of this perspective is a critique of Rawls and Habermas's implicit understanding of rationality. Rawls and Habermas seem to believe that people's comprehensive doctrines and collective self-understandings are largely formulated rationally. As long as people observe the distinction between private and public justification (Rawls) or have a safe forum where they can engage in critical deliberation (Habermas), people can consider alternative positions impartially, free from contextual skews and personal biases. In opposition, soft agonists maintain that "rational" deliberations are inevitably embedded in fluid, *contentious* environments where people understand their identities in terms of how they differ from others.[55] Rational discourse is not so much a resource that people use to formulate their comprehensive doctrines and to pursue consensus, as it is a resource that the powerful employ, knowingly or unknowingly, to construe "others" as "irrational," and their own identity and

---

[53] Hamilton et al., *Federalist*, 6.

[54] William E. Connolly, *The Ethos of Pluralization* (Minneapolis: University of Minnesota Press, 1995), xiv.

[55] William E. Connolly, *Identity\Difference: Democratic Negotiations of Political Paradox: Expanded Edition* (Minneapolis: University of Minnesota Press, 2002), 64. [Hereafter Connolly, *I\D*.]

values as "rational" – the impartial, timeless results of correct reasoning.[56] For example, Connolly points to how both the American Left and Right in the 1950s understood homosexuality to be a defect. With the former understanding homosexuality to be a sickness, and the latter, a moral fault, the left and right merely differed over the means through which this deviance should be addressed; the former favoured doctors, and the latter, the church and the police.

Soft agonists maintain that the only way to rectify such domination is for the oppressed to join and pressure the powerful into recognizing their marginalized identities. Connolly recognizes the possibility that the oppressed might "decline into warring fragments." However, according to him, as the oppressed come to recognize that identity formation consists of differentiation, they will increasingly recognize that the majority has conspired to demonize or ignore them – that for all their differences, they suffer from related crimes, strive for recognition, and can only win recognition by standing together. In Connolly's words, members of different oppressed groups can come to share in "an ethos from multiple sources ... a majority assemblage" whereby they support one another's objectives for various reasons:

[A] majority assemblage is a mobile constellation in which some support the programs in question out of dire economic need, some out of particular self-interest, some because they are implicated with others who need these programs, some because they endorse such programs in exchange for assemblage support for others ethnically or materially crucial to them, some because they believe that the negatives of steep inequality will eventually undermine the good life they now participate in, some because they seek to meet responsibilities flowing from this or that creed, and most out of some mixture of these diverse considerations.[57]

The oppressed can thereby reveal to the powerful that identity formation is indeed a process of antagonistic differentiation, and prompt the powerful into developing new lenses through which they view other perspectives – lenses defined by humility, empathy, and respect. In short, the dynamics of unmanaged pluralism offer the possibility of an *agonistic* politics whereby society is transformed into a "collective assemblage," defined by "a democratic ethos of generalized respect for multifarious ways of being,"[58] that acts in the name of expanding recognition.

The soft agonistic perspective is compelling at first glance because its foundational conception of epistemic truth is plausible. The doctrine of impartial rationality seems suspect when we consider the plethora of definitions of "common sense" which have existed across history. Values and identities are likely not, a priori, waiting to be discovered, but rather *generated* by people in

---

[56] Thomas McCarthy, "The Critique of Impure Reason: Foucault and the Frankfurt School," *Political Theory* 18(3) (1990): 438.

[57] Connolly, *The Ethos of Pluralization*, 95.   [58] Connolly, *The Ethos of Pluralization*, 94–96.

response to contingent contexts – specific individual experiences, cultures, understandings of history, material circumstances, and the like.[59] So, as Iris Marion Young notes, "blindness to difference ... perpetuates cultural imperialism by allowing norms expressing the point of view and experience of privileged groups to appear neutral and universal ... [and] often produces an internalized devaluation by members of ... [underprivileged] groups."[60] In addition, as I shall note when developing my notion of role-based constitutional fellowship, the privileged and the dominant often pretend that undue hierarchies do not exist, so forceful exertions of power by the underprivileged and the oppressed are vital in the general effort to redress those hierarchies.

Still, there is good reason to believe that this perspective underestimates the need to actively cultivate a sense of unity, both (1) between the oppressed and the dominant *and* (2) among the oppressed themselves. First, soft agonism prescribes a politics of pluralization *while* accepting the basic legitimacy of the liberal democratic framework. So, in order for the oppressed to embark on this brand of power politics, not only must they feel sufficiently oppressed; they must also have enough faith in the liberal democratic framework so as to be inclined to seek greater recognition *within* that framework. This implies that the oppressed must be willing to practice self-restraint so as to not jeopardize the survival of liberal democracy. Yet whether they will practice this self-restraint depends on whether their oppressors do respond in the desired manners. If the oppressed feel *too* oppressed – and if their oppressors seem intransigent – then they might conclude that reconciliation is not possible and that there are no viable paths to pursue greater recognition within the liberal democratic framework. They might even conclude that liberal democracy is actually *the problem*. For instance, deeming more moderate reforms like the Civil Rights Act and the Voting Rights Act inadequate responses to racial and economic injustice, African American revolutionary parties and nationalist groups encouraged African Americans to violently overthrow the capitalist system.[61] Therefore, insofar as soft agonism accepts the basic legitimacy of

---

[59] Note, however, that Rawls might deny that he does in fact adhere to an a priori conception of human rationality. Given his constructivism and contractarianism, Rawls might counter that, under his scheme, the political conception of justice is indeed rooted in a society's particular public political culture and, thus, varies from society to society.

[60] Iris Marion Young, *Justice and the Politics of Difference* (Princeton: Princeton University Press, 2011), 165–166.

[61] Garret Albert Duncan. *Encyclopaedia Britannica*, s.v. "Black Panther Party." Chicago: Encyclopedia Britannica, 2018. www.britannica.com/topic/Black-Panther-Party (accessed August 17, 2018). In Chapter 7, I shall argue that these more radical approaches do have roles to play in the effort to identify and rectify injustices, but only as parts of a broader division of labour *alongside* more conciliatory approaches.

the liberal democratic framework and aims to work within it, its proscribed politics of pluralization jeopardizes that framework.[62]

Second, a politics of pluralization relies on the development of a shared ethos or majority assemblage among the oppressed. However, the way in which identities are constituted hinders the development of such a shared ethos. Here are just three such obstacles:

(a) In order to develop a shared ethos, the oppressed must identify a common source of their grievances – something against which they can unite. However, members of different oppressed groups might (rightfully or wrongfully) identify different sources of their grievances. Members of the LGBTQ+ community might identify the heterosexual majority as the cause of its grievances, but this does not imply that members of an oppressed religion, race, or culture will identify the heterosexual majority as the source of their respective grievances. Indeed, in the United States, arguably the most oppressed racial-ethnic group (African Americans) has consistently lagged behind other racial-ethnic groups in its support for same-sex marriage.[63] Members of an oppressed religion might identify the exclusivist majority religion as the problem instead, just as racial-ethnic minorities might identify the racial-ethnic majority. This means that the given oppressed identity might fail to have the *numbers* required to forcefully demand recognition. Different oppressed groups might identify different oppressors and demand recognition from those oppressors – but not together.

(b) People often identify with powerful *and* oppressed identities simultaneously. A poor, straight Christian African American man might identify with both powerful and oppressed identities: as a straight Christian man, he is powerful; yet as a poor African American, he is oppressed.[64] This

---

[62] This is not to say that the oppressed are unjustified in losing hope in the possibility of reconciliation and in liberal democracy. However, the soft agonist vision aims to both encourage such power politics and preserve liberal democracy. So, this possibility is a problem.

[63] A Pew Research Center survey indicates that, between 2007 and 2017, African Americans were 10–15 percent less likely than whites and Hispanics to support same-sex marriage. ("Support for Same-Sex Marriage Grows, Even Among Groups that Had Been Skeptical," Pew Research Center: U.S. Politics & Policy, June 26, 2017, www.people-press.org/2017/06/26/support-for-same-sex-marriage-grows-even-among-groups-that-had-been-skeptical/ (accessed August 17, 2018).)

[64] It can be argued that this overlap between powerful and oppressed identities manifests itself in electoral results (at least in the US context). For example, in the 2016 US presidential election, race was the most significant predictor of voting preferences among women. Women of colour voted for Democratic candidate Hillary Clinton at significantly higher rates than their white counterparts ("2016 Election Exit Polls," *The Washington Post*, November 29, 2016, www.washingtonpost.com/graphics/politics/2016-election/exit-polls/.). Assuming that women and racial minorities are more likely victims of oppression than men and whites, and assuming that oppressed identities tend to support the Democratic Party over the Republican Party, it can be

undermines the likelihood of collective action. If people do not primarily identify as members of a handful of groups, but rather as *individuals* who have "authentic" collections of memberships unique to themselves, then their capacity for sustained collective action might diminish.[65] Their identification with others risks being at once many and shallow.

(c) The oppressed might develop particularistic resentments against *one another*. For example, rather than fight their oppressors, different segments of the working class might be manipulated into resenting and fighting one another. Writing about Reconstruction, W. E. B. Du Bois argues that Southern elites successfully employed a "carefully planned and slowly evolved method" to undercut working class solidarity. By affording the white working class a "psychological wage ... public deference and titles of courtesy because they were white," elites "drove such a wedge between the white and Black workers that there probably are not today in the world two groups of workers with practically identical interests who hate and fear each other so deeply and persistently and who are kept so far apart that neither sees anything of common interest."[66]

People, in short, have identities that resemble patchworks; social cleavages cut across various powerful and oppressed identities. These overlaps undermine the development of a shared ethos among the oppressed. So, even if attempts to manage difference and disagreement are counterproductive, soft agonism must concede that the emergence of such a shared ethos cannot be left to chance or unmanaged pluralism alone.

Now, it is possible that in response to this coordination problem, the oppressed might deviate from the soft agonist notion of *unmanaged* pluralism and seek strategies to better ensure that a shared ethos does indeed emerge. For example, following Mouffe and Ernesto Laclau, the oppressed can employ a left populist strategy. By designating a common enemy in "the establishment," the oppressed can unite in a "chain of equivalence." So the theory goes, such a chain preserves their differences, yet also allows them to make their demands more forcefully as "one people," thereby pushing liberal democracy to become more inclusive.[67]

Yet such a populist strategy jeopardizes a key component of the soft agonist vision: the possibility that increased mutual recognition, empathy, and respect

---

argued that white women voted for Clinton at lower rates, in part, because they are both dominant (white) and oppressed (female), rather than simply oppressed (e.g., Black and female).

[65] Mark Lilla, *The Once and Future Liberal: After Identity Politics* (New York: HarperCollins, 2017).

[66] W. E. B. Du Bois, *Black Reconstruction in America*, ed. Henry Louis Gates Jr. (Oxford: Oxford University Press, 2007), xvi.

[67] Chantal Mouffe, *For a Left Populism* (New York: Verso, 2018).

will emerge from confrontation. After all, designating members of privileged and dominant groups members of the establishment – and, by extension, *morally corrupt enemies* – might help unite the oppressed, but it is hardly conducive to mutual recognition. As a result of the contestation that might ensue, their oppressors might make concessions, yet the state of mutual forbearance which would emerge is not the sort of mutual recognition, empathy, and respect envisioned by soft agonists. Rather, as we shall see immediately below, such mutual forbearance is more akin to a stalemate where antagonism bubbles under the surface and where shifts in the balance of power might inspire either side to exert itself, potentially instigating a fresh spiral of mutual aggression.[68]

In short, even if the sorts of disruption soft agonism envisions are necessary to redress undue hierarchies, in order for antagonism to transform into mutual recognition, the oppressed and the dominant need to feel a sense of unity so that they can stick together when the going gets rough. Soft agonism depends on the cultivation of a shared ethos *among* the oppressed, as well as mutual recognition *between* the oppressed and the dominant.

Hard Agonism

Hard agonists like Mouffe agree with the soft agonistic critique of discursive democracy. However, they reject the notion that political confrontation can counterintuitively lead to greater mutual recognition, empathy, and respect. Instead, hard agonists insist that the most we can do is structure political confrontation so that citizens compete as *adversaries* rather than as *enemies*.[69]

Hard agonism draws its conceptual foundations from the writings of Carl Schmitt. It might be tempting to dismiss hard agonism simply on the basis of this association. After all, Schmitt was an unrepentant Nazi. However, hard agonists contend that at least during the Weimar Republic, Schmitt critiqued liberal democracy as a friend of sorts.[70] Indeed, they insist that Schmitt's concepts can be refashioned to further liberal democracy and even progressive

---

[68] Note that such a left populist strategy is not the only possible approach to unite a plurality of oppressed groups. For instance, Çigdem Çidam argues that the practices of political friendship as understood by the likes of Danielle Allen (to be discussed) and Jill Frank can facilitate such cooperation. Yet such an approach effectively concedes that soft agonism depends on political friendship among the oppressed – and still leaves open the question of how unity can emerge *between* the oppressed and the dominant. See Çidam, Çigdem, "Unruly Practices: Gezi Protests and the Politics of Friendship," *New Political Science* 39(3) (2017): 369–392 and Jill Frank, *A Democracy of Distinction* (Chicago: University of Chicago Press, 2005).

[69] Note that my discussion here does not interrogate the full corpus of Mouffe's political theory. For an account of the evolution of her political thought, see Mark Wenman, *Agonistic Democracy: Constituent Power in the Era of Globalisation* (Cambridge: Cambridge University Press, 2013), 180ff.

[70] Ellen Kennedy's introduction to Carl Schmitt, *The Crisis of Parliamentary Democracy*, trans. Ellen Kennedy (Cambridge, MA: The MIT Press, 1986); Gopal Balakrishnan, *The Enemy: An Intellectual Portrait of Carl Schmitt* (New York: Verso, 2000); Andreas Kalyvas, *Democracy*

causes. So, rather than condemn hard agonism merely for its association with Schmitt, I shall demonstrate why it is futile – and dangerous – to pursue such a reformed Schmittianism.

According to Schmitt, the political is structured by a permanent antagonism between "friends" and "enemies." A "state" or "people" is defined not by some shared pursuit of the good life or by a set of economic relations, but rather by its juxtaposition against an existential alien or enemy. One does not necessarily hate one's enemies, and one is not always in a state of *active* warfare. However, the *possibility* of conflict is a permanent condition of politics, so one must always be ready to "negate" the life of the other if necessary.[71] A people denies this reality at its own peril, for the friend–enemy distinction must express itself. If it is not expressed externally, then it will be expressed internally.[72]

Mouffe accepts the necessity of the friend–enemy distinction. However, she maintains that it does not follow that the friend–enemy or us–them distinction must be drawn externally along state borders, nor that the state must be authoritarian.[73] This is because, according to Mouffe, the frontier can instead be drawn internally in a way that both avoids civil war and promotes liberal democracy. The key mechanism to facilitate this is *commonality*: even though political competitors might disagree about how to define liberal democratic principles like freedom and equality,[74] as long as they do accept those principles, they can compete *agonistically* rather than *antagonistically* – as *adversaries* who recognize one another's political legitimacy and who are fellow members of a *conflictual consensus*, rather than as *mere enemies* who aim to destroy one another. For example, they can compete to realize their preferred "interpretations of the ethico-political principles: liberal-conservative, social-democratic, neo-liberal, radical-democratic, and so on."[75] Not only can such an agonistic politics help ensure that marginalized and oppressed voices are not forgotten; it also can enhance liberal democracy's long-term stability. By allowing the friend–enemy distinction to be expressed, hard agonism prevents the *suppression* of that distinction – a suppression that will ultimately result in "an explosion of [even more intense] antagonisms that can tear up the very basis of civility."[76]

---

and the Politics of the Extraordinary: Max Weber, Carl Schmitt, and Hannah Arendt* (Cambridge: Cambridge University Press, 2009).

[71] Carl Schmitt, *The Concept of the Political: Expanded Edition*, trans. George Schwab (Chicago: The University of Chicago Press, 2007), 28ff.

[72] Schmitt, *The Concept of the Political*, 45ff.

[73] Given Schmitt's understanding of liberalism and democracy, which I do not discuss here, some characterize Schmitt as promoting an "anti-liberal presidential democracy." See Reinhard Mehring, "Carl Schmitt and the Politics of Identity" in *Key Thinkers of the Radical Right: Behind the New Threat to Liberal Democracy*, ed. Mark Sedgwick (Oxford: Oxford University Press, 2019), 43.

[74] Chantal Mouffe, *The Democratic Paradox* (New York: Verso, 2000), 104.

[75] Mouffe, *The Democratic Paradox*, 57, 102–103.   [76] Mouffe, *The Democratic Paradox*, 104.

Now, there is great insight in Mouffe's distinction between adversaries and enemies. (Indeed, I incorporate a version of this distinction into my account of role-based constitutional fellowship, except I crucially determine that adversaries must share in a sort of trust to remain adversaries.) Likewise, her argument that citizens will become disillusioned when mainstream political vehicles do not allow them to express their demands and passions is instructive. She attributes the challenges Western liberal democracies currently face – in particular, the resurgence of support for right populist movements – to the fact that mainstream parties have lost the support of many of their historic constituencies:

In many European countries, this [centrist] consensus has led to the implementation of a type of democracy that eliminates anything to do with people's power, the very constituent dimension of the democratic idea. When there's no longer a fundamental difference between the programmes of right and left-wing parties, citizens think their vote won't make a difference. They feel excluded by the elites in power, and that creates a fertile ground for parties that present themselves as the voice of the people against the "Establishment."[77]

We do not need to accept Mouffe's condemnation of centrism – or her wholesale embrace of Schmitt's friend–enemy distinction – to appreciate this insight. If citizens do not feel represented, then democracy will feel more like oligarchy. Indeed, as we shall see, just as role-based constitutional fellowship aims to heed Connolly's advice that social differences must be expressed in some form, fellowship also aims to heed Mouffe's warning that political disagreements cannot be artificially suppressed.

Still, we should reject Mouffe's efforts to refashion Schmitt's authoritarian vision for progressive purposes. First, Mouffe's conflictual consensus is only viable when citizens have already committed themselves to liberal democracy. If citizens do not share such a commitment, then they will consider one another enemies, not adversaries. What this means is that Mouffe's agonistic project, ironically, suffers from an initiation problem reminiscent of that which troubles the Rawlsian and Habermasian projects. How should citizens be encouraged to become committed to liberal democracy? This is a vital question. If hard agonism cannot provide a plausible answer, beyond simply letting history run its course, then its ability to transform political opponents into adversaries can only be a matter of happenstance. It will always threaten to devolve into an explosion of antagonisms that can tear up the very basis of civility. The viability of hard agonism, in short, depends either on a shared *principled* acceptance of liberal democracy (not unlike Rawls and Habermas's visions) or on things that are foreign to itself, such as norms and habits of civility that might have emerged over time.

[77] Iñigo Errejón and Chantal Mouffe, *Podemos: In the Name of the People* (London: Lawrence & Wishart, 2016), 98–99.

Second, commonality does not do enough to prevent the internal frontier from becoming antagonistic rather than agonistic. We can see why this is the case by comparing Schmitt's antagonism with Mouffe's agonism. As we have seen, Schmitt defines the political in essential terms of enmity. He does not develop his conceptual categories by deriving law-like statements from empirical regularities. Instead, he "penetrates empirical variations in group competition ... to discover the ever-present possibility of a deadly conflict in which any or all may eventually fall."[78] Extreme conditions are not worst-case scenarios; they define what is normal: "The exception is more interesting than the rule. The rule proves nothing; the exception proves everything."[79] In Jacques Derrida's words,

As soon as war is possible, it is effectively taking place. Whether the war takes place, whether war is decided upon or declared, is a mere empirical alternative in the face of an essential necessity: war is taking place; it has already begun before it begins, as soon as it is characterized as *eventual* ... And it is *eventual* as soon as it is possible.[80]

So, friends are only ever friends because they have a common enemy.

From an empirical standpoint, Schmitt's analysis is too dichotomous. Warfare might be a latent possibility in all human relations, but it is not the only possibility. So too are the possibilities of indifference, caution, curiosity, cooperation, love, and friendship. "Normal politics" is defined less by possible warfare than by ambiguity – a plurality of possibilities. Even though a polity *can* draw upon external enmity to maintain internal unity, it need not *depend* on external enmity to do so. Citizens can appeal instead to norms, a civic culture, economic relations, religion, associational life, and/or political principles.

We can, however, read Schmitt's theory alternatively as an ideological project that aims to influence how we think, not to make accurate diagnoses. In advancing the friend–enemy or us–them distinction, Schmitt downplays the need to cultivate positive forms of unity and encourages us to *overlook* the resources that might be available to do so. Indeed, even though Schmitt emphasizes the possibility that non-political antagonisms (e.g., religious, moral, economic, aesthetic) can become so strong that they become political antagonisms,[81] Schmitt *obscures* the possibility that non-political resources can be mobilized to cultivate friendship. He makes it seem like the non-political can only be imported to intensify the political antagonism – not to diminish it. The fact that he makes it seem like external enmity is the *only* way to secure

---

[78] Gerald M. Mara, *Between Specters of War and Visions of Peace: Dialogic Political Theory and the Challenges of Politics* (Oxford: Oxford University Press, 2019), 26.

[79] Carl Schmitt, *Political Theology*, trans. George Schwab (Chicago: The University of Chicago Press: 2005), 15.

[80] Jacques Derrida, *The Politics of Friendship*, trans. George Collins (New York: Verso, 2005), 86.

[81] Schmitt, *The Concept of the Political*, 36–37.

internal unity suggests that he intends for the distinction to facilitate certain ideological goals – namely an authoritarian government that can do what it takes to maintain public order and realize the will of the people, including by suspending the constitution.[82]

The trouble with hard agonism thereby emerges. On the one hand, it maintains Schmitt's ideological binary – the friend–enemy distinction. On the other hand, by insisting upon an internal frontier, hard agonism robs that distinction of its capacity to unify; the friend–enemy distinction now describes the relations of different groups of citizens, not the relations between different peoples.[83] So, agonism imports Schmitt's antagonism into the domestic sphere.

This is by design. However, just like how Schmitt disparages alternative mechanisms to foster unity, hard agonism also condemns alternative mechanisms to cultivate unity on the grounds that they will inhibit the expression of antagonism and lead to the explosion of even more intense antagonisms. Indeed, if hard agonism does rely on things that are foreign itself, such as norms and habits of civility, to sustain itself, then it must condemn those things as well on the grounds that they might inhibit the expression of the friend–enemy distinction.[84] As a result, with commonality the only explicit mechanism left to foster basic unity among citizens and to transform antagonism into agonism – and a rather weak mechanism at that – not only is an agonistic politics bound to be more fragile than a Schmittian politics of external antagonism; such an agonistic politics is also bound to be more fragile than a politics that avails itself to alternative mechanisms to cultivate unity, particularly if that alternative politics manages to allow for differences and disagreements to be expressed.

Consider the following conversation between Mouffe and Iñego Errejón, the leader of a Spanish left populist party that explicitly draws inspiration from Mouffe:

CM: Well, as for that friend–enemy passion you talk about, I would prefer to refer to its agonistic form of battle between adversaries.
IE: Well, it's friend–enemy because supporters occasionally kill each other. It's undesirable, but violence constitutes the ultimate possibility, it is part of the clash.

---

[82] Schmitt, *Political Theology*, 7.
[83] This is not to say that external enmity cannot exist. Indeed, Mouffe also argues in favour of a multipolar international system on the grounds that such an arrangement will facilitate the agonistic expression of the friend–enemy distinction among nation states (Chantal Mouffe, *On the Political* (New York: Routledge, 2005), 90–118.). However, if my argument here holds, then the fragility of democratic agonism in the domestic sphere will make it harder for the nation state to demand from citizens the sacrifices required to struggle against other nation states, if the circumstances demand such sacrifices.
[84] To this point, the Rawlsian and Habermasian visions that Mouffe condemns can be interpreted as attempts to formalize the norms of civility. See Colin Farrelly, *Justice, Democracy and Reasonable Agreement* (London: Palgrave Macmillan, 2007).

CM: They may kill each other, yes, but luckily it's not usual. And one tries to avoid it.
IE: But that's where the intensity comes from. Passion comes from the intensity of the clash. I feel part of the intensity of the clash. I feel part of the same thing, of an "us," along with many people who chant like me.
CM: But, Iñigo, in agonistic battles there is also passion between the adversaries.
IE: Yes, but I think that passion always entails the possibility of antagonism. Agonism among opponents is an antagonism between enemies that has been institutionalised.[85]

Mouffe maintains that it is "not usual" for political opponents under agonism to kill each other, but can opponents really be considered adversaries who recognize one another's legitimacy if the passion which fuels their confrontations is underlined by the possibility of death? Such a state of affairs seems more like a state of straight-up antagonism, albeit one where the parties involved do not constantly engage in physical violence. At most, this state of affairs can be considered a fragile modus vivendi. Yet hard agonism aspires to something more than a modus vivendi: hard agonism yearns for a state of basic *mutual recognition* where the parties involved view one another as legitimate, not a state of mutual forbearance that can erupt at any moment, or that can collapse should the balance of power shift. So, even on its own terms, hard agonism does not offer an adequately secure basis for liberal democracy. In order for adversaries to remain adversaries, they must share more than mere commonality.

AIMING TOO HIGH, AIMING TOO LOW

In this chapter, I have shown that the two predominant broad approaches to the question of difference and disagreement in contemporary democratic political theory fall short. Discursive approaches aim too high. They focus on securing higher standards of legitimacy but do not provide persuasive accounts of how to safeguard basic liberal democracy, except via historical happenstance. Meanwhile, realist approaches aim too low, overestimating the ability of institutions to channel antagonism and underestimating the need to actively cultivate a sense of unity to prevent the expression of difference and disagreement from spiralling out of control.

Through these discussions, we have begun to refine our understanding of what it will take for liberal democracy to harness the benefits of difference and disagreement and avoid unduly squashing difference and disagreement, yet also sidestep the potential perils of difference and disagreement. Namely, liberal democracy must be supported by a sense of unity that is oriented toward the preservation of liberal democracy but does not suppress the expression of difference and disagreement. In the next chapter, we shall begin to consider what such a sense of unity might look like.

[85] Errejón and Mouffe, *Podemos*, 62–63.

3

Fellowship's Forefather

Moving beyond Aristotelian Political Friendship

How can liberal democracy harness the benefits of difference and disagreement and avoid unduly squashing difference and disagreement, yet also prevent the expression of difference and disagreement from overheating and spiralling out of control? In Chapter 2, I demonstrated that the prevailing orientations in contemporary democratic political theory aim either too high or too low. Discursive approaches focus on attaining higher standards of legitimacy but do not provide persuasive accounts of how to safeguard basic liberal democracy. Meanwhile, realist approaches overstate the ability of well-designed institutions to channel antagonism, and underestimate the need to actively cultivate a sense of unity. On this basis, I argued that citizens ought to be encouraged to share a sense of unity that is oriented toward the preservation of liberal democracy but does not suppress the expression of difference and disagreement.

In this chapter, I begin to explore what such a sense of unity might look like. Specifically, I consider Aristotle's notion of political friendship, as discussed in the *Nicomachean Ethics* (NE) and the *Politics* (POL).[1] This might seem to be an unexpected place to begin. After all, Aristotle wrote over 2,000 years ago. However, I argue that the problem of difference and disagreement is *the* central concern of Aristotelian political friendship. According to Aristotle, when citizens are political friends, they might still have differences and disagreements. They have different class interests, and they tend to understand justice in

---

[1] The in-text citations refer to: Aristotle, "Eudemian Ethics," in *The Complete Works of Aristotle, Volume 2: The Revised Oxford Translation*, ed. Jonathan Barnes, 1922–1981 (Princeton: Princeton University Press, 1984); Aristotle, *Nicomachean Ethics*, trans. Robert C. Bartlett and Susan D. Collins (Chicago: University of Chicago Press, 2011); Aristotle, "Poetics," in *The Complete Works of Aristotle, Volume 2: The Revised Oxford Translation*, ed. Jonathan Barnes, 2316–2340 (Princeton: Princeton University Press, 1984); and Aristotle, *Politics*, trans. Carnes Lord (Chicago: University of Chicago Press, 1984).

different ways. However, rather than engage in factional conflict, they share a commitment to further the common advantage of the polity and, providing that the regime of the polity is "correct" or not excessively "deviant," aim to play their part in preserving the regime. So, even though Aristotle's notion of political friendship is obviously dated, I consider it because doing so helps to refine our understanding of what sort of unity citizens ought to share.

By engaging with Aristotle, I determine that the sort of unity we are looking for should assume the form of a "culture of trust" where citizens who have differences and disagreements tend to believe that their fellow citizens *probably* value the continuation of their civic relationship and are committed to supporting social and political arrangements which can allow them to continue that relationship: liberal democracy. More than not suffocate the expression of difference and disagreement, this culture of trust must not stymie debate over the meaning of (in)equality and (in)justice, even if such debate might seem to undermine that trust.

I also show, however, that such a liberal democratic culture of trust seems to presuppose a broad shared commitment to liberal democracy. If this is the case, then this culture of trust seems to face an initiation problem, not unlike that which beleaguers Rawls and Habermas's visions. Accordingly, I argue that one of two things follow. First, citizens should be encouraged to develop a culture of trust on the basis of something other than a shared commitment to liberal democracy, such as on national identity. If citizens care about one another's fates on this basis, then they might, further down the line, come to view liberal democracy and social inclusion to be expressions of that trust. Second, citizens should instead be able to contribute to a liberal democratic culture of trust without realizing it, at least initially. By advancing these arguments, I pave the way for my discussions of liberal nationalism in Chapter 4 and of role-based constitutional fellowship in the remainder of the book.

In what follows, after briefly reviewing the conceptual fundamentals of Aristotle's notion of friendship (or *philia*), I show that Aristotle understands political friendship to be a sort of "utility friendship," oriented toward the preservation of correct regimes and the moderation of deviant regimes, that can counteract civic aggression.[2] I then discuss the limitations of Aristotle's understanding of political friendship, thereby motivating the remainder of this book.

FOUNDATIONS OF ARISTOTLE'S *PHILIA*

Aristotle understands friendship (*philia*) to be a relationship characterized by a lasting sense of reciprocity and mutual affection (*NE*.1155b30). Friends do not

---

[2] In advancing my interpretation of Aristotle, I omit important nuances, particularly in regards to how political friendship differs from other sorts of utility friendship. For a more comprehensive discussion, see Eric Cheng, "Aristotelian Realism: Political Friendship and the Problem of Stability," *The Review of Politics* 81(4) (2019): 549–571.

merely have good will toward one another; they also act on that mutual affection (*NE*.1166b30–1167a10). At first glance, this seems like a common-sensical definition. However, Aristotle characterizes a variety of relationships as friendships – "equal" and "unequal friendships," superficial and intimate friendships. Indeed, we today would not classify many of these relationships as friendships.

First, Aristotle describes equal friendships where the friends involved share the same underlying sort(s) of affection and function(s). He identifies three primary sorts of equal friendships: pleasure, utility, and virtue friendships (*NE*.1155b20–30). Friends of utility are friends because they derive advantage from one another (e.g., business partners); friends of pleasure, because they derive pleasure from one another (e.g., sexual partners); and friends of virtue, because they love one another for their intrinsic goodness (*NE*.1156b10). Aristotle construes utility and pleasure friendships as *incidental* because they dissolve once the friends involved are no longer useful or pleasurable to one another (*NE*.156a20). In contrast, he construes virtue friendships as *complete* because they are durable, and because they are shared among good people who wish one another well for one another's sake (*NE*.1156b10). Indeed, Aristotle deems virtue friendship necessary for a happy life of human flourishing; if one does not love any other people as "other selves," then one's happiness is "disfigured" (*NE*.1099b1–5).[3]

Second, Aristotle describes unequal friendships where the friends involved have different functions, exhibit different sorts of affection, and merit different degrees of affection (*NE*.1158.b15–25). He identifies a range of such friend-ships – notably, those between fathers and sons, and those between husbands and wives.

FOR THE PURPOSES OF COUNTERACTING CIVIC AGGRESSION

There is a temptation to believe that Aristotle likens political friendship to virtue friendship.[4] After all, Aristotle declares, "Living well ... is the end of the city ... A city is a partnership of families and villages in a complete and self-sufficient life. The political partnership must be regarded, therefore, as being for the sake of noble action, not for the sake of living together" (*Pol*.1281a2–3). It would seem, then, that political friendship is a form of friendship that promotes

---

[3] For a discussion on why virtue friendships are the greatest of "external goods" – goods "exter-nal" to oneself that one needs in order to live a life of flourishing – see Nancy Sherman, "Aristotle on Friendship and the Shared Life," *Philosophy and Phenomenological Research* 47(4) (1987): 589–613.

[4] Alexander Nehamas, *On Friendship* (New York: Basic Books, 2016); Ann Ward, *Contemplating Friendship in Aristotle's Ethics* (Albany: State University of New York Press, 2016); John von Heyking, *The Form of Politics: Aristotle and Plato on Friendship* (Montreal and Kingston: McGill-Queen's University Press, 2016).

human flourishing, without which one's happiness is disfigured – and that it is inappropriate to discuss Aristotelian political friendship in the context of contemporary liberal democracy. This is because the notion of virtue friendship is tied to a particular conception of the good life and of the moral universe, while the promise of liberal democracy lies partly in the fact that it can accommodate a plurality of conceptions of the good life and of the moral universe. It seems that citizens of a liberal democracy ought not to be encouraged – indeed, forced – to partake in a thick social unity that is grounded in a specific ethical worldview.

Yet there is good reason to believe that Aristotle actually understands political friendship to be a sort of *utility* friendship. For one thing, as a matter of numbers, it is not possible to share in many virtue friendships. Aristotle maintains that only the best of people are capable of wishing one another well for one another's sake and of viewing others as "other selves." Moreover, the formation of virtue friendship requires time and *intimacy* – that people develop love, trust, and the "habits formed by living together (*sunētheia*)" (*NE*.1156b25, 1158a11–21). So, virtue friendship is not scalable and cannot come close to describing the bonds shared by the inhabitants of a small city state like Ancient Athens (40,000), let alone a modern nation state.

For another thing, Aristotle states that political friendship is oriented toward the pursuit of the advantageous.[5] This does not mean that Aristotle reduces political friendship to business transactions or partnership – that Aristotle wishes for citizens to only share *thin* social bonds.[6] In fact, Aristotle explicitly notes that a set of ongoing market exchanges, regulated by a common set of laws ensuring just transactions, does not make a city (*Pol*.1280b20). However, it does mean that, for Aristotle, when citizens are political friends, they are *like-minded (homonoia)* (*NE*.1155a25–28). Political friends do not simply agree on just anything; they agree on how to approach practical issues of common concern, and they act on those shared judgments – on how to further the common advantage of the polity. Like-minded citizens agree on matters like whether a political office should be created, whether an alliance should be

---

[5] Note that for Aristotle, the joint pursuit of the advantageous is an expression of man's social-political nature or *telos*: man is a social-political being because of his unique capacity for speech, and speech *"serves to reveal the advantageous and the harmful*, and hence also the just and the unjust ... and partnership in these things is what makes a household and a city [emphasis added]" (*Pol*.1253a1–19).

[6] Some interpretations of Aristotle do come close to suggesting that this is the case, pointing to passages in the *Eudemian Ethics* that seem to suggest this. See Kazutaka Inamura, *Justice and Reciprocity in Aristotle's Political Philosophy* (Cambridge: Cambridge University Press, 2015); Bernard Yack, *The Problems of a Political Animal: Community, Justice, and Conflict in Aristotelian Political Thought* (Berkeley: University of California Press, 1993); and Douglas B. Rasmussen and Douglas J. Den Uyl, "Aristotelianism, Commerce, and the Liberal Order," in *Aristotle and Modern Politics: The Persistence of Political Philosophy*, ed. Aristide Tessitore (Notre Dame: University of Notre Dame Press, 2002), 278–306.

formed, or, critically, as we shall see, what regime type should prevail (*NE*.1167a20–30).

It is therefore fitting for us to consider Aristotle's notion of political friendship, for it seems, at least at first glance, to describe the sorts of civic bonds we are seeking here: a sense of unity that can help preserve the regime in the face of difference and disagreement. That is, Aristotle considers political friendship because he fears what might happen if any city becomes "filled with enemies" (*Pol*.1284b30). He worries about what might happen when citizens organize themselves into factions and develop mutual animosity – how clashes between competing material interests and divergent conceptions of justice can render politics a succession of destabilizing coups and attempts to change the regime type of the city (*Pol*.1301b5ff).

Indeed, as an empirical matter, Aristotle observes that the most common regime types of his day – democracy and oligarchy – are prone to factional conflict precisely because their citizens do not agree on what constitutes justice and thereby lack like-mindedness: some citizens believe that the regime type in question is just and ought to be preserved, while others believe that the regime type is unjust and ought to be overturned. In democracies, the poor rule on the basis of "numerical equality," while those denied a share in office (the wealthy) demand that the regime be ruled on the basis of "proportional equality."[7] Meanwhile, in oligarchies, the wealthy rule on the basis of proportional equality, while those shut out of office (the poor) demand that the regime be ruled on the basis of numerical equality (*Pol*.1301b30–1302a5).

THE GENERAL DEFINITION OF POLITICAL FRIENDSHIP

What does it mean, exactly, for citizens to be political friends? What does it take for them to be like-minded and to prevent their differences and disagreements from spiralling out of control? Certainly, for Aristotle, it demands that they have some sort of virtue. He maintains that the base cannot be like-minded, for they only look to maximize their self-interests; they obstruct the pursuits of others, and they refuse to perform their share of public service. Not only do the base neglect the commons; they instigate factional conflict, for they shun just action and seek instead to coerce others into acting in various ways (*NE*.1167b10–16).

I submit that, for Aristotle, political friends (1) have political virtue and (2) recognize one another as having political virtue. First, political friends are politically virtuous. This does not mean that they are capable of partaking in virtue friendship; typically, they are not. Rather, it means that political friends recognize that their respective individual advantages are bound up with the

---

[7] According to proportional equality, those who "merit" more goods deserve more goods. In contrast, according to numerical equality, everyone ought to have the same amount of goods.

common advantage of the polity, and that they are capable of doing their part to help further that common advantage. This involves committing themselves to the *regime type* of the polity and fulfilling their respective roles within the regime, provided that the regime type in question is "correct" or not excessively "deviant" (discussed later). After all, there is arguably no greater cause of factional conflict – no greater internal threat to the common advantage – than disagreement over what regime type should prevail. As Aristotle notes, "although citizens are dissimilar, preservation of the partnership is their task, and the regime is [this] partnership; hence the virtue of the citizen must necessarily be with a view to the regime" (*Pol.*1276b28).

Second, according to Aristotle, as a sort of friendship – a sort of reciprocal relationship – political friends must recognize in one another political virtue. Certainly, they need not and cannot possibly love one another as "other selves" (as do virtue friends). However, they must recognize that they are each committed to the common advantage and capable of doing their part in furthering that common advantage, even if difference and disagreement might persist. Only so can they sustain a commitment to the long-term common advantage, for only so can they have a sense that others are committed to the common advantage as well. To be a political friend is not to engage in unilateral altruism, self-sacrifice, or (in some cases) disarmament. Rather, to be a political friend is to fulfill one's end of a bargain.

POLITICAL FRIENDSHIP IN ACTION

Given that different sorts of regime types exist, what this all means is that political friendship manifests itself differently in different regime types. After all, the demands of the common advantage that grounds political friendship vary from regime type to regime type: the actions required to further the common advantage of a kingship differ from those required to further the common advantage of an aristocracy, and those actions differ from those required to further the common advantage of a polity. It also means that the manners in which political friends exhibit political virtue vary according to regime type *and* according to their respective statuses within the regime type. As Aristotle notes, "the virtue of the citizen must necessarily be with a view to the regime. If, then, there are indeed several forms of regime, it is clear that it is not possible for the virtue of the excellent citizen to be single, or complete virtue" (*Pol.*1276b31–36).

In the context of correct regimes, political friendship helps to ensure that political rule furthers the common advantage, not merely factional interests and the private interests of rulers. Aristotle famously declares three sorts of regimes (kingship, aristocracy, and polity or timocracy) "correct" regimes on the grounds that they are ruled for the sake of the common advantage, and three other sorts of regimes (tyranny, oligarchy, and democracy) "deviant" on the grounds that they are ruled for the sake of their rulers' private advantages. Each of the three correct regimes can be ruled for the common advantage when their citizens are committed to the common advantage of those regimes and are capable of sustaining that commitment in manners appropriate to each of those regimes (*NE*.1161a10) – in manners befitting their respective statuses within those regimes or friendships. For instance, it is more likely that a kingship will indeed be ruled for the common advantage when a king rules over his subjects as a responsible father cares for his children and as a shepherd cares for his sheep, and when his subjects obey him as good children obey their fathers. Likewise, it is more likely that a polity or timocracy will be ruled for the common advantage when citizens rule and are ruled in turn on an equal basis, not unlike how good brothers can be equal and decent to one another – just as it is more likely that an aristocracy will be ruled for the common advantage if political rule is distributed according to merit, not unlike how a good husband and a good wife distribute their household responsibilities according to who is better suited to which task (*NE*.1160b23–1161a9).

Meanwhile, in the context of deviant regimes, according to Aristotle, political friendship can help make those regimes less bad. Specifically, political friendship can help reduce factional conflict in oligarchies and democracies so as to make them *moderate* oligarchies and democracies. On Aristotle's account, oligarchies and democracies are prone to factional conflict precisely because their citizens lack political virtue and are not political friends. Given that the rich possess all the gifts of fortune (money, strength, friends), usually from birth, they probably only know how to rule as arrogant oligarchic masters seeking self-aggrandizement, rather than as virtuous aristocrats who recognize the need to distribute prerogatives on the basis of virtue (*Pol*.1294a10). Meanwhile, given that the poor tend to be needy and humble, they are typically only capable of being ruled, in extreme cases, as slaves (*Pol*.1295b6–20). As a result, there is a danger that oligarchies and democracies might devolve into cities of contemptuous masters and envious slaves, either extreme oligarchies or extreme democracies – tyrannies. Such cities do not qualify as cities at all, for cities involve "the element of affection" (*philikon*); enemies do not wish to even go on a journey together (*Pol*.1295b24).

Certainly, Aristotle is under no illusions that political friendship can easily emerge in such conditions. Nor is Aristotle optimistic about the prospect that these extreme oligarchies and democracies will transform into polities. Nonetheless, he maintains that a degree of political friendship – or, perhaps more accurately stated, the presence of some citizens who are capable of partaking in political friendship – can at least help other citizens obey the law, even if they are not quite politically virtuous friends. Specifically, Aristotle argues that the "middling element" can be mobilized to ensure that those deviant regimes become less deviant: "where the multitude of middling persons predominates either over both the extremities together or over one alone, there a lasting polity is capable of existing" (*Pol*.1296b38). Unlike the modern middle class – eager to acquire more and become rich, yet anxious about falling into poverty in a context of regularized social mobility[8] – Aristotle's middling element refers to a rather stable social and psychological state: members of the middling element are moderate in both possessions and character. The middling element is the "readiest to obey reason" (*Pol.*1295b6), is the most capable of ruling and being ruled, and is "alone without factional conflict" (*Pol.*1296a6–8).

The middling element can help deviant regimes become less deviant because it can induce an "element of affection." Specifically, when the middling element is the largest part of the city or is "added" to one of the others in order to prevent the regime from becoming an extreme oligarchy or democracy, civic aggression can be diluted: "[W]hen the middling element is numerous, splits over the regime occur least of all" (*Pol.*1296a6–8). This is because the middling person can act "as a sort of arbiter" for citizens who would otherwise not tolerate being ruled by "the other" (the rich by the poor, the poor by the rich): "the most trustworthy person everywhere is the arbiter" (*Pol.*1297a1–5). The middling element can moderate the ruling rich (in oligarchies) or the ruling poor (in democracies) so that the rulers recognize that their conceptions of justice are indeed only "partial" conceptions,[9] and so that they rule with some view to the common good. With rulers ruling neither as arrogant and contemptuous masters nor as malicious and envious slaves seeking vengeance, citizens who are denied political power have more reasons to obey the law, rather than revolt. In this manner, political friendship can indirectly help deviant regimes become less deviant.

LIBERAL DEMOCRACY AND POLITICAL EQUALITY

I have skipped over many important nuances of Aristotle's discussion of political friendship. Nonetheless, we now have a sense of what political friendship represents: a sort of unity whereby citizens have the requisite virtues to do their part in furthering the common advantage of the polity – including upholding the polity's regime type, provided that that regime is either correct or not excessively deviant. So, political friendship seems, on a basic level, to be the sort of unity we identified toward the end of Chapter 2 as worth striving toward.

Of course, there are good reasons why we must not simply aim to rehabilitate Aristotle's notion of political friendship without revision. For one thing, liberal democracy was not on the horizon when Aristotle theorized. So, we would have to develop a brand of political friendship that is appropriate for liberal democracy – and, with that, an understanding of the political virtues and/or practices needed to sustain liberal democracy.

---

[8] I paraphrase the formulation offered by Alexis de Tocqueville, *Democracy in America*, ed. J. P. Mayer (New York: Harper Perennial Modern Classics, 2006), 636.

[9] Recall that the poor tend to understand justice to consist of the rule of numerical equality, and the rich, of the rule of proportional equality (*Pol.*1301b30–1302a5).

For another, political friendship for Aristotle can be shared among political unequals – say, between a king and his subjects (kingship), or between the wise and the rest (aristocracy). Yet such conceptions of citizenship clearly contradict the political equality that undergirds contemporary liberal democracy. So, in the context of contemporary liberal democracy, efforts would also need to be made to ensure that the sense of unity citizens experience does not interfere with ongoing debates over the meaning of political equality and with efforts to more perfectly realize equality. If that unity is not realized in this manner, then it might fuel civic aggression: liberal democracy *promises* citizens that they will be treated like political equals, so some citizens might, in the name of justice, reject that sense of unity (and perhaps liberal democracy itself) if they deem that unity an unduly conservative source of social cohesion whose primary function is to *stymie* greater equality – to *consolidate* political inequality.

Still, my discussion of Aristotle reveals that in our effort to discern how to better preserve liberal democracy, we must consider how citizens ought to behave toward one another, and that we must aspire toward a sort of unity that does not inhibit debate over the content of political (in)equality and (in) justice. In the remainder of this book, I shall explore how we can work toward such a sense of unity. Accordingly, in the rest of this chapter, I shall lay the groundwork for my subsequent discussions. Specifically, I identify two additional limitations to Aristotelian political friendship. First, I show that Aristotelian political friendship relies on the mutual recognition or *verification* of political virtue among citizens, and that Aristotelian political friendship therefore runs into a problem of scale. Accordingly, I argue that the unity we ought to aspire toward must take the form of a more abstract "culture of trust" (to be defined). Second, given that the unity we ought to aspire toward represents an ideal that is premised on a commitment to liberal democracy, I argue that a plausible account of how to cultivate that unity must redress "the problem of initiation." I thereby pave the way for my discussions of liberal nationalism and role-based constitutional fellowship; both aim to overcome this problem.

UNITY THROUGH A SCALABLE CULTURE OF TRUST

The first limitation of Aristotelian political friendship has to do with scale. Now, there is disagreement among readers of Aristotle about whether political friends need to know one another. Some insist that even if political friends are not intimate with one another, they must be *personally* acquainted with one another: how else can they recognize one another as politically virtuous?[10] In contrast, others maintain that political friends do not need to know one another

---

[10] A. W. Price, "Friendship and Politics," *Tijdschrift voor Filosofie*, 61ste Jaarg.(3) (1999): 542; P. E. Digeser, *Friendship Reconsidered: What It Means and How It Matters to Politics* (New York: Columbia University Press, 2016), 109–111.

at all, nor do they need to share close emotional bonds: political friends "work through the public processes of the state's social and political, legal, and educative institutions."[11] Indeed, some even suggest that political friendship is a virtue.[12] The stakes of this disagreement are high. If the former interpretation holds, then the circle of political friendship can only be so wide; if the latter holds, then the circle of political friendship can extend much further.

My own sense, as a matter of textual interpretation, is that there are limits to how wide the circle of Aristotelian political friendship can extend. As we have seen, as a matter of basic definitions, friendship is a reciprocal relationship that involves mutual recognition; it is unclear why political friendship should be exempt from this basic definitional requirement, if it is indeed a sort of friendship. Indeed, it seems odd to declare citizens political friends if those citizens do not have at least some sense that their fellow citizens are indeed committed to further the common advantage and willing to do what it takes to fulfill that commitment. To this point, Aristotle himself insists that "a city could not come into being from ten human beings, yet when there are ten times ten thousand, it is no longer a city either" (*NE*.1170b31–32). The figure "ten times ten thousand" is obviously not to be taken literally. However, by mentioning it, Aristotle indicates that there are limits to how many people can share in political friendship together.

The chief question we need to ask when answering the question of how wide the circle of political friendship can extend, then, is this: to what extent can *strangers* be political friends? Given that most citizens in even a small city state will not know one another personally, how can strangers nonetheless come to recognize one another as politically virtuous?

Aristotle is ambiguous on this point. However, one possibility is that political friendship can be realized through a series of networks, not unlike those present in democratic Athens as described by Josiah Ober. On Ober's account, Athens was organized into a series of participatory districts (demes), united by a citywide council (a "master network of local networks"). As a result, Athens had the *feel* of a face-to-face society, even though it was never literally a face-to-face society: "virtually every Athenian had access to a network of personal contacts ... every Athenian was connected to every other Athenian by only one or two 'degrees of separation.'"[13] Perhaps, when such intertwining networks exist, strangers can use those networks to recognize one another as political virtuous, just as Athenians were able to use such networks to draw on the collective resources and knowledge of Athens as a whole.

---

[11] Sibyl A. Schwarzenbach, *On Civic Friendship: Including Women in the State* (New York: Columbia University Press, 2009), 54.

[12] Danielle S. Allen, *Talking to Strangers: Anxieties of Citizenship since* Brown *v.* Board of Education (Chicago: University of Chicago Press, 2004), 120.

[13] Josiah Ober, *Athenian Legacies: Essays on the Politics of Going Together* (Princeton: Princeton University Press, 2005), 41.

An immediate potential concern with this approach concerns the ability of such networks to reach across social cleavages. If these networks are developed, but not to the extent that they can transcend social cleavages and collectively encompass the entirety of society, then those networks can end up serving as sources of misunderstanding and faction. In Robert Putnam's terms, such networks would serve to *bond*, but not to *bridge*; they would "reinforce exclusive identities and homogeneous groups . . . [thereby] undergirding specific reciprocity and mobilizing solidarity . . .," but without establishing links "to external assets . . . [and] generat[ing] broader identities and reciprocity."[14] This concern seems particularly salient in the context of contemporary liberal democracy: liberal democracies are far larger than ancient city states and are defined by a greater number of social cleavages. So, if citizens in contemporary liberal democracies do form networks, but only among their own respective racial, ethnic, religious, cultural, economic, and political groups, then those networks will serve primarily as "echo chambers" and sources of mutual distrust, not as forums to form political friendship.

The degree to which such fragmentation is actually a threat is somewhat unclear. Take the case of political polarization. On the one hand, there is evidence that people are increasingly clustering into homogeneous communities. Bill Bishop famously finds that Americans have steadily "sorted" themselves into increasingly ideologically homogeneous communities over the past 50 years.[15] Recent election results, which indicate that American cities are voting overwhelmingly Democratic, and rural areas, Republican, seem to support Bishop's findings.

On the other hand, Ana Tanasoca notes that just because a particular area seems to be homogeneous does not mean that its members do not encounter at least some forms of difference. For one thing, people who vote the same ways still disagree on particular issues; fellow Democrats disagree wildly over economic policy or over the role of religion in politics. So, Bishop's "ideologically homogenous" communities are not necessarily echo chambers.[16] For another, except for strident partisans, people generally do not tend to choose their friends and acquaintances only on the basis of their political preferences; they also make those choices on the basis of shared interests, passions, and employment considerations. So, people tend to discuss politics *incidentally* rather than purposefully. Given that they have not purposefully sorted themselves according to their partisan affiliations, they end up encountering at least some degree of disagreement in the workplace and even in their neighbourhoods. As

---

[14] Robert D. Putnam, *Bowling Alone: The Collapse and Revival of American Community* (New York: Simon & Schuster, 2000), 22–23.

[15] Bill Bishop, *The Big Sort: Why the Clustering of Like-Minded America Is Tearing Us Apart* (New York: Houghton Mifflin Books, 2008).

[16] Ana Tanasoca, *Deliberation Naturalized: Improving Real Existing Deliberative Democracy* (Oxford: Oxford University Press, 2020), 163.

a result, informal networks – in particular, those defined by "weak ties" – can "facilitate the flow of information across different clusters within the larger community network."[17]

I am inclined to say that the potential for networks to divide rather than to bridge is probably more pronounced in some contexts than others. Tanasoca rightfully points out that ideologically homogeneous communities are likely never devoid of difference and disagreement. Even in the 2020 US Presidential Election, Wyoming and Vermont, the reddest and bluest states, voted 30 percent Democratic and 30 percent Republican, respectively. Yet there are also times when informal networks cannot withstand political disagreement, even if those disagreements come up incidentally rather than purposefully. Indeed, since the rise of Donald Trump in 2016, Democrats and Republicans increasingly view the opposing party as an existential threat and each other as "close-minded," "immoral," and "dishonest."[18] Eighty percent of Americans *generally* now report having "just a few" or "no" friends across the aisle.[19] So, it is reasonable to say that the threat of fragmentation is a serious concern but not inevitable.

Putting this dispute aside, even though Tanasoca might be right to insist that concerns over the potentially divisive ramifications of network fragmentation are overblown, it is still unclear whether such networks can facilitate the mutual recognition of political virtue as fluidly as they can facilitate the transfer of knowledge and viewpoints. For one thing, these networks allow citizens to readily call upon specific pieces of information and to have access to expertise *when necessary* or *desired*, whereas friendship demands some degree of *sustained attention*: "many friendships the lack of contact dissolves" (*NE*.1157b13). For another, even though it is less vigorous than virtue friendship, political friendship does concern the common advantage of a polity – something that is supposed to last and that cannot be "rendered in a short time" (unlike the trade of services) (*NE*.1158a18). So, even though political friendship does not require citizens to develop the habit of living together (as does virtue friendship), it likely requires citizens to "acquire [some sort of] experience of the other person" (*NE*.1158a14–15). Knowledge of whether fellow citizens are politically virtuous cannot be transferred in the manner that different political perspectives and knowledge of how to perform a certain task can be transferred. It is one thing for Democrats and Republicans to be exposed to one another's perspectives; it is another for them to be able to come to the conclusion that supporters of the opposing party are committed to the common advantage and are not existential threats.

---

[17] Tanasoca, *Deliberation Naturalized*, 156ff.
[18] "Partisanship and Political Animosity in 2016," Pew Research Center, June 22, 2016, www .pewresearch.org/politics/2016/06/22/partisanship-and-political-animosity-in-2016/.
[19] "Few Trump or Biden Supporters Have Close Friends Who Back the Opposing Candidate," Pew Research Center, September 18, 2020, www.pewresearch.org/fact-tank/2020/09/18/few-trump-or-biden-supporters-have-close-friends-who-back-the-opposing-candidate/.

Therefore, we have good reason to believe that the sort of unity we are aspiring toward must not rely on the *verification* that specific fellow citizens are politically virtuous. Instead, since most fellow citizens are strangers, that unity must, by necessity, be more abstract. Now, this does not mean that citizens ought to be discouraged from cultivating a sense of unity with some *specific* fellow citizens. Nor does it mean that that more abstract sense of unity can sustain itself if citizens do not verify that at least *some* of their fellow flesh-and-blood citizens are politically virtuous. Indeed, even if the unity we seek here cannot depend wholly on personal familiarity, that unity must still embody a sort of reciprocity: even those citizens who are politically virtuous will not be inclined to continue acting politically virtuously if they believe that most of their fellow citizens are not politically virtuous and do not act in ways that further the common advantage. As Putnam observes, people are unlikely to engage in "cooperative forms of behaviour" if they do not observe others doing the same:

[I]f I'm the only member of a committee, it's not a "committee," and if no one else comes to a meeting on a bond issue, it is not a "meeting," even if I show up. Knowing that, I may well back out, too. In other words, it is precisely those forms of civic engagement most vulnerable to coordination problems and free riding – those activities that brought citizens *together*, those activities that most clearly embody social capital – that have declined most rapidly.[20]

Rather, by insisting that citizens must share in a more abstract sort of unity, I mean to say that that unity must assume the form of what we can call a more generalized *culture of trust* where citizens judge one another as *probably* "valu[ing] the continuation of [their] [civic] relationship,"[21] despite the fact that they are, for the most part, strangers. In this culture of trust, even though citizens personally know *some* flesh-and-blood citizens who do value their civic relationship in this manner, they generally do not know who *specifically* values the continuation of their civic relationship. Likewise, citizens are aware that some citizens either do not do their part in upholding the relationship or actively try to undermine that relationship. Nonetheless, when such a culture of trust exists, due to one reason or another – for example, their personal experiences with some fellow citizens, or the collective stories they tell themselves as members of the same country – citizens believe that most of their fellow citizens do value the continuation of their civic relationship. More than that, citizens believe that most of their fellow citizens are committed to social

---

[20] Putnam, *Bowling Alone*, 45. Along these lines, I will later argue that in order to cultivate such unity, citizens must engage in the appropriate practices with subsets of the citizenry that can plausibly be described as somewhat representative of the citizenry as a whole.

[21] Russell Hardin, *Trust and Trustworthiness* (New York: Russell Sage Foundation, 2002), 1.

and political arrangements that can allow them to indeed continue their civic relationship, despite their differences and disagreements: liberal democracy.[22] That is, citizens who share in this culture of trust believe that their fellow citizens value the rule of law, individual rights, the freedom and fairness of elections, and crucially – as we shall see in Chapter 5 – the notion of equal citizenship. In other words, the unity we must strive toward should take the form of a general social climate where people feel that they are in it together to support liberal democracy, and treat one another accordingly. I shall argue that role-based constitutional fellowship (with the help of liberal nationalism) is the path through which this climate can emerge.

THE PROBLEM OF INITIATION

The second limitation to Aristotelian political friendship arises from the fact that political friendship does represent a sort of ideal. Now, it certainly is not a sort of "high-aiming" ideal in the vein of Rawls's overlapping consensus or Habermas's discursive democracy. As we saw, the overlapping consensus and discursive democracy are accounts of what the more fully legitimate liberal democracy looks like. In contrast, Aristotelian political friendship is more akin to what I have called a "negative ideal" – certainly, a North Star of sorts, but one that is intended to help prevent certain social and political evils from arising (e.g., to combat the corrosion of correct regimes) or, when those evils have arisen, to make bad situations less bad (e.g., to moderate deviant regimes). So, we can expect that the demands of such a negative ideal would be less vigorous than the demands of those more ambitious ideals.[23] For example, a liberal democratic sort of political friendship would likely demand that citizens accept the ideal of political pluralism, that political disagreement is legitimate; this is

---

[22] The phrase "value the continuation of the relationship" appears in Russell Hardin's discussion of trust. There, Hardin advances a notion of *encapsulated interest* whereby "I trust you because I think it is in your interest to take my interests in the relevant matter seriously in the following sense: You value the continuation of our relationship, and you therefore have your own interests in taking my interests into account" (Hardin, *Trust and Trustworthiness*, 1). Hardin's definition captures some of what I have in mind here. Indeed, I consider liberal nationalism in Chapter 4 in part because it offers a way to "mix" citizens' interests together. However, I am moved to define the "culture of trust" we ought to aspire toward as also encompassing a shared commitment to liberal democracy because a commitment to liberal democracy does not necessarily follow from the encapsulation or mixing of interests. Indeed, there are societies abound where *enough people* encapsulate one another's interests for society to function, yet where some members of society are excluded from that trust and where liberal democracy is absent.

[23] Similarly, as we have seen, within Aristotle's thought, the demands of political friendship are less vigorous than the demands of virtue friendship. In fact, in some regimes, being politically vigorous makes one *less capable* of participating in virtue friendship. The king's subjects exhibit political virtue by obeying, but this sort of "political virtue" hardly prepares them to be the "best of men," capable of partaking in virtue friendship.

less demanding than adherence to the ideals of public reason or of communicative action.

Still, political friendship does constitute an ideal of sorts. Even though political friendship constitutes a path to prevent difference and disagreement from corroding (not excessively-bad) regimes, it seems vulnerable to the charge that it does not offer a path to encourage citizens whose differences and disagreements have already overheated to act in accordance to the ideal of political friendship. Indeed, it does not seem adequate to ask such citizens to simply unilaterally decide to act in accordance to this ideal, even if their fellow citizens do not reciprocate. For example, it does not seem likely that many citizens will agree to act in accordance to the ideal of political pluralism if they know that other citizens will not do the same. In other words, it seems that political friendship suffers from a problem of initiation.

Aristotle recognizes this challenge. Recall his remarks on the middling element. The middling element is the readiest to obey reason and alone without factional conflict – oriented toward the common advantage, not its own private, factional interests. In a deviant regime, this element can work toward inducing the element of affection. It can act like an arbiter between warring factions, and it can encourage the ruling class to develop a less-partial conception of justice. So, in contexts defined by factional conflict, Aristotle does not simply recommend that some citizens behave like political friends unilaterally. Instead, he encourages them to work with whatever faction is preeminent. Although the goal is to make that ruling faction govern more in the spirit of political friendship, we can expect that the practice of getting the ruling faction to rule more with a view to the common advantage – indeed, in a manner that is acceptable to the ruled – will be anything but straightforward. Especially given that "the middling element is often few" (*Pol.*1296a23), the middling element would likely have to compromise and be strategic so as to maximize its influence on the ruling class.

Of course, as I have noted, members of the modern middle class tend to be different in temperament and outlook than members of Aristotle's middling element. So, it seems unreliable to depend on a certain class of citizens with alleged psychological features to initiate political friendship. However, we can envision that in promoting a liberal democratic sort of political friendship in contexts where there are many autocratic citizens or where many citizens lack the capacities necessary to support liberal democracy, we might encourage those citizens who have committed themselves to liberal democracy to do something similar. We might urge those citizens to try to find opportunities to compromise with other citizens, for such compromises might encourage autocratic citizens to moderate and, unbeknownst to themselves, begin to accept the ideal of political pluralism.[24]

---

[24] This is just a hypothesis. There is evidence that such compromises can sometimes help initiate or fortify liberal democracy. For example, in Tunisia (which was far from a liberal democracy), a compromise between secular liberals and Islamist fundamentalists in the aftermath of the Arab

Nonetheless, what these difficulties reveal is that even though Aristotelian political friendship is thinner than Rawls's political liberalism and Habermas's discursive democracy, political friendship has a similar vulnerability: it is grounded in a narrow set of conceptual resources – namely in citizens' commitment to the particular regime type (e.g., liberal democracy). Citizens can become political friends if they see one another doing their part in sustaining (and improving) the regime, yet they can only begin this process if they are already committed to the common advantage and/or the regime type. In other words, the sense of unity (and trust) we must aspire toward seems to *presuppose* a broad commitment to liberal democracy, yet how can that sense of unity get off the ground and running if citizens are not already committed to liberal democracy?

I submit that one of two things (or both) follow(s). First, even if the sort of unity we are aspiring toward must ultimately be grounded in a principled commitment to liberal democracy, that unity must be grounded in other resources as well – non-political resources. That way, citizens can be more inclined to care about one another's fate, even if they do not initially share a commitment to liberal democracy. The hope, then, is that citizens will gradually develop a commitment to liberal democracy as they come to view liberal democracy to be somehow connected to those resources, and that the culture of trust citizens share will increasingly accommodate difference and disagreement. As we shall see in Chapter 4, this is what theories of "liberal nationalism" try to achieve.

Second, that sense of liberal democratic unity must have a plausible chance at self-initiation; citizens must be able to contribute to it without realizing that they are doing so. Citizens might not necessarily "buy into" either the need for that sort of unity or the apparatus that can foster that unity. Nonetheless, if citizens can act in the appropriate manners, then that unity might emerge, and citizens will increasingly understand their civic relations in terms of that unity. This promise, I shall argue, is what role-based constitutional fellowship has to offer.

GUIDEPOSTS FOR THE PATH FORWARD

Through my engagement of Aristotle's notion of political friendship, I have refined our understanding of what it would take for liberal democracy to better harness the benefits of difference and disagreement and avoid unduly squashing difference and disagreement, yet also sidestep the potential perils of difference and disagreement. Citizens must share in a sense of unity, and that sense of

Spring helped to establish a regime that reasonably approximates liberal democracy – and to moderate those Islamists. See Noah Feldman, *The Arab Winter: A Tragedy* (Princeton: Princeton University Press, 2020). However, there are distinct dangers to such compromises. I discuss these dangers later during my discussion of role-based constitutional fellowship.

unity should assume the form of a culture of trust whereby they believe that their fellow citizens probably value the continuation of their civic relationship and are committed to supporting social and political arrangements that can allow them to continue that relationship: liberal democracy. Crucially, this culture of trust must not suffocate the expression of difference and disagreement and must not achieve unity by silencing debate over the meaning of political (in)equality and (in)justice.

How can such a culture of trust emerge and be sustained? I determined that such a culture must be supported by certain political virtues and/or practices. Yet an initiation problem emerges: how can a culture of trust which seemingly *presupposes* a broad commitment to liberal democracy get off the ground and running in the first place if citizens are not already committed to liberal democracy, or if they do not have the political virtues required to sustain (and improve) liberal democracy? Accordingly, I argued that one of two things must occur. First, citizens might be encouraged to develop a culture of trust on the basis of something other than a shared commitment to liberal democracy so that they can be more inclined to care about one another's fates. Further down the line, citizens might then come to view liberal democracy and social inclusion to be expressions of the trust they feel. Second, citizens might contribute to a *liberal democratic* culture of trust without realizing it, at least initially.

In the remainder of this book, I explore these two potential paths to cultivate a liberal democratic culture of trust. In Chapter 4, I consider liberal nationalism. Liberal nationalism proposes a path whereby citizens can come to care about one another's fates vis-à-vis their common nationality, and whereby they can eventually come to view liberal democracy and social inclusion to be expressions of that collective identity. Then, beginning in Chapter 5, through my notion of role-based constitutional fellowship, I hope to show that citizens can act like constitutional fellows by fulfilling various normative roles without realizing it, at least initially. My contention is that as citizens act in these manners, they will gradually act less *like* constitutional fellows and more *as* constitutional fellows. Role-based constitutional fellowship, then, offers a culture of trust that goes far enough to sustain liberal democracy amidst difference and disagreement, but not so far as to squash that difference and disagreement in the process.

4

Broadening the Base

The Necessity and Dilemmas of Liberal Nationalism

In order for liberal democracy to harness the benefits of difference and disagreement and avoid unduly squashing difference and disagreement, yet also sidestep the potential perils of difference and disagreement, citizens should be encouraged to share a sense of unity. I have argued that this sense of unity should assume the form of a culture of trust where citizens believe that their fellow citizens probably value the continuation of their civic relationship, and where citizens are committed to supporting social and political arrangements that can allow them to continue that relationship: liberal democracy. This culture of trust must not artificially suppress the expression of difference and disagreement, and must not silence debate over the meaning of political (in)equality and (in)justice.

Yet how can such a liberal democratic culture of trust be initiated? In this chapter, I consider one approach that encourages citizens to develop a preliminary culture of trust on the basis of something other than a shared principled commitment to liberal democracy. According to so-called liberal nationalists like David Miller and Yael Tamir, citizens should be encouraged to identify as *co-nationals*. When citizens share an emotional connection to a *national community* – to a pre-political community that is defined by common descent, culture, language, and/or history – they can develop what Keith Banting and Will Kymlicka call a sense of "bounded solidarity." That is, citizens can come to share "a set of *attitudes* and *motivations* . . . of mutual acceptance, cooperation and mutual support in time of need . . . [that goes beyond] self-interest . . . [and that is] rooted in an ethic of membership."[1] While liberal nationalists do acknowledge that nationality can assume exclusivist and autocratic forms, they

---

[1] Keith Banting and Will Kymlicka, "Introduction" in *The Strains of Commitment: The Political Sources of Solidarity in Diverse Societies*, ed. Keith Banting and Will Kymlicka (Oxford: Oxford University Press, 2017), 3–6.

maintain that it can propel citizens to care about one another's fates. Citizens can then *gradually* develop inclusive and liberal democratic understandings of their nationality. As a result, even if the culture of trust citizens share might not be *premised* on a commitment to liberal democracy from the get-go, that culture of trust can over time come to embody that commitment. Likewise, even if that culture of trust might initially squash difference and disagreement, that culture of trust can mature in a way that enables it to better accommodate difference and disagreement.

I argue that liberal democrats must take liberal nationalism seriously because it can help a liberal democratic culture of trust overcome the problem of initiation, and because the failure to engage the nation will put the liberal democratic project at a competitive disadvantage against autocratic and xenophobic brands of nationalism. I also show, however, that liberal nationalism cannot adequately ensure that bounded solidarity will become liberal democratic, socially inclusive, and capable of accommodating difference and disagreement. First, liberal nationalism handcuffs its own ability to prevent citizens from developing or sustaining exclusivist, racially or ethnically laden understandings of their national identity, and from undermining liberal democracy in an effort to enforce that homogeneity. I trace this difficulty to the fact that liberal nationalists intend for liberal nationalism to be a way to "strike a balance" between liberal democracy and nationality, rather than a way to help the nation better *serve* liberal democracy. Second, liberal nationalism does not provide citizens with the resources and the capacities necessary to prevent their differences and disagreements from corroding any preliminary sense of trust or unity that might have emerged from their shared civic-national identity. I trace this difficulty to the fact that liberal nationalism only augments citizens' ability to *tolerate* their differences and disagreements, not to actually work through those differences and disagreements. On this basis, I deem it necessary to explore another approach to the cultivation of a liberal democratic culture of trust – one whereby citizens can indeed work through their differences and disagreements, and whereby they can (at least initially) contribute to that culture of trust without realizing it: role-based constitutional fellowship.

In what follows, I first show why we ought to take liberal nationalism seriously by critiquing an alternative approach to bounded solidarity that abstains from appealing to the nation: constitutional patriotism. I then advance my principal critiques of liberal nationalism.

BOUNDED SOLIDARITY WITHOUT THE NATION?

Perhaps the strongest argument in favour of the liberal nationalist approach consists of a negative critique of liberal nationalism's primary alternative: constitutional patriotism. Like liberal nationalism, constitutional patriotism aspires toward an inclusive, liberal democratic sort of bounded solidarity. However, constitutional patriotism abstains from engaging with the resources of the national community. Rather, constitutional patriotism is grounded more narrowly in the foundational political principles of the liberal democratic state. Constitutional patriotism does so because sidestepping the resources of the nation makes it easier for the polity to encompass a variety of "ethical communities [, each] integrated around different conceptions of the good"[2] – different religions, races, ethnicities, even nationalities. After all, the nation is often intertwined with race and ethnicity: fellow nationalists often have a common ethnicity or "racial appearance,"[3] so a bounded solidarity that involves the nation might unduly exclude.

It might seem at first glance that constitutional patriotism is simply a sort of Rawlsian constitutional consensus. However, whereas a Rawlsian constitutional consensus is (in theory) sustained by a mutual recognition among citizens that they are committed to liberal democracy, constitutional patriotism is instead sustained by the collective practice of developing a shared understanding – a shared story – of how the country came to embrace liberal democracy. As Jürgen Habermas puts it, citizens discuss in the political culture how to best interpret the foundational political principles of the liberal democratic state in light of their country's particular history – how the country came to accept liberal democracy – and this shared activity can foster solidarity while reinforcing citizens' loyalty to liberal democracy.[4] So, constitutional patriotism is more robust than Rawls's constitutional consensus.[5]

Still, in order to be motivated to partake in such discussions, citizens must already be the sorts of people who are at least predisposed to become committed to liberal democracy. If they do not possess the beginnings of such a commitment, then either they will not be motivated to even begin deliberating

---

[2] Jürgen Habermas, "Struggles for Recognition" in *The Inclusion of the Other: Studies in Political Theory*, ed. Ciran Cronin and Pablo De Greiff (Cambridge, MA: The MIT Press, 2000), 224.

[3] Eric Kaufmann, *White Shift: Populism, Immigration, and the Future of White Majorities* (New York: Abrams Press, 2019), 8.

[4] Jürgen Habermas, "The European Nation-State: On the Past and Future of Sovereignty and Citizenship" in *The Inclusion of the Other: Studies in Political Theory*, ed. Ciran Cronin and Pablo De Greiff (Cambridge, MA: The MIT Press, 2000).

[5] This means that constitutional patriotism is not so abstract that it is motivationally inert. Martha Nussbaum remarks that constitutional patriotism "is so moralized and so abstract that one can't have any confidence that it would work in real life," that it demands an "unlearning [of] partiality ... [that citizens learn] not to find special value or delight in a particular," and that it therefore falls prey to the "problem of 'watery motivation' ... [that] To make people care, you have to make them see the object of potential care as in some way 'theirs'" (Martha C. Nussbaum, *Political Emotions: Why Love Matters for Justice* (Cambridge, MA: The Belknap Press of Harvard University Press, 2013), 219–222.). Constitutional patriotism, however, does *not* aim to have citizens "unlearn partiality." Even though it is rooted in abstract political principles, constitutional patriotism demands that citizens of a given state develop a *particular* collective interpretation of those principles. So, Canadians' interpretations of those political principles necessarily differ from Germans', for Canada and Germany arrived at liberal democracy through different paths.

how to interpret those principles or they will participate in such deliberations unproductively – perhaps, destructively. Habermas himself recognizes that constitutional patriotism can only succeed if citizens are first committed to liberal democracy and willing to ensure that their substantive ethical, cultural, and religious values do not contradict those political principles: those principles must become "enduringly linked with the motivations and convictions of the citizens."[6]

What this means is that constitutional patriotism – like the other approaches to the cultivation of unity or trust that we have considered thus far – suffers from an initiation problem. Constitutional patriotism is more convincing as an approach to *strengthen* citizens' commitments to liberal democracy than as an approach to *instil* such a commitment. Constitutional patriotism proposes a clear procedure through which citizens' *pre-existing* substantive political commitments can be developed into a sense of solidarity. Yet it is less clear how this virtuous circle can be kick-started. Constitutional patriotism's viability depends on whether citizens are already somewhat committed to liberal democracy. The more those principles are contested or absent, the less plausible constitutional patriotism becomes.

Can constitutional patriotism overcome this initiation problem? Well, there are two conceivable paths through which constitutional patriotism can be initiated. First, constitutional patriotism can potentially be realized via evolution; constitutional patriotism can become increasingly viable over time. In this scenario, some citizens might come to value liberal democracy intrinsically. Meanwhile, others might only value liberal democracy instrumentally for its ability to secure a social environment where they can pursue their various interests, yet they might also develop habits conducive to liberal democracy's survival. This is not unlike how people, on David Hume's account, came to view certain conventions of bodily security and property (which were conducive to their interests and pursuits) as the rules of justice.[7]

The trouble with this path is that those citizens who only value liberal democracy instrumentally are bound to revoke their provisional commitment to liberal democracy and change their behaviour and habits accordingly, should liberal democracy appear to stop "delivering the goods" (e.g., on the economy). This, of course, is not wholly unreasonable; all regimes should be judged in part on whether they actually "work." Yet the deeper issue is that these citizens are ripe fruit to be seduced by autocratic and likely exclusivist nationalist forces. After all, constitutional patriotism cannot simply become viable on its own merits; it must also be more appealing than alternative brands of bounded solidarity – in particular, autocratic ones. So, should liberal democracy appear to falter, and should liberal democrats fail to lay claim to the nation, those

---

[6] Habermas, "Struggles for Recognition," 225.
[7] David Hume, *A Treatise of Human Nature*, ed. David Fate Norton and Mary J. Norton (Oxford: Oxford University Press, 2000), III.

citizens will likely gravitate away from constitutional patriotic narratives toward racially or ethically laden autocratic nationalist narratives – narratives that construe liberal democracy and social inclusion as the causes of those problems, and autocratic and xenophobic alternatives as the solutions. Indeed, it becomes easier for autocratic nationalists to accuse liberal democrats of caring more about non-citizens (e.g., refugees) and about people who do not "look" like "real" citizens than about citizens, and of supposedly trying to "import liberalism from without" by means of international "cooperation" and supranational institutions like the European Union – in a word, of being "globalists."[8]

Second, constitutional patriotism can potentially be realized via revolution: special social-political circumstances might be conducive to constitutional patriotism's birth, seemingly out of nowhere. For example, the collapse of Nazism shocked West Germans, who had been spellbound by a deeply autocratic and xenophobic brand of nationalism, into either embracing liberal democratic principles or, more typically, grudgingly consenting to have those principles imposed onto them by outside forces.[9] With many Nazi sympathizers compelled to suppress their political and nationalistic attitudes in public, proponents of liberal democracy were able to teach German youth about the inhumanity of the Holocaust and about the dangers of autocratic and xenophobic nationalism, even if the more conservative of those forces – notably, the Christian Democratic Union and the Christian Social Union – did maintain broadly socially conservative outlooks. This explains why some have characterized constitutional patriotism as an especially *German* perspective. As Jan-Werner Müller observes, "Habermas himself ... stressed that ... Only after the ultimate evil of Nazism had Germany, at least its Western part, finally and fully embraced the Enlightenment and firmly anchored itself in the West ... [']only through the shock of this moral catastrophe.'"[10]

The worry here, however, is that constitutional patriotism seems to depend on the rawness of historical memory. Constitutional patriotism sustains itself,

---

[8] To this point, Habermas suggests that a sort of constitutional patriotism can be developed on a supranational level to encourage Europeans to feel more like citizens of the European Union. See Jürgen Habermas, "An Exploration of the Meaning of Transnationalization of Democracy, Using the Example of the European Union" in *Critical Theory in Critical Times: Transforming the Global Political and Economic Order*, ed. Penelope Deutscher and Christina Lafront (New York: Columbia University Press, 2017), 3–20.

[9] Following World War II, many Germans believed that the Nuremberg Trials and the general effort to "de-Nazify" the German citizenry was merely victors' justice. See Susan Neiman, *Learning from the Germans: Race and the Memory of Evil* (New York: Farrar, Straus and Giroux, 2019).

[10] Jan-Werner Müller, *Constitutional Patriotism* (Princeton: Princeton University Press, 2007), 33. [Hereafter Müller, *CP*.]

at least in part, through citizens' memory of past nationalistic misadventures. Yet memory fades. Even an astute reader of history, by virtue of not having actually lived through the salient historical event(s), cannot understand those events as immediately as can someone who lived through those events.[11] Indeed, the further removed those events are from the present, the more memory of those events must be constructed. No longer the manifestations of personal experience, and no longer communicable through oral history alone, the memory of such fateful events must first be preserved via culture (e.g., texts, monuments) and institutions (e.g., practice, observance), after which it can be reinterpreted so as to express liberal democratic values.[12]

In a sense, this constructed sort of memory is a superior sort of memory – unblemished by partiality and enhanced by hindsight. As Hannah Arendt suggests, a story's meaning or *truth* can only fully reveal itself to "the backward glance of the historian": "What the storyteller narrates must necessarily be hidden from the actor himself, at least as long as he is caught in its consequences because to him the meaningfulness of his act is not in the story that follows."[13] The difficulty, however, is that how memory is constructed – how events are (re-)interpreted and truths drawn – depends on *who* does the constructing. In order for this more distant sort of memory to support constitutional patriotism, it must be constructed by liberal democrats.

A paradox thereby emerges. The further removed autocratic and xenophobic nationalistic misadventures are from the present, the more memory of those misadventures must be constructed. Yet the further removed those misadventures are, the less taboo it becomes for autocratic and xenophobic political actors to assert their own interpretations of those events – and those interpretations will certainly be filled with nostalgia and victimhood, not guilt. In 2017, the Alternative für Deutschland achieved the German far right's best electoral result since the fall of the Nazis, in part, because it successfully promoted a coherent reactionary narrative that reaches back to the Nibelungen, Faustian,

---

[11] To this point, recent surveys indicate that Canadians and Americans lack basic knowledge of the Holocaust. Over 40 percent of Canadians and 30 percent of Americans cannot correctly name one concentration camp, and over 50 percent of Americans wrongly believe that the Nazi Party came to power via force. Among American "millennials," over 40 percent believe that the Holocaust claimed the lives of fewer than two million Jews, and two-thirds cannot say what Auschwitz was. See "New Survey by the Azrieli Foundation and the Claims Conference Finds Critical Gaps in Holocaust Knowledge," Claims Conference, 2018, www.claimscon.org/study-canada/ (accessed February 21, 2019) and "New Survey by Claims Conference Finds Significant Lack of Holocaust Knowledge in the United States," Claims Conference, 2018, www.claimscon.org/study/ (accessed February 21, 2019).

[12] Jan Assmann and John Czaplicka, "Collective Memory and Cultural Identity," *New German Critique* 65 (1995): 125–133.

[13] Hannah Arendt, *The Human Condition*, ed. Margaret Canovan (Chicago: University of Chicago Press, 1998), 192.

and Kyffhaüser myths, all the while conveniently omitting Nazism, to construe Germany as a sleeping empire, waiting to be reborn.[14]

Therefore, even though it is reasonable to put the resources of the nation on probation and to pursue constitutional patriotism in contexts like Germany, forgoing those resources typically makes it more difficult to initiate and sustain liberal democratic bounded solidarity. On this basis, we can see how liberal nationalism is, in most contexts, more viable. Indeed, as Kymlicka and Banting note,

[i]n many contexts, a common national identity emerged within a core ethnic group before the society developed into a liberal-democratic constitutional order. The English, Danes, Dutch, Czechs, Germans, and Portuguese viewed themselves as nations even when they were ruled by monarchs or aristocrats under constitutional orders that were neither liberal nor democratic. These societies have now established liberal-democracies, but they viewed themselves as co-nationals before they were co-authors of a liberal-democratic order. Indeed, they often demanded democracy in the name of their (pre-existing) nation, as a form of national liberation or national self-determination or national advancement.[15]

Why, then, should we move toward role-based constitutional fellowship? Why is liberal nationalism problematic when pursued by itself? Let us now turn our attention to answering these questions.

TO "BALANCE" OR TO "PRIORITIZE"?

Liberal nationalists typically aim to strike a "balance" between liberal democracy and nationalism.[16] Liberal nationalists acknowledge that a nationalism untempered by liberal democracy is dangerous – that nationalism's "most extreme expression ... [is] Nazism and fascism." At the same time, liberal nationalists insist that without nationalism, liberal democracy too is dangerous: an extreme liberal democracy manifests itself as "brutal neoliberalism" or individualistic "globalism"[17] whereby everyone is left to fend for himself or herself – and whereby liberalism (i.e., individual rights) becomes untethered from democracy (i.e., the rule of the people). In short, liberal nationalists believe that liberal democracy and nationalism need each other to be their best selves, and that the promotion of both can lead to a sort of unity reminiscent to that which we are looking for here: an inclusive culture of trust that can help accommodate difference and better secure liberal democracy. If the two are

---

[14] Julian Göpffarth, "How Alternative für Deutschland is trying to resurrect German nationalism," *New Statesman*, September 28, 2017, www.newstatesman.com/world/europe/2017/09/how-alternative-f-r-deutschland-trying-resurrect-german-nationalism.

[15] Banting and Kymlicka, *The Strains of Commitment*, 17–18.

[16] Yael Tamir, *Why Nationalism* (Princeton: Princeton University Press, 2019); David Miller, *On Nationality* (Oxford: Oxford University Press, 1995). [Hereafter Miller, *ON*.]

[17] Tamir, *Why Nationalism*, 23, 54.

allowed to develop individually without the moderating influence of the other, then dehumanizing results will follow.

Yet the failure to prioritize liberal democracy over the nation – to discern how the nation can be (re-)conceptualized and mobilized to *serve* liberal democracy – makes liberal nationalism more susceptible to exclusivist and autocratic consequences than its proponents realize. We can see why this is the case by considering two iterations of liberal nationalism.

"Legitimate" National Identity

Miller distinguishes between national identities that are "the result[s] of political imposition" and national identities that emerge and evolve "more or less spontaneously" through open discussion.[18] The former are illegitimate because they are typically constructed on top of blatant historical falsehoods and are employed by autocrats to satisfy a narrow set of interests. The latter, in contrast, are legitimate. First, even though these national identities might have mythical qualities, they are typically based on fundamentally indisputable facts and only "fill in the blanks" when no direct evidence is available. Second, even though national identities are usually inherited rather than chosen, they need not be doctrinaire; citizens can reflect on and revise their national identities through debate in the national public culture. "To the extent that the process involves inputs from all sections of the community, with groups openly competing to imprint the common identity with their own particular image," Miller remarks, "we may justifiably regard the identity that emerges as an authentic one."[19] According to Miller, legitimate national identities are likely the sorts of national identities that will become "stripped of elements that are repugnant to the self-understanding of one or more cultural groups" – inclusive.[20] In particular, these national identities will likely shed themselves of any racial or ethnic criteria that might lead the racial-ethnic majority to deny minorities equal political standing.

Is this the case? Now, Miller's liberal nationalism does permit the use of civic education to encourage citizens to embrace their nation's identity. However, such civic education regimes may only propagate understandings of national identity that have *already been endorsed* by an enduring and sizeable majority of the national community: "where some cultural feature – a landscape, a musical tradition, a language – *has become a component part of national identity*, it is justifiable to discriminate in its favour if the need arises" [emphasis added].[21] Liberal nationalism does not permit civic education regimes like that which prevailed in Maoist China. There, "an attempt was made by a small political clique to impose a uniform definition of Chinese identity upon the

---

[18] Miller, *ON*, 40.   [19] Miller, *ON*, 40.   [20] Miller, *ON*, 142.   [21] Miller, *ON*, 195.

mass of the people, involving a deliberate attempt to destroy traditional Confucian moral values and replace them with Maoist ideology."[22]

The case of Maoist China is an extreme case. Still, we can extract from all this the following general principle: the more that elites employ the resources of civic education to impose a specific understanding of national identity that has not been endorsed by an enduring and sizeable majority of citizens, the less that national identity can be considered legitimate. This is not to say that elites may not help shape their common national identity; as citizens themselves, they may. It is also not to say that elites will not have some special influence on the debate as a result of their political standing. Rather, it is to say that open public debate cannot be truly "open" if elites participate in that debate with the aid of resources like civic education that their fellow interlocutors cannot access. National identity cannot be considered as having "evolved more or less spontaneously"[23] if elites rig the debate in their favour.

Yet it is only a possibility that an inclusive liberal democratic national identity will emerge from open debate. It is also a distinct possibility that "open" debate will result in distinctly exclusivist and autocratic understandings of national identity. After all, according to Miller, the state may not issue regulations over the direction in which national identity evolves; it may only issue regulations to *consolidate* understandings of national identity that continue to be endorsed by an enduring and sizeable majority of the national community. Miller's framework therefore admits a self-contradictory possibility: its openness implies certain liberal democratic rights (e.g., to free thought and expression) in the name of open debate; yet the given national identity becomes less legitimate if certain actors use the power of the state to guide that debate in a liberal democratic direction that has not yet been endorsed (or is no longer endorsed) by an enduring and sizeable majority of the nation – indeed, to ensure that citizens remain committed to the very rights that make open debate possible.

Of course, uncertainty is not something that beleaguers only liberal nationalism. Politics is always about possibilities only, and possibilities are always accompanied by risk. So, perhaps contingency and uncertainty are simply things liberal nationalism shares with any political creed. Yet the issue here, more precisely stated, is not the mere *possibility* that open discussion might yield exclusivist and autocratic results per se. Rather, the issue is that liberal nationalism's commitment to strike a balance between liberal democracy and nationality prevents it from doing more than it does to minimize the risk of this possibility. The appeal of liberal nationalism lies in the possibility of liberal democracy and inclusion, but its notion of legitimacy is not grounded in liberal democracy and inclusion. As a result, liberal nationalism is forced to condemn the very measures that can help further its aspirations. In other words, liberal

---

[22] Miller, *ON*, 41.   [23] Miller, *ON*, 40.

nationalism is more beholden to fortuitous social preconditions that are conducive to the sort of evolution it desires than it should be.

The case of English Canada illustrates this predicament. English Canadians
long understood their national identity to be rooted in Canada's membership in
the British Commonwealth[24] and, accordingly, endorsed an ethnically laden
conception of that identity. Many once condemned the American melting pot
for failing to adequately control immigration and preserve a "distinct culture."[25] However, beginning in the 1960s, the government enacted policies to
facilitate the incorporation of newcomers and minorities into Canada's economic, social, and political life in an effort to "de-centre"[26] this historic
conception. Among these policies were a "point-based" immigration system
and an official policy to "promote the understanding that multiculturalism is a
fundamental characteristic of the Canadian heritage and identity and that it
provides an invaluable resource in the shaping of Canada's future."[27] Fifty
years later, Canadians understand their national identity much differently.
Surveys indicate that Canadians who have the strongest sense of Canadian
identity tend to be more sympathetic to diversity and immigration than those
who have weaker senses of Canadian identity.[28] Whereas roughly two-thirds of
Canadians in 1977 believed that immigration levels were too high, one-third
believe the same today.[29]

There are complexities to the English Canadian case that I shall return to
later. However, the point I would like to make here is that under Miller's
criteria of legitimacy, Canada's current mainstream understanding of national
identity is *less legitimate* than its historic conception. This is because even
though it is no longer tethered to ethnicity, the current mainstream understanding of Canadian national identity is not a consensus at which Canadians arrived
through open and spontaneous debate; it was imposed onto a general citizenry
by political elites through *proactive* social policy. This is a rather puzzling
conclusion for a framework that derives its normative appeal from the possibility of greater inclusion and liberal democracy.

---

[24] George Grant, *Lament for a Nation: The Defeat of Canadian Nationalism*, ed. Andrew Potter (Montreal and Kingston: McGill-Queen's University Press, 2005), 33.

[25] Sarah V. Wayland, "Immigration, Multiculturalism and National Identity in Canada," *International Journal on Group Rights* 5 (1997): 40.

[26] Keith Banting, "Is There a Progressive Dilemma in Canada? Immigration, Multiculturalism and the Welfare State," *Canadian Journal of Political Science* 43(4) (2010): 811. [Hereafter Banting, "Progressive Dilemma."]

[27] "Canadian Multiculturalism Act," Government of Canada, 1985, https://laws-lois.justice.gc.ca/eng/acts/c-18.7/page-1.html (accessed September 1, 2019).

[28] Banting, "Progressive Dilemma," 811.

[29] "Focus Canada – Spring 2019: Canadian Public Opinion about Immigration and Refugees," Environics Institute for Survey Research, April 2019, www.environicsinstitute.org/docs/default-source/project-documents/focus-canada-spring-2019/environics-institute—focus-canada-spring-2019-survey-on-immigration-and-refugees—final-report.pdf?sfvrsn=8dd2597f_2.

National Solidarity and "Diversity"

The exclusionary potential of liberal nationalism is even clearer in Tamir's iteration.

For Tamir, it is vital that citizens feel that they are part of a "great chain of being" and that they have a sense of control over their own fates. Identifying the nation as one place where citizens can derive a sense of comfort and belonging, she worries about what will happen if the individualism which undergirds liberal democracy (liberalism in particular) is allowed to overwhelm the nation and proliferate unchecked. In the short run, citizens will find themselves in an increasingly globalized, "neoliberal" world of pervasive competition where national governments no longer have any control over the material well-being of their citizens.[30] In such a world, people no longer feel that they are bound together by a place, and they no longer feel that they have any say in collective decision making. Instead, they find themselves left to fend for themselves in a hyper-individualistic world of "nowheres" and "somewheres" – a world where the winners of the winner-take-all global economy jet-set from cosmopolitan megacity to cosmopolitan megacity, and where the somewheres are left to rot in rapidly degrading, racially or ethnically homogeneous rural communities. In the long run, they will also find themselves in an increasingly illiberal world, for the somewheres will increasingly view xenophobic, autocratic nationalist political movements as worthy vehicles to – desperately – express their frustrations and reclaim a sense of control:

The vulnerable are not territorially concentrated and they do not share a distinct language, culture, or history, so they tend to define themselves in sentimental terms. They cling to a nostalgic memory of the "good old days" when their nation gave them a sense of dignity. Being unable to be proud of themselves, they emphasize the shortcomings of others that disrupted the traditional way of life that afforded them a comfortable social place. Consequently, their self-definition is grounded in exclusionary ideas, often sliding into xenophobia, racism, and misogyny, negative perspectives that help them cope with their hardships.[31]

Therefore, Tamir argues that liberal democrats must strike a balance between liberal democracy and nationalism: only so can liberal democracy provide citizens with the sense of belonging and control they crave, and only so can the appeal of xenophobic and autocratic nationalism be blunted. Besides reversing globalization and enacting nationalistic social democracy ("state patriotism"),[32] this involves striking a balance between diversity and social cohesion. (By "diversity," Tamir refers to a wide range of difference.) Reaching this balance will demand reducing the number of immigrants and minorities:

---

[30] Tamir, *Why Nationalism*, 94.   [31] Tamir, *Why Nationalism*, 130.
[32] Tamir, *Why Nationalism*, 176–177.

Rather than asking who is for or against diversity, maybe it's time to stop and think not in *for* and *against* terms but in terms of degrees: how much diversity can be taken in while retaining social cohesion? How fast can a society adjust to demographic changes? Who carries the burden of such changes, and can these be more evenly distributed? The mere fact of asking these questions could sow the seeds of a new discourse that does not position people against one another but tries to offer applicable solutions.[33]

The practical impulse behind Tamir's brand of liberal nationalism is understandable. However, it accommodates racially or ethnically laden notions of national identity in a manner that can lead to autocratic results. By Tamir's own admission, her proposal is informed by the observation that, in many countries, "diversity [has] intensifie[d] the spread of native sentiments and harsh laws on immigration."[34] Increased diversity undermined many citizens' (racially or ethnically laden) understandings of national identity – right at the time when neoliberalism began to take root; immigrants and minorities became the perfect scapegoats for economic hardship. So, unlike Miller, who hopes to decouple race or ethnicity and nationality, Tamir aims to conserve a(n) *racial-* or *ethno-*national sense of identity that can accommodate the presence of *some* minorities and immigrants. She aims to satiate citizens' desire for belonging and control without completely capitulating to autocratic and xenophobic nationalism.

On the face of it, Tamir's vision is problematic because it seems to trade away the core liberal democratic notion of equal citizenship in a bid to pacify the shrinking and anxious racial-ethnic majority or plurality. Certainly, as a good liberal, Tamir does maintain that "the fact that they [minorities] do not share the ruling ethos, culture, or language ... [should] not be used against them."[35] However, this nod toward diversity is an exception to the rule – an expression of an ethos of *hospitality*, not an expression of solidarity. We should only accommodate diversity insofar as doing so does not undermine internal cohesiveness, and internal cohesiveness is grounded in exclusionary features. So, under Tamir's vision, cultural, linguistic, religious, ethnic, or racial minorities would be considered *others* in perpetuity – others whose rights are protected and for whom the majority must develop empathy, but others nonetheless.

Of course, Tamir might concede that her brand of liberal nationalism does promote an ethos of hospitality. However, given the growing appeal of xenophobic and autocratic nationalism, she can still insist that such an arrangement is necessary for the survival of the broad liberal democratic project. The deeper issue, however, is that this arrangement might not be able to quell the anxieties of the "somewheres" as successfully as Tamir anticipates.

---

[33] Tamir, *Why Nationalism*, 164–165.   [34] Tamir, *Why Nationalism*, 162–163.
[35] Tamir, *Why Nationalism*, 179.

The root of the problem lies in a misunderstanding of what it means for majority racial and ethnic groups to express "in-group solidarity." Empirical scholars define in-group solidarity as a sense of camaraderie or attachment people feel toward fellow group members (e.g., fellow whites), and maintain that "such attitudes are not synonymous with prejudice ... [or] strong out-group animosities."[36] Pointing to social psychological research, Tamir notes that "membership in a group necessarily leads individuals to express in-group favoritism, but actual dislike or hostility toward the out-group is closely related to the feeling of being subject to 'an imposed unjust distribution of resources.'"[37] So, she maintains that a "balance" between diversity and social cohesion can give members of the racial-ethnic majority or plurality less to complain about as they become tempted to look for scapegoats to explain their hardships.

There is evidence, however, that even if economic hardship (or more typic-ally, the *perception* of impending economic hardship)[38] can catalyze the out-group attitudes Tamir notes, in-group solidarity among some members of the racial-ethnic majority or plurality is steeped in racial-ethnic hierarchies from the get-go; these attitudes are actually *not* merely "inward-directed." For example, Ashley Jardina finds that white Americans who have higher levels of racial identity tend to believe that it is very or extremely important for "true American[s]" to not just have American citizenship but also to be Christian, to have American ancestry, to have been born in America, and to have spent most of their lives in America.[39] These white Americans are proud of the achievements of their race, recognize that their race affords them special privileges and status, and – importantly – do not feel any guilt over the fact the other racial-ethnic groups lack those privileges. Moreover, these white Americans are untroubled by the thought that those privileges might come at the expense of other racial-ethnic groups.[40] These white Americans express befuddlement at why they should not be able to celebrate their heritage – they accuse critics of White Heritage Month of practicing "reverse discrimination"[41] – and they are particularly prone to believe that "more political or economic power for out-group members, like Blacks and Latinos, means less power for their groups."[42]

What this indicates is that even though members of the racial-ethnic majority or plurality who have a sense of in-group solidarity might not actually harbour prejudices against other groups, they are often nonetheless motivated to

---

[36] Ashley Jardina, *White Identity Politics* (Cambridge: Cambridge University Press, 2019), 35.
[37] Tamir, *Why Nationalism*, 49.
[38] Research indicates that support for xenophobic and autocratic nationalism is more of a middle-class phenomenon than a lower-class phenomenon. See Jardina, *White Identity Politics*; Kaufmann, *Whiteshift*; John B. Judis, *The Populist Explosion: How the Great Recession Transformed American and European Politics* (New York: Columbia Global Reports, 2016).
[39] Jardina, *White Identity Politics*, 123–125.   [40] Jardina, *White Identity Politics*, 130ff.
[41] Jardina, *White Identity Politics*, 136ff.   [42] Jardina, *White Identity Politics*, 139ff.

perpetuate their racial-ethnic status and to maintain their special privileges. These whites do not turn to xenophobic and autocratic nationalism because they feel like there is nowhere left for them to turn. Rather, they turn to such nationalism because they view it as a way to preserve their status and privileges.[43]

Tamir's brand of liberal nationalism therefore encounters two opposing challenges. On the one hand, it does admit some diversity. So, unless that diversity is kept at minimal levels – certainly, lower than current levels – it will threaten members of the racial-ethnic majority or plurality who have a sense of in-group identity, not just those who have out-group prejudices. On the other hand, by not seeking to detach race or ethnicity from national identity, Tamir's liberal nationalism reinforces existing racially or ethnically laden nationalistic attitudes. This risks emboldening those members of the racial-ethnic majority or plurality who have a sense of in-group identity to assert themselves, particularly when they feel that their sense of national identity is under threat. In short, Tamir's liberal nationalism opens the door to some diversity all the while provoking citizens who oppose that diversity.

Given these difficulties, I submit that liberal democrats must avoid being trapped in this manner and that they must fully commit themselves to promote a fully inclusive national identity that is detached from race and ethnicity. Now, such a commitment does not entail that liberal democrats must "drum up" as much diversity as quickly as possible. Indeed, as we shall see later in this book, I deem it important to account for the possibility of backlash, and I acknowledge that there is virtue in caution. However, such a commitment does demand that liberal democrats work toward reducing the degree to which members of the racial-ethnic majority or plurality harbour a sense of in-group solidarity, not to mention out-group prejudices. In other words, in order to adequately make room for difference, liberal democrats must prioritize liberal democracy over the nation, and not merely seek a balance.

NAGGING DIFFERENCES AND DISAGREEMENTS

Liberal nationalists can, of course, concede that the demands of liberal democracy must take precedence over the demands of the nation while remaining nationalists, insofar as being nationalists involves accepting the need to engage with the nation constructively in some fashion. Indeed, some argue that if "cosmopolitanism ... [is] defined by contrast with its real enemies – xenophobia, intolerance, injustice, chauvinism ...," then liberal nationalism should, to the greatest extent possible, be structured in a manner that furthers "the universal values of freedom and equality" so that it can properly be described

---

[43] Kaufmann, *Whiteshift* finds similar attitudes in many other liberal democratic societies.

as "involv[ing] a *redefinition* of cosmopolitanism."[44] This is the sort of liberal nationalism that we *should* take seriously, for it can help the project of liberal democratic trust overcome the problem of initiation.

Still, I maintain that it is necessary to move toward role-based constitutional fellowship. Even though such a liberal nationalism can contribute to a preliminary sense of unity, it does not equip citizens with the resources and techniques required to negotiate their differences and disagreements in manners that serve to deepen that initial unity.

Consider how liberal nationalist solidarity is structured. Liberal nationalism is modelled on the normative dynamics of groups. When people are members of a group (e.g., a team, a school) and share a durable sense of group identity, not only do they develop a sense of group loyalty and prioritize the group's interests; they also afford one another's interests special consideration and expect one another to reciprocate.[45] There are two reasons, according to liberal nationalists, for why this is the case. First, as a result of their shared group identity, people increasingly recognize that their interests and those of the group are not necessarily at odds, and they come to find that their shared group membership enhances their sense of self-esteem.[46] So, contributing to the group becomes a form of goal-fulfillment. Second, group members come to expect that they will benefit from their group membership. This is not to say that they are chiefly motivated by self-interest; the expected costs of group participation likely exceed the expected benefits. Rather, it is to say that the conflict between the personal goals of group members and the goals of the group become softened, and ethical behaviour for imperfect altruistic agents, easier, because "the act of making a contribution is not a pure loss ... [and helps] sustain a set of relationships from which [group members] stand to benefit to some degree."[47]

What this means is that liberal nationalism offers a mediated sort of solidarity. Citizens A and B care about each other not primarily because they are fellow human beings, but rather because they are members of the same national community. So, even though national solidarity does offer certain positive resources to hold citizens together – Citizens A and B can share a devotion to the national soccer team, or they can celebrate the same national myths – solidarity depends, in part, on whether citizens judge one another as fulfilling their civic-national responsibilities.[48]

This is not a problem in and of itself. Yet complications arise from the nation's unique characteristics. Namely, as Benedict Anderson explains, given

---

[44] Will Kymlicka, *Politics in the Vernacular* (Oxford: Oxford University Press, 2001), 22.

[45] Miller, *ON*, 67; Tamir, *Why Nationalism*, 58ff.   [46] Tamir, *Why Nationalism*, 63.

[47] Miller, *ON*, 67.

[48] This is not to say that liberal nationalism depends on the absence of free-riders. Rather, it is to say that liberal nationalism depends on a culture of trust where some might free-ride but where most are judged (or assumed) by their fellow citizens to be responsible citizens.

the modern nation's size (among other things), citizens must rely heavily on their faculties of imagination to form an image of that community.[49] This leads to ambiguity regarding what sorts of responsibilities citizens must fulfill in order to be judged by their fellow citizens as responsible. Accordingly, Miller explains that citizens must participate in an ongoing process of public debate in the national public culture, during which they can develop and revise a set of ideas about the nation's "ethos" or "character"; this set of ideas "fix[es] responsibilities."[50] In other words, liberal nationalism is compromised when citizens do not judge one another, by and large, to be responsible citizens, according to criteria that they determine together.

Liberal nationalism is therefore at its most secure when the need for public discourse is minimized, for the lack of such a need indicates that citizens have already arrived at a consensus on what their civic-national responsibilities look like. Perhaps surprisingly, this does not mean that citizens must have the exact same understanding of what the national community stands for – its ethos. Indeed, it might be better for parts of that ethos to be left ambiguous. After all, solidarity can be reinforced when citizens see the nation as their own, on their own terms.[51] So long as those different understandings do not radically diverge,[52] citizens can experience solidarity on the basis of the overlap between their various understandings of the nation's ethos and the set of responsibilities that follow.

The case of English Canada, again, is instructive. Surveys indicate that English Canadians share a broad understanding of the core components of Canadian identity: among them, certainly, the Charter of Rights and Freedoms, the Royal Canadian Mounted Police,[53] the national flag, and the national anthem; and, to a lesser extent, Medicare, Bilingualism, hockey, the military, and First Nations.[54] These surveys also indicate that, beyond those core items, different Canadians identify contrasting national symbols, *and* that those symbols are not necessarily sources of contestation. In particular, although more right-leaning than left-leaning Canadians identify rural symbols like pickup trucks, resource towns, and snowmobiles to be national symbols, those symbols

---

[49] Benedict Anderson, *Imagined Communities* (London: Verso, 2016).   [50] Miller, *ON*, 68.

[51] This echoes Aristotle's justification of polity. A polity is relatively stable because it is composed of both democratic and oligarchic elements: the poor support the regime because they can interpret it as a democracy, while the rich also support the regime because they can interpret it as an oligarchy. See Aristotle, *Politics*, 1294b13ff.

[52] Examples of radically divergent understandings of the nation are white nationalist and multicultural understandings of America. Examples of less divergent understandings are those based on "conservative" and "liberal" interpretations of America's founding principles.

[53] Given recent controversies surrounding the use of force on Indigenous Canadians, the RCMP's status as a core component of English Canadian national identity might be waning.

[54] Greg Quinn, "Survey Finds We Like the Charter of Rights More than Hockey," *Calgary Herald*, October 1, 2015, https://calgaryherald.com/news/national/canadians-like-hockey-they-love-the-constitutional-bill-of-rights.

are relatively politically latent; the Conservative Party has largely not used them to rally its base and construe its opponents as un-Canadian. So, Canadians can develop solidarity on the basis of whether they observe one another to be fulfilling the responsibilities that flow from those core components of Canadian identity, while right-leaning Canadians can strengthen their allegiance to Canada through those rural symbols.[55]

Yet we cannot expect liberal nationalism to always be at its most secure. Often, the nation's ethos is contested, and ambiguities serve as sources of division. Indeed, although the national symbols cherished by right-leaning English Canadians are relatively politically latent, those cherished by left-leaning Canadians are more divisive – for example, the Canadian Broadcasting Corporation and Margaret Atwood.[56] The status of the crown jewel of left-leaning Canadians' conception of national identity, diversity, is ambiguous. On the one hand, English Canada is by all accounts far removed from the British, Christian, and Caucasian society that it once was. Only around 15 percent of Canadians (including French Canadians) believe that it is very important for Canada to be a Christian country.[57] In 1977, two-thirds of Canadians believed that immigration levels were too high; today, one-third believe the same.[58] On the other hand, Conservative Party supporters are more likely to believe that there are too many non-white immigrants than their Liberal counterparts (69 percent to 15 percent),[59] and more right-leaning than

---

[55] Note that French Canada has different normative dynamics. Specifically, many Quebeckers believe that Quebec constitutes its own nation or "distinct society." This nationalism, distinct from *Canadian* nationalism, long expressed itself in calls for separation from Canada. In 1995, nearly half of registered voters in Quebec voted to separate from Canada. Since then, the separatist movement has lost steam, but skepticism toward immigration and multiculturalism has risen decidedly.

[56] Consider the following statement by right populist Doug Ford: "I don't even know her. If she walked by me, I wouldn't have a clue who she is ... Tell her to go run in the next election and get democratically elected. And we'd be more than happy to sit down and listen to Margaret Atwood" (Paul Moloney, "Doug Ford Blasts Margaret Atwood over Libraries, Says 'I Don't Even Know Her,'" *The Star*, July 26, 2011, www.thestar.com/news/gta/2011/07/26/doug_ford_blasts_margaret_atwood_over_libraries_says_i_dont_even_know_her.html).

[57] Bruce Stokes, "What It Takes to Truly Be 'One of Us': In US, Canada, Europe, Australia and Japan, Publics Say Language Matters More to National Identity than Birthplace," Pew Research Center, February 2017, www.pewresearch.org/global/wp-content/uploads/sites/2/2017/02/Pew-Research-Center-National-Identity-Report-FINAL-February-1-2017.pdf, 27.

[58] "Focus Canada – Spring 2019: Canadian Public Opinion about Immigration and Refugees," Environics Institute for Survey Research, April 2019, www.environicsinstitute.org/docs/default-source/project-documents/focus-canada-spring-2019/environics-institute—focus-canada-spring-2019-survey-on-immigration-and-refugees—final-report.pdf?sfvrsn=8dd2597f_2.

[59] "Increased Polarization on Attitudes to Immigration Reshaping the Political Landscape in Canada," Ekos Politics, April 15, 2019, www.ekospolitics.com/index.php/2019/04/increased-polarization-on-attitudes-to-immigration-reshaping-the-political-landscape-in-canada/.

left-leaning Canadians consider being born in Canada important to being Canadian (24 percent to 15 percent).[60] Similarly, half of Conservative Party supporters think that current immigration levels are too high, while three-quarters of Liberal Party supporters have a positive view of immigration.[61]

In such circumstances, citizens need to engage in public discourse. So, liberal nationalism does not only depend on the fact of common membership to generate fellow feeling; it also depends on the ability of citizens to reach an accommodation of their differences and disagreements. This is not to say that they must eliminate all their differences and disagreements. Nor is it to say that they must reach the same understanding of their national identity. Rather, it is to say that they must somehow understand their differences and disagreements to be the bases of *good faith* disagreements about what it means to be a good Canadian – not the basis of a more existential struggle between those who love Canada and those who wish to do Canada harm. If this does not occur, then it becomes more likely that they will allow their outstanding differences and disagreements to generate animosity.

For instance, Eastern and Western English Canadians might share a devotion to the Charter, and they might both do what is necessary to uphold its rights and freedoms. However, if Western Canadians cannot understand that Eastern Canadians' opposition to the oil sands are motivated by a genuine concern about climate change, and if Eastern Canadians cannot appreciate that Western Canadians value resources towns as important parts of their national identity, then their disagreements over climate change policy risk overwhelming any solidarity that might have emerged from their shared devotion to the Charter. Western Canadians would accuse Eastern Canadians of trying to destroy Western Canadians' way of life, while Eastern Canadians would accuse Western Canadians of trying to destroy the planet.

On this score, the trouble with liberal nationalism is twofold. First, it is unclear whether the necessary public discourse will even begin to take place.

---

[60] Stokes, "What It Takes to Truly Be 'One of Us,'" 20.

[61] "Focus Canada," Environics Institute, 3. It is possible, however, that this potentially potent divide is more of an urban-rural divide than a left-right divide: Canada's version of right populism attracts and caters to many ethnic minorities (Daniel Silver, Zack Taylor, and Fernando Calderón-Figueroa, "Populism in the City: The Case of Ford Nation," *International Journal of Politics, Culture, and Society* 33(4) (2010): 1–21). Supporting this hypothesis is evidence that recent immigrants, who tend to cluster around cities like Toronto and Vancouver, are more likely to vote Conservative than immigrants of previous generations (Darrell Bricked and John Ibbitson, *The Big Shift: The Seismic Change in Canadian Politics, Business, and Culture and What It Means for Our Future* (Toronto: HarperCollins, 2014)). Alternatively, some argue that the Conservative Party has been incentivized to moderate and court "ethnic voters" because antagonism between Quebec nativists and English Canadian nativists has fractured the stronger anti-immigration sentiments found in rural and smaller urban areas. See Joshua Gordon, Sanjay Jeram, and Clifton van der Linden, "The Two Solitudes of Canadian Nativism: Explaining the Absence of a Competitive Anti-immigration Party in Canada," *Nations and Nationalism* 26(4) (2019): 902–922.

Under liberal nationalism, the nation's common public culture is the venue where citizens can shape their collective understanding of national identity. Often, however, it is more appropriate to speak of common public culture*s*. Citizens might not share in *one* common public culture, but rather participate in rival public cultures. When this occurs, national identity serves to divide rather than to unite – to *bond* Eastern Canada together and Western Canada together, but not to *bridge* the divide between the two.[62] So, a sort of problem of social cleavages persists.

Second, a sense of solidarity does not, by itself, empower citizens with the techniques and/or virtues required to adequately manage their differences and disagreements. Yes, such solidarity might help citizens recognize that their long-term interests align, and it might inform a civic education regime that can narrow citizens' differences and disagreements. Miller maintains that children should be expected to assimilate a "core body of material,"[63] while Tamir praises the "heroic efforts" of past national education regimes to bring "classes closer together, allowing discourse across different groups, making the nation-state the first political entity grounded in a social-cultural alliance that gives place to the people as well as the elites."[64]

Yet it does not follow that citizens will be able to actually adequately manage their outstanding differences and disagreements. Rather, it only follows that citizens will be motivated to *tough it out* when the going gets rough. There is a limit, however, to how much the mere recognition that their long-term interests align can compel citizens to continue toughing it out. Even loyalty has a breaking point. Indeed, while national education can narrow the range of citizens' differences and disagreements, it can only persist as a source of unity so long as citizens continue broadly supporting it – and this requires citizens to reach some accommodation of their outstanding differences and disagreements. If citizens fail to do this, then that national education regime risks becoming a site of confrontation rather than a source of consolidation.

For example, US public school curricula have become arenas of heated debate between creationists and global warming skeptics on the one hand and the self-described proponents of science on the other hand. With the former also typically advocating for religiously laden initiatives like school prayer and prohibitions on abortion, and the latter, the separation of church and state, these confrontations can be understood as proxies for the unresolved differences which exist between how the American Left and Right understand national identity.

In short, liberal nationalism alone cannot empower citizens with adequate resources to deal with their differences and disagreements in manners that allow them to deepen any initial sense of unity or trust which might have

---

[62] Robert D. Putnam, *Bowling Alone: The Collapse and Revival of American Community* (New York: Simon & Schuster, 2000), 22.
[63] Miller, *ON*, 142.   [64] Tamir, *Why Nationalism*, 86.

emerged from their shared civic-national identity. Nor can liberal nationalism reliably facilitate the development of a shared set of criteria by which citizens can judge whether their fellow citizens are acting responsibly. As a result, in cases where such basic unity has eroded, civic-national identity can, paradoxically, *raise the stakes* of citizens' differences and disagreements. In the absence of basic unity, efforts to encourage citizens to love their country can lead citizens to interpret their differences and disagreements as problems of civic-national identity, even if they have nothing to do with civic-national identity.

Nowhere is this clearer than in the United States. Americans are exceptionally proud about their country (and loud about it). Yet given the breakdown of trust and the rise of negative partisanship, not only do the American Right and Left consider each other to be wrong programmatically; they also consider each other existential threats to the country. No longer does the left consider the right as "merely" xenophobic and heartless toward the poor, and no longer does the right consider the left as merely tax-and-spenders and hostile to success; they now consider each other un-American.

TOWARD ROLE-BASED CONSTITUTIONAL FELLOWSHIP

Liberal nationalists outline an approach to the promotion of a socially inclusive, liberal democratic culture of trust that mobilizes citizens' emotional attachment to the national community. I argued that liberal nationalism should be taken seriously, not just because it can help overcome the problem of initiation, but also because it can help the liberal democratic project better compete against autocratic and xenophobic brands of nationalism. I also showed, however, that liberal nationalism handcuffs its own ability to prevent citizens from developing or sustaining racially or ethnically laden understandings of their national identity. Moreover, I demonstrated that liberal nationalism only provides citizens with resources to tolerate their differences and disagreements, and that there is a significant risk under liberal nationalism that citizens will not be able to deepen any preliminary sense of unity or trust which might have emerged from their shared civic-national identity. As a result, I submit that even though we usually should incorporate liberal nationalism into the general effort to promote a liberal democratic culture of trust, liberal nationalism risks perpetuating undue social hierarchies (particularly between different races or ethnicities) and, counterintuitively, further aggravating citizens' differences and disagreements.

Given these difficulties, in the remainder of this book, I advance a notion of role-based constitutional fellowship. I argue that role-based constitutional fellowship offers liberal democracy the best path through which citizens can work through their differences and disagreements. That is, role-based constitutional fellowship can help initiate and sustain a virtuous circle whereby citizens work through their differences and disagreements in ways that contribute to a culture of trust, and whereby that emerging culture of trust in turn makes it easier for citizens to indeed work through their differences and disagreements. As part of my discussion, I show that citizens under role-based constitutional fellowship can contribute to a liberal democratic culture of trust, even if some citizens might seem to act in ways that contradict the spirit of trust production. I also show that it is possible for citizens to fulfill at least some of the "roles" implied by constitutional fellowship without necessarily realizing it and without necessarily "buying into" the entire apparatus of constitutional fellowship, at least at first. So, role-based constitutional fellowship can also help the liberal democratic culture of trust overcome the problem of initiation in a manner that is distinct from – but not incompatible with – the manner implied by liberal nationalism.

5

Three Dimensions of Trust

We have been refining our understanding of what it would take for liberal democracy to harness the benefits of difference and disagreement and avoid unduly squashing difference and disagreement, yet also prevent the expression of difference and disagreement from "overheating," damaging liberal democratic norms and institutions, and leaving liberal democracy vulnerable to the growing influence of its enemies. I have shown that citizens should be encouraged to share in a sense of unity, and that this unity should assume the form of a culture of trust. Under this culture of trust, citizens believe that their fellow citizens *probably* value the continuation of their civic relationship, and they are committed to supporting social and political arrangements that can allow them to continue that relationship: liberal democracy. This culture of trust must not suffocate the expression of difference and disagreement, and it must not stymie debate over the meaning of political (in)equality and (in)justice. In addition, this culture of trust must somehow be able to emerge or sustain itself in contexts where the value of liberal democracy might not be as widely accepted or appreciated as liberal democrats might hope. On this basis, I argued in Chapter 4 that liberal nationalist efforts to fuse liberal democracy with non-political resources like the nation can help counteract the problem of initiation. I also argued, however, that liberal nationalism only provides citizens with resources to tolerate their differences and disagreements and that there is a significant risk that citizens will not be able to deepen any preliminary sense of unity or trust that might have emerged from their shared civic-national identity.

In the remainder of this book, I shall argue that liberal democracy can more successfully realize and sustain a culture of trust if citizens act in accordance to – and gradually come to understand their civic relations in terms of – a metaphor of citizenship that I call "role-based constitutional fellowship." Under role-based constitutional fellowship, citizens do not cultivate trust by practicing the same set of techniques. Rather, citizens first recognize (or act in manners that are consistent with the recognition) that trust assumes different complexions in different contexts and that different solutions are required to overcome the different barriers to trust that exist in these different contexts. Second, citizens observe a series of divisions of labour to overcome these different barriers. Therefore, citizens might seem to behave in contradictory manners, and they might not even recognize, at first, that they are indeed fulfilling the various normative roles entailed by role-based constitutional fellowship. However, when citizens do fulfill these roles, it becomes more likely that they will overcome those barriers, develop a culture of trust, and come to view themselves explicitly as constitutional fellows – partners in the effort to preserve liberal democracy.

What this all means, concretely, is that role-based constitutional fellowship consists of a series of divisions of labour to cultivate trust within and between different spheres of activity: (1) trust within the formal political sphere; (2) trust within the general citizenry; and (3) trust between the formal political sphere and the general citizenry. First, when trust exists within the formal political sphere, political competitors treat one another as adversaries to be defeated rather than as enemies to be destroyed. The primary barrier to trust here is the "institutionalized enmity problem" – the tendency for competitors to indeed treat one another as enemies. I argue that the cultivation of trust here demands a division of labour between "principled pragmatists" and "principled purists." Principled pragmatists can develop a sense of reciprocity by performing compromises, while principled purists can more stubbornly refuse to compromise in order to keep principled pragmatists honest and compel pragmatists to compromise for the sake of the public good, not their own private interests. Such a division of labour would not just help political actors avoid competing as enemies but also help prevent political actors from evolving into a self-serving club and trust from becoming a symbol of corruption.

I also note, however, that it is not always appropriate to cultivate political trust. Specifically, when some mainstream liberal democratic political actors have forged "unholy alliances" with autocratic political forces, it is instead necessary for those who stand outside of those unholy alliances – the defenders of liberal democracy – to discern the most effective ways to defeat those alliances so as to disincentivize further participation in those alliances. Still, should the defenders of liberal democracy win, they should seek to entice those former liberal democrats back into the liberal democratic fold, and to try to begin re-establishing trust. This will involve compromise.

Second, when trust exists within the general citizenry, citizens at large treat one another in manners befitting their equal citizenship, despite their various differences. I show that in the liberal democratic context, this means that citizens who trust one another believe that their fellow citizens largely do not wish to have special, unequal privileges of citizenship as a result of their differences and that fellow citizens do wish to redress undue social hierarchies. So, the primary barrier to trust here is what I call "the social domination problem" – the tendency for those undue hierarchies to indeed aggravate distrust among citizens who have differences.

It is unlikely that such trust can come to encompass all citizens. After all, some – whom I call "proud oppressors" and "harder complicit oppressors" – either relish such hierarchies or feel threatened by efforts to redress those hierarchies. Still, I argue that such trust can gradually emerge through a division of labour among the oppressed, the underprivileged, and their allies (who are members of privileged and dominant groups) between two broad sets of practices: "shouting back" and "talking." Specifically, the practice of shouting back can compel the privileged and the dominant to pay attention to various instances and patterns of injustice, while the practice of talking can cultivate trust with "unwitting, well-intentioned oppressors" and "softer complicit oppressors." When citizens talk, they ideally engage in transparent discourse where they identify and rectify injustices together. More typically, when citizens talk, they adhere to (and revise) the conventions of good manners. Through this balance of shouting back and talking, citizens can realize a culture of trust that accommodates the gradual rectification of undue hierarchies.

As part of my discussion of trust among citizens at large, I clarify the role of the allies of the underprivileged and the oppressed. In addition to talking and shouting back when appropriate, allies ought to strive to fulfill a mediating role by "listening well." Allies can listen well to the underprivileged and the oppressed so as to afford the underprivileged and the oppressed a degree of recognition in contexts where recognition is all too rare. Likewise, allies can listen well to unwitting oppressors and softer complicit oppressors so as to provide a softer touch and assure unwitting oppressors and softer complicit oppressors that they (oppressors) are not merely being condemned as bad people. In these manners, allies can persuade the underprivileged and the oppressed to maintain faith that progress within the liberal democratic framework is possible. Likewise, allies can dissuade unwitting oppressors and softer complicit oppressors from aligning politically with proud oppressors and harder complicit oppressors.

Third, when trust exists between the formal political sphere and the general citizenry, citizens at large believe that political actors largely do try to further the public good. So, the primary barrier to trust here is what I call the "representative cynicism problem" – the tendency for citizens at large to believe that political actors are largely in it for themselves, individually and as a class. Accordingly, I argue that in order to cultivate trust here, political actors should refrain from excessively demonizing their opponents, explain why they might have compromised (but only after the fact), and avoid promulgating fantastical understandings of politics. Meanwhile, citizens can prepare themselves to return these good faith efforts by reflecting on how they act hypocritically in their own lives as well – for example, in business, in the job market, and even at school. Citizens will more likely do this preparatory work and adopt a less cynical posture toward politics if political actors act in the manners I outline.

To prepare for my detailed discussion of role-based constitutional fellowship in Chapters 6–8, this short chapter introduces fellowship's conceptual foundations. I articulate what trust looks like in the formal political sphere, in the general citizenry, and between these two spheres of activity, and I identify the three primary barriers to trust production.

SELF-INITIATION AND THE CHARGE OF ELITISM

Let me make three preliminary remarks before we get started. First, although Chapters 6–8 make reference to some of the political institutions and associational contexts that can encourage citizens to act like constitutional fellows, I defer my full account of these institutions and contexts until Chapter 9. However, role-based constitutional fellowship has a structure that is conducive to its own realization, and it contains devices that can motivate citizens to act in accordance to its recommendations. Importantly, the various divisions of labour that role-based constitutional fellowship proposes take advantage of what we can call the "natural distribution of personality types." Some political actors are more disposed to be pragmatists, and others, purists. Likewise, some citizens are more disposed to shout back; others, to talk; and others still, to engage in either practice in different contexts. In addition, role-based constitutional fellowship mobilizes salutary hypocrisy (to be discussed) but does not embrace hypocrisy wholesale. It recognizes the inevitably of some forms of hypocrisy and aims to make the most out of them but also takes into account the distrust ordinary citizens tend to feel toward hypocrisy. So, the recommendations put forth by role-based constitutional fellowship are not incompatible with the imperatives of competitive politics and social contestation.

Second, although role-based constitutional fellowship is a sort of ideal that can serve as a model with which we can evaluate practice, I intend for role-based constitutional fellowship, over time, to become a source of motivation for more and more citizens. Importantly, however, the performance of some of the roles I articulate does not necessarily require that citizens "buy into" the entire framework of role-based constitutional fellowship; citizens might, without even realizing it, contribute to the sort of trust and normative goals that fellowship aspires toward. Moreover, as we shall see, role-based constitutional fellowship recognizes that different actions are required in different contexts. For example, fellowship holds that there are times when the threat of authoritarianism is too pressing and that trust building is only appropriate after those threats have been defeated. Therefore, even though role-based constitutional fellowship is a sort of reciprocity, fellowship stands a better chance at overcoming the sorts of first-mover problems that beleaguer many theories of democratic reciprocity.

Third, role-based constitutional fellowship observes a structural distinction between the formal political sphere and the general citizenry. So, some might object to role-based constitutional fellowship on the grounds that it implies a division between *elites* and *masses*.[1] However, I maintain that the distinction between the formal political sphere and the general citizenry is apt, for it reflects empirical distinctions between political and extra-political associations.[2] Political associations are embedded within or oriented toward state power. They include political parties, lobbies, pressure groups, and watchdog groups. Extra-political associations, in contrast, are embedded within or oriented toward either social media (e.g., norms, customs, traditions, language) or, in the case of economic associations, markets. These associations include families, schools, religious groups, unions, and firms. Although what happens within these associations has political implications, their focuses lie elsewhere. So, even though the distinction between the formal political sphere and the general citizenry is neither impermeable nor immutable,[3] we have good reason to believe that the normative dynamics and hurdles to trust production within and between these different spheres are distinct.[4] Moreover, as we shall see, given that the formal political sphere is defined by explicit competition, the elimination of this distinction risks rendering society *as a whole* more explicitly competitive and prone to strife.

TRUST WITHIN THE FORMAL POLITICAL SPHERE

Different spheres of activity have different normative dynamics. Practices that produce trust in one sphere might produce distrust in another, and the trust that exists in one sphere might contribute to distrust *between* those spheres. So, trust has different complexions in different contexts.

A culture of trust involves trust among political actors. Now, political actors engage in explicit competition. Politicians compete to win offices, to enact their preferred policies, and to further the interests of their constituents and/or supporters. Interest and pressure groups jockey for influence, and social

---

[1] Joseph A. Schumpeter, *Capitalism, Socialism, and Democracy: Third Edition* (New York: HarperCollins, 2008).

[2] Mark E. Warren, *Democracy and Association* (Princeton: Princeton University Press, 2001), 54, defines associations as organizations "whose force is derived primarily from associational relations – that is, relations based on normative influence," not money or power. Note that the distinction I am drawing here between the formal political sphere and the general citizenry roughly parallels the distinction between the state and the public sphere that appears in Jürgen Habermas, *Between Facts and Norms*, ed. William Rehg (Cambridge, MA: MIT Press, 1998), 329ff and Jean Cohen and Andrew Arato, *Civil Society and Political Theory* (Cambridge, MA: MIT Press, 1992), 29ff. I make reference to Habermas's discussion in Chapter 2.

[3] Indeed, during "populist" moments, just when the disparities between the two seem to have fossilized, the norms and sometimes crude language of the agitated citizenry flood into the political sphere.

[4] This is not to say that the production or corrosion of trust in one sphere does not affect the status of trust in the other. For example, as we shall see later, the presence of trust in the general citizenry can spill over into the formal political sphere or, at least, constrain the degree to which political competition can engage in negative partisanship.

movements try to harness the energy of citizens at large to influence political actors. Although *public policy* can be positive-sum and does not necessarily involve "difference-splitting compromise," electoral competition is zero-sum: one candidate's victory entails another's loss.[5] So, we can say that when political actors value the continuation of their relationship, they compete as *adversaries* with a sense of respect and self-restraint, and cooperation is possible: "you might be able to win over an adversary today and turn him or her into an ally tomorrow."[6]

The challenge of trust production among political actors involves counteracting the tendency of political competition to become modeled on warfare. When political actors understand political competition in these terms, they treat one another as *enemies* who are illegitimate and corrupt. Accordingly, they try to destroy one another, even if doing so propels them to harm the rule of law, to undermine the freedom and fairness of elections, and/or to solicit the help of hostile foreign actors. I call this tendency the "institutionalized enmity problem."[7]

TRUST WITHIN THE GENERAL CITIZENRY

A culture of trust also involves trust among citizens at large. Although they can sometimes view their social relations in zero-sum terms, particularly when they understand their social relations in partisan terms,[8] citizens typically do not engage in zero-sum competition. So, when they trust one another, they do not compete with a sense of self-restraint; rather, they treat one another in manners befitting their equal citizenship, despite their differences. For example, in diverse societies, when trust exists, minorities feel that the majority treats them like political equals, and vice versa (and different groups of minorities feel similarly about one another as well). So, citizens who trust one another believe that their fellow citizens do not wish to have special, unequal privileges of citizenship as a result of their differences.

Yet these sorts of differences are rarely "mere" differences; they are often structured hierarchically and can be understood to be forms of *domination*. Sometimes, domination is explicit – a conscious project, sustained by base

---

[5] Matthew Yglesias, "Positive-Sum Policy vs Zero-Sum Politics," Think Progress, May 20, 2010, https://archive.thinkprogress.org/positive-sum-policy-vs-zero-sum-politics-270234a8391c/.

[6] Michael Ignatieff, *Fire and Ashes: Success and Failure in Politics* (Cambridge, MA: Harvard University Press, 2013), 151.

[7] As I noted in Chapter 2, I incorporate the agonistic distinction between adversaries and enemies into role-based constitutional fellowship but deem the agonistic approach to keeping adversaries adversaries inadequate.

[8] Shanto Iyengar and Sean J. Westwood, "Fear and Loathing across Party Lines: New Evidence on Group Polarization," *American Journal of Political Science* 59(3) (2015): 690–707, find that when presented with job candidates with identical résumés, US partisans tend to pick the candidate whose party affiliation matches their own.

passions like cruelty, prejudice, and subconscious insecurities. White suprema-cists and homophobes maintain their identities by juxtaposing themselves against "the inferior" and seek to legally codify those hierarchies. However, domination can also be perpetuated unwittingly through the well-intentioned or disinterested, everyday actions and norms of law-abiding citizens who benefit from those hierarchies and who might harbour implicit or unconscious biases, but who would otherwise not wish to further injustice.[9] For example, in the United States, the fact that Blacks and Latinos work in menial jobs dis-proportionately serves to enhance the statuses of those they serve, even if those who are served might wish to make the business and professional classes more inclusive.

As a result, the challenge of trust production among citizens at large – of promoting a broad sense that fellow citizens take their political equality ser-iously – does not consist merely of a broad acceptance of difference. It also demands, at the very least, that citizens find a way to demonstrate to one another that they take the persistence of undue social hierarchies seriously, *even if* they might disagree about which hierarchies are justified or unjustified and even if some of them might unwittingly behave in ways that hinder the rectification of those hierarchies. So, the challenge of trust production among citizens at large involves counteracting the tendency of the persistence of undue social hierarchies to encourage citizens – in particular, the underprivileged and the oppressed – to believe that their fellow citizens do not take injustice seriously. I call this problem the "social domination problem."

There are two things we should note here. First, just because we must deal with the persistence of undue social hierarchies for the sake of cultivating trust does not mean that we should not deal with the persistence of those hierarchies for the sake of rectifying those hierarchies. However, as I argued in Chapter 1, insofar as we believe that liberal democracy does secure important goods and that it is worth preserving, it is important to consider how we can identify and rectify undue social hierarchies in manners that help to preserve liberal democ-racy. So, if redressing the potential perils of difference and disagreement depends on the cultivation of a culture of trust, then we must discern how to identify and rectify undue social hierarchies in ways conducive to the produc-tion of trust.

Second, this social realm is not solely a realm of structural domination. It is also a realm of economic competition where businesses compete with one another for profits, and workers for jobs. Economic competition is less likely than political competition to be zero-sum; the pie can grow, and everyone can potentially gain. For our current purposes, however, it is more vital that we address the hurdles to trust that emerge from domination. First, empirical

---

[9] Iris Marion Young, *Justice and the Politics of Difference* (Princeton: Princeton University Press, 2011), 52.

research suggests that successful economic cooperation is not the catalyst but rather the result of a pre-existing, extra-economic culture of trust.[10] So, the persistence of social domination or unreconciled social differences can inhibit economic cooperation. Second, as Marxists and neorepublicans note, economic relations can be interpreted in terms of domination. So, the lack of underlying trust between owners and workers can undermine institutional arrangements that mitigate economic domination. Even in Sweden, as industrial jobs and the power of labour have declined, business leaders have sought to weaken the country's social democratic institutions.[11] So, it is more urgent to address the distrust that emerges from social domination.

TRUST BETWEEN THE POLITICAL SPHERE AND THE GENERAL CITIZENRY

Finally, a culture of trust involves trust between political actors and citizens at large. When such trust exists, citizens at large believe that political actors largely do try to further the public good. When such trust is absent, citizens believe that political actors are largely in it for themselves, individually and as a class. I call the tendency of citizens at large to arrive at such negative assessments of political actors the "representative cynicism problem."

Producing such trust can be challenging, not just because such trust depends in part on the perception that public policies are indeed furthering the public good, but also because that which produces trust among political actors might lead citizens to distrust them. For example, the willingness of political actors to sacrifice their principles in order to compromise can produce trust among them. This is because compromise is a form of reciprocity – an agreement where the parties involved agree to get less than they each believe they deserve for the sake of making some improvements. In the words of Amy Gutmann and Dennis Thompson, compromise can demonstrate a desire to find "mutually acceptable ways not only of resolving disagreements but also of living with the disagreements that inevitably remain ..."[12] – to deescalate and prevent divorce. As Alan Simpson observed about the Simpson-Bowles Commission on deficit reduction, "members were willing to take on their sacred cows and fight special interests ... if they saw others doing the same and if what they were voting

[10] See Luigi Guiso, Paola Sapienza, and Luigi Zingales, "Does Culture Affect Economic Outcomes?," *Journal of Economic Perspectives* 20(2) (2006): 23–48. Robert D. Putnam, *Bowling Alone: The Collapse and Revival of American Community* (New York: Simon & Schuster, 2000).

[11] Lucio Baccaro and Chris Howell, *Trajectories of Neoliberal Transformation: European Industrial Relations since the 1970s* (Cambridge: Cambridge University Press, 2017), 149.

[12] Amy Gutmann and Dennis Thompson, *The Spirit of Compromise: Why Governing Demands It and Campaigning Undermines It* (Princeton: Princeton University Press, 2012), 34.

for solved the country's problems."[13] Yet political actors negotiate in secret because they know that compromises, if conducted publicly, would not be able to get off the ground.

This reticence suggests that political actors worry – with cause – that their constituents and supporters will resist compromise. Surveys indicate that even though Americans support compromise in principle, they tend to oppose *specific* compromises. The more they care about an issue, the less likely they will support compromise. Crises (e.g., impending economic collapse) can soften this resistance, yet many Americans revert to their earlier postures once those threats subside.[14] This might or might not be a good thing. What matters, for our purposes, is that the cultivation of trust among political actors does not necessitate the emergence of trust among citizens at large toward political actors. In fact, it indicates that cooperation and trust among political actors might inspire distrust *between* political actors and citizens at large. After all, even when citizens at large expect political actors to compromise, it is difficult for political actors to discern just how much citizens at large wish for them (political actors) to compromise. More than that, when political actors do trust one another, they can forget that the purpose of compromise is to find a way for the *polity* – and not just political actors – to move forward together. As a result, they can end up either "tabling" issues that are controversial yet important to citizens or striking compromises that undermine their constituents' long-term interests – sowing the seeds for future crises of trust, should those compromises become perceived as undermining ordinary citizens. In Joseph Carens's words:

They do give their peers a sympathetic hearing. They pay attention to their interests and to their beliefs. But they seek to keep debate and negotiation within the political community. This maximizes the flexibility and freedom of each of them. Thus, they have a bias towards interpreting all conflicts as conflicts of interest. They dislike and fear issues (such as abortion) that animate and divide the public, since these issues can have important but unpredictable effects on their chances for reelection ... [but] the policy that enhances the politician's chances of reelection may not be the policy that best meets the needs of the immediate community he serves (to say nothing of the larger community). This leads to a[n] [injurious] kind of logrolling.[15]

Political actors sometimes try to re-establish trust with their supporters by never compromising. Yet such stubborn sincerity inevitably undermines the possibility of trust among themselves.[16]

---

[13] Alan Simpson and Erskine Bowles, "Our Advice to the Debt Supercommittee: Go Big, Be Bold, Be Smart," *Washington Post*, September 30, 2011, www.washingtonpost.com/opinions/our-advice-to-the-debt-supercommittee-go-big-be-bold-be-smart/2011/09/30/gIQAPzjBBL_story.html.

[14] Gutmann and Thompson, *The Spirit of Compromise*, 25–27.

[15] Joseph H. Carens, "Compromises in Politics," *Nomos* 21 (1979): 138.

[16] Of course, some political actors refuse to compromise simply because they are intransigent. It is unlikely that those political actors will compromise and cooperate, even if trust among political actors broadly exists.

NOW ONTO THE DETAILS

We now have a good understanding of the broad contours of role-based constitutional fellowship. When citizens are constitutional fellows, they share in a culture of trust. Generally speaking, when this culture of trust exists, citizens believe that their fellow citizens probably value the continuation of their civic relationship and that they are committed to social and political arrangements conducive to that relationship: liberal democracy. Given that different spheres of activity have different normative dynamics, however, this trust assumes different complexions in different contexts. First, when trust exists in the formal political sphere, political competitors treat one another as adversaries rather than enemies. Second, when trust exists among citizens at large, citizens who have differences and disagreements treat one another in manners befitting their equal citizenship and believe that their fellow citizens take the persistence of undue social hierarchies seriously. Third, when trust exists between these two spheres, citizens at large believe that political actors largely aim to further the public good, not their (political actors') own self-interests, individually and as a class.

In Chapters 6–8, I shall describe how my "role-based" account of constitutional fellowship can potentially self-initiate and overcome the three major hurdles to the cultivation of such trust: the institutionalized enmity problem in the formal political sphere, the social domination problem in the general citizenry, and the representative cynicism problem between the formal political sphere and the general citizenry.

6

Principled Pragmatists, Principled Purists, and the Liberal Democratic Front

In this chapter, I show how trust can emerge in the formal political sphere. As we saw in Chapter 5, when trust exists here, political competitors compete as *adversaries* with a sense of respect and self-restraint, rather than as *enemies* to be destroyed.[1] In order for political actors to share in trust, they must overcome the institutionalized enmity problem. This problem refers to the tendency for formal political competition to devolve into de facto or actual warfare.

I argue that a division of labour among political actors who are committed to liberal democracy is needed between *principled pragmatists* and *principled purists*. Principled pragmatists can develop a sense of reciprocity by performing compromises, while principled purists can more stubbornly refuse to compromise in order to keep those principled pragmatists honest. This sense of reciprocity can help counteract the tendency of these political actors to compete as enemies while making it easier for them to form liberal democratic fronts to repel autocratic threats when necessary. I also argue, however, that a different approach is needed should some mainstream liberal democrats forge "unholy alliances" with autocratic political actors (and become *former* liberal democrats). In these cases, it is instead necessary for those who stand outside those alliances to discern the most effective ways to defeat those alliances, and to show that partaking in those alliances is politically costly. Still, the purpose of such contestation should be to restore conditions where trust building among liberal democratic competitors can begin once again. Should the defenders of liberal democracy win, they should – cautiously – seek to entice those former liberal democrats back into the liberal democratic fold: this will involve compromise.

---

[1] As I noted in Chapter 2, I value the hard agonistic distinction between adversaries and enemies, but deem the hard agonistic approach to keeping adversaries inadequate.

In what follows, I first elaborate on what it means for formal politics to be modelled on warfare, and I demonstrate that the production of trust here likely depends on practices that we would not normally associate with the production of trust. Specifically, I show that the practices of "salutary hypocrisy" can more reliably facilitate cooperation and compromise among political actors than those practices that we would normally associate with trustworthiness: the practices of sincerity. Second, I argue that the desired sort of trust can emerge through a division of labour between principled purists and principled pragmatists. Third, I note that there are contexts where enough distrust exists among mainstream political actors that this division of labour is not plausible. In these contexts, autocrats can succeed in turning liberal democrats against each other, and even convert some of those liberal democrats into autocrats. Fourth, I argue that in these contexts, a different approach is needed whereby those liberal democrats who stand outside those unholy alliances must instead discern the most effective strategies and tactics to defeat those alliances. However, I insist that the purpose of such confrontation should be to recover conditions where the division of labour between principled pragmatists and principled purists is viable once again.

COUNTERINTUITIVE APPROACHES TO THE PRODUCTION OF TRUST

Overcoming the institutionalized enmity problem involves preventing the metaphor of warfare from taking over. When political actors consider one another enemies, they deny the legitimacy of disagreement and are willing to undermine liberal democratic norms and institutions to win. So, even though competition is valuable for liberal democracy (see Chapter 1), it is necessary to stop politics from becoming a "permanent campaign" where political actors, coordinating with "war rooms," constantly stand on principle, condemn their opponents at every turn, and construe compromise as a violation of integrity.[2] Given that smart institutional design and "commonality" cannot, by themselves, reliably channel competition to prevent such a politics (see Chapter 2), the question at hand is this: how can trust emerge among political competitors?

One potentially attractive answer is that political actors should be encouraged to pursue a politics of sincerity. After all, as a matter of "commonsensical" morality, we typically associate trustworthiness with sincerity. People can be trusted when they mean what they say, act in accordance to what they claim to believe, and demonstrate a concern for others – when they do not act deceptively. Now, this does not mean that we typically only trust those who act as if they are in an "ideal speech condition" regulated by the ideals of

[2] Amy Gutmann and Dennis Thompson, *The Spirit of Compromise: Why Governing Demands It and Campaigning Undermines It* (Princeton: Princeton University Press, 2012), 160ff.

"communicative action" (discussed in Chapter 2) – those who abstain from appealing to emotions, "framing" claims misleadingly, and using rhetoric.[3] Nor does it mean that we only trust people who treat all their listeners the same or who are fully transparent. Indeed, we do not begrudge people for treating their friends differently than strangers (and for expecting more from friends than strangers);[4] and in the context of personal friendships, people would be well advised to practice an "indirection of intention." As Sandra Lynch explains, duties of friendship might exist, yet it is unbefitting to let friends feel that one fulfills those duties out of a sense of obligation, rather than affection.[5] Rather, to say that we tend to associate trustworthiness with sincerity is to say that we typically trust those whose *characters* we deem sincere.

Unsurprisingly, then, some proponents of political friendship argue that in order for a culture of trust to emerge, citizens who have differences and disagreements should demonstrate to one another that they care to treat one another as citizens of equal standing. For instance, Danielle Allen recommends that citizens should recount the processes by which they arrive at successful proposals and reveal the moral maxims to which they hold themselves in order to demonstrate that they adhere to a "rule of law approach" to politics, not "an approach that affords themselves special privileges." Citizens can also "disarm" the negative emotions caused by loss by determining which losses are only "apparent" and which losses are "actual," just as they can refrain from treating one another as "passive and submissive students . . . suffering in silence while being told what to do."[6] In these manners, the privileged and the dominant can demonstrate that they take the interests of the underprivileged and the oppressed seriously, and that they (the privileged and the dominant) wish to realize a state of affairs where the underprivileged and the oppressed are indeed treated as having equal standing.

Yet according to theorists of political hypocrisy, even if such displays of sincerity can generate trust among citizens at large (discussed in Chapter 7), relying on such displays to cultivate trust in the formal political sphere is a fool's errand at best. Political actors are bound to act in untrustworthy manners. If this is the case, then it seems more worthwhile to encourage political actors to identify "salutary" forms of hypocrisy. That is, even though

---

[3] Elizabeth Markovits, "The Trouble with Being Earnest: Deliberative Democracy and the Sincerity Norm," *The Journal of Political Philosophy* 14(3) (2006): 253.

[4] To this point, according to Bernard Yack, in order for citizens to be political friends, it is important for people to distinguish between intimate friends and political friends. To confuse intimate friends for political friends is to expect more from political friends – and to make the production of civic trust more difficult (Bernard Yack, *The Problems of a Political Animal: Community, Justice, and Conflict in Aristotelian Political Thought* (Berkeley: University of California Press, 1993), 110ff).

[5] Sandra Lynch, *Philosophy and Friendship* (Edinburgh: Edinburgh University Press, 2005).

[6] Danielle S. Allen, *Talking to Strangers: Anxieties of Citizenship since* Brown v. Board of Education (Chicago: University of Chicago Press, 2004), 145–154.

we might distrust hypocrisy, certain forms of hypocrisy might actually be more conducive to cooperation and compromise in the competitive environment of formal politics than demonstrations of sincerity. So, hypocrisy can, counter-intuitively, facilitate the production of trust among political actors.

Noting that "hypocrites" were Ancient Greek stage actors who played parts, David Runciman defines hypocrisy as "the construction of a persona ... that generates some kind of false impression ... the wearing of masks."[7] It is a type of deception that might involve, yet is distinct from, lying.[8] Like lying, hypocrisy involves misrepresentations of how things "really are." However, whereas a liar misrepresents the truth, a hypocrite misrepresents his or her character. A hypocrite might claim to support a cause while undermining that cause. Moreover, while lying is always purposeful – one does not lie when one misrepresents the truth out of false belief – hypocrisy need not be purposeful. One can unwittingly be a hypocrite. The environmentalist can drive a Hummer to the local farmer's market without realizing the irony of his or her behaviour.

According to this perspective, politics is not friendship, where people share interests and care about one another. Yet in ordinary circumstances, it is also not warfare; unlike enemies, political competitors do depend on one another and tend not to resolve their differences forcefully. Rather, politics-as-usual is defined by "relations of dependence among people with conflicting interests." Interests overlap, but do not coincide: people must cooperate in order to attain what they need and want, yet they must also compete and are prone to distrust one another. As Ruth Grant notes,

Even a powerful prince, for example, will find himself at various times in need of allies and supporters. His dependence on them makes it necessary for him to flatter them and to appear to be trustworthy. He needs their voluntary cooperation because he is not in a position to coerce their compliance. Yet he cannot simply expect that their cooperation will be forthcoming, because their interests do not coincide with his own and no altruistic motive is at work. Only a very foolish prince would rely on lifelong loyalties, true friendships, or trust.[9]

So, whereas both friends and enemies are, in their own ways, sincere – friends sincerely care about one another, while enemies are sincerely hostile toward one another – political actors tend to misrepresent their characters; politics is defined by hypocrisy. Political actors tend to be hypocrites not because they constitute an especially "two-faced" class of human beings, but rather because the normative dynamics of politics-as-usual compels them to be so. They feel a

---

[7] David Runciman, *Political Hypocrisy: The Mask of Power, from Hobbes to Orwell and Beyond* (Princeton: Princeton University Press, 2008), 31.

[8] Note that not all lies are deceptive. In the case of "bald-face lies," the listener knows that the speaker is lying, and the speaker knows that the listener knows that he or she (the speaker) is lying.

[9] Ruth W. Grant, *Hypocrisy and Integrity: Machiavelli, Rousseau, and the Ethics of Politics* (Chicago: The University of Chicago Press, 1997), 21.

need to seem better than they actually are, not just so that they can pursue shared goals together when their interests overlap, but also so that they can deceive one another and win when their interests conflict – when the victory of one entails the loss of another, such as during elections.

If this is the case, then demonstrations of sincerity cannot possibly produce trust among political actors. It is easy to see why one would think that displays of sincerity of character and concern for others would produce trust, yet such disclosures can only produce trust if they actually reveal the right sort of sincerity – sincerity of concern, not sincerity of hostility. These disclosures undermine trust when they reveal that the speakers make exceptions for themselves, or that speakers who claim to be motivated by compassion or by a sense of common cause are in fact motivated by narrow self-interest. The problem, from the standpoint of theorists of political hypocrisy, is that the adversarial dimensions of politics pressure political actors to make exceptions for themselves and to be at least partially motivated by narrow self-interest, even if they wish things were otherwise. To encourage motivated political actors to cultivate trust by pursuing a politics of sincerity is to encourage them to unilaterally act *as if* most of their political competitors *already* act in trustworthy manners, regardless of whether those competitors reciprocate. That is, to urge a politics of sincerity is to encourage political actors to seek cooperation and to compete with a sense of restraint, even if their opponents do not reciprocate.

One can object that the goal should nonetheless be to "nudge" the "non-ideal" world of political hypocrisy toward the "ideal" world of political sincerity: even if there are political actors who do to act untrustworthily, we are better off if some political actors act trustworthily, and we can expect that more and more political actors will follow suit as such behaviour becomes more prevalent. After all, game theory suggests that in a repeated prisoner's dilemma, the incentive to defect will diminish (although not disappear) if there are enough people willing to cooperate, punish defectors, and resume cooperation once defectors no longer defect.[10]

Yet if the structural features of zero-sum electoral competition persist, then so too will the adversarial dimensions of politics. So, it is likely that even those political actors who do try to practice a politics of sincerity would reverse course should there be too many defectors, or should there be no first mover. Efforts to nudge might then even be counterproductive, for those disappointed by these efforts might end up writing off not just a politics of sincerity as naïve, but also politics-as-usual and the hypocrisy it entails as irredeemably corrupt. As a result, they might turn toward an understanding of politics as warfare – one that is more sincere, but also more transparently antagonistic and hostile.

[10] Robert Axelrod, *The Evolution of Cooperation* (New York: Basic Books, 1984).

The evolution of the American Left over the course of Barack Obama's administration arguably bears this out. During his first presidential campaign in 2008, Obama espoused a message of unity, that there are no "Blue" or "Red" States," but only the *United* States, and vowed to change "the ways of Washington."[11] Having promised a better sort of politics, Obama (in the eyes of many on the left) tried to govern in this spirit, seemingly offering pre-emptive compromises to Republicans and even going so far as to suggest to his Chief of Staff, Rahm Emanuel, that health care reform ought to be negotiated in "as open and transparent a process as possible . . . [where] everyone will have a seat at the table . . . Not . . . behind closed doors."[12] With the Republicans refusing to reciprocate[13] – and Obama seemingly reluctant to adopt a more confrontational approach, despite the fact that the "compromises" he struck seemed more like capitulations – many on the left bemoaned Obama's apparent weakness and naïveté as indicative of how politics-as-usual inevitably favours bad-faith actors.[14] Worse still, some accused Obama and Democrats of being closet Republicans and corporate shills – of using the veneer of the rhetoric of a politics of sincerity to be the "good cops" to the Republicans' "bad cops."[15] So, the failures of attempts to practice a politics of sincerity can, ironically, intensify citizens' frustrations with business-as-usual and lead to a more antagonistic politics.

What this all goes to suggest is that if hypocrisy is inevitable, then it is necessary to make the most out of it. We should not simply stop worrying about hypocrisy. However, rather than wish hypocrisy away, we should instead identify forms of hypocrisy that can help political actors compete and cooperate simultaneously as *quasi-friends* – to build coalitions. It is easier to build coalitions when political actors cater their arguments to their audiences, conceal their true motives, hide what they think about their audiences, and care to appear better than they are. In other words, even though we might tend to

---

[11] Barack Obama, "Barack Obama's Campaign Speech," *The Guardian*, February 10, 2007, www .theguardian.com/world/2007/feb/10/barackobama.

[12] Barack Obama, *A Promised Land* (New York: Random House, 2020), 381.

[13] Senate Republican leader Mitch McConnell famously announced near the beginning of Obama's tenure that the top Republican priority was to deny Obama a second term. See Jonathan Capehart, "Republicans Had It in for Obama before Day 1," *The Washington Post*, August 10, 2012, www.washingtonpost.com/blogs/post-partisan/post/republicans-had-it-in-for-obama-before-day-1/2012/08/10/0c96c7c8-e31f-11e1-ae7f-d2a13e249eb2_blog.html.

[14] Sam Youngman, "Angry Left to Obama: Stop Caving on Agenda," *The Hill*, November 18, 2010, https://thehill.com/homenews/administration/129323-angry-left-to-obama-stop-caving. For a counterargument emphasizing how Obama in fact "seized" power over policy, see Ross Douthat, "There Will Be No Trump Coup," *New York Times*, October 10, 2020, www.nytimes .com/2020/10/10/opinion/sunday/trump-election-authoritarianism.html.

[15] Luke Savage, "The Real Barack Obama Has Finally Revealed Himself," *Jacobin*, November 27, 2019, https://jacobinmag.com/2019/11/obama-socialism; Max Mastellone, "Exposing the Parties and Pitching Solidarity," *Counterpunch*, June 2, 2017, www.counterpunch.org/2017/ 06/02/exposing-the-parties-and-pitching-solidarity/.

frown upon hypocrisy, hypocrisy can help political competitors get things done together. From these collective endeavours, political competitors can come to believe that they do indeed value the continuation of their civic relationship.

Indicatively, Grant likens political hypocrisy to good manners. Yes, manners can express a commitment to respect others – to "bridge the gap" between what one believes one should be like and what one actually is like. As Karen Stohr notes, "I may not be able to summon up the gratitude that I should be feeling, but I can at least say the right words and act as I should."[16] However, one can exhibit "the pretense of sympathetic concern or respect for others" for purposes of expediency. Should this occur, one neither treats others according to what they merit nor reveals one's true feelings about them. Rather, one treats them "as respectable ... regardless of whether they personally merit respect" by adhering to "conventional forms." Manners might be phony, yet they "prevent conflict by treating people who are not good or respectable as if they were and by supporting habitual restraints on self-interested behavior."[17] Analogously, the failure to act hypocritically can facilitate a politics that is more honest and sincere, but also more antagonistic – a politics of open hostility. So, hypocrisy can be salutary.

A DIVISION OF LABOUR BETWEEN PRINCIPLED PRAGMATISTS AND PURISTS

There are limits to the possibilities of salutary hypocrisy. Indeed, in Chapter 8, I shall demonstrate that even though the adversarial dimensions of the formal political sphere encourage hypocrisy, people's general distrust of hypocrisy – even salutary forms of hypocrisy – will inform how citizens judge political actors. As a result, either these judgments will constrain the degree to which political actors can in fact act hypocritically, or political actors will have to justify their apparent hypocrisy in the appropriate manners. Still, given the aforementioned discussion, we can say that trust can emerge among political actors if some of them practice principled hypocrisy, for the production of trust is a function of salutary hypocrisy, given explicit competition. So, some political actors should strive to be *principled pragmatists* who are willing to settle for half measures – not merely to further their own narrow self-interests but to pursue justice (as they each understand it).

Now, principled pragmatists do not all have to be committed to the same substantive political principles. For example, liberals, conservatives, and social democrats can all be principled despite their disagreements over what the just society looks like. Similarly, principled pragmatists do not have to be "moderate" in their political persuasions and policy preferences. Indeed, many of the

---

[16] Karen Stohr, *On Manners* (New York: Routledge, 2012), 83.
[17] Grant, *Hypocrisy and Integrity*, 32–33.

most renowned pragmatists – from Republicans Ronald Reagan and John McCain to Democrats Ted Kennedy and Tip O'Neill – were not moderate, let alone centrist, and they often disagreed sharply. Reagan and McCain were firm (and sometimes strident) proponents of supply-side economics, and Kennedy and O'Neill, activist government.[18]

Rather, being a principled pragmatist entails two things. First, although no savvy political actor can ever eschew strategic considerations – even the most noble politician is of no use if he or she is an ex-politician – being a principled pragmatist entails that he or she always maintain a view to the common good when making political choices, and that he or she avoid harming liberal democracy if possible. Second, being a principled pragmatist means that one is open to striking compromises – agreements where one agrees to get less than one believes he or she deserves to get for the sake of making some improvements. To name two prominent examples, O'Neill and Reagan led their parties to pass (1) the 1986 Tax Reform Act that lowered tax rates for the wealthy and corporations while closing loopholes, shelters, and deductions;[19] and (2) the 1983 Social Security Amendments to both raise the retirement age and increase payroll taxes on the self-employed in order to shore up Social Security.[20]

Such compromises can help build trust. This is because compromise is a form of reciprocity. Compromises demonstrate a willingness to perform sacrifices for the sake of finding mutually acceptable ways of living together, despite people's differences and disagreements.[21] Political actors who compromise agree that it is better to give up a little bit of what they each value in order to find a path forward together than to either divorce or allow their disagreements to fuel further antagonism. The more these political actors compromise, the more they will come to trust one another; and the more they trust one another, the more they will be inclined to adopt a "problem-solving orientation," rather than an "individualistic orientation."[22] They will be less inclined to view one another's interests as hurdles to be overcome, and the objective of negotiations, to secure concessions; and more inclined to seek solutions that are mutually satisfying

---

[18] I recognize that Reagan engaged in race-baiting throughout his political career. Still, we can consider him a principled pragmatist for his willingness to compromise on Tax Reform and Social Security.

[19] Stuart E. Eizenstat, "Back to the Future: Reagan, Trump and Bipartisan Tax Reform," Brookings Institute, September 27, 2017, www.brookings.edu/blog/fixgov/2017/09/27/back-to-the-future-reagan-trump-and-bipartisan-tax-reform/.

[20] Paul C. Light, "The Crisis Last Time: Social Security Reform," Brookings Institute, March 5, 2005, www.brookings.edu/opinions/the-crisis-last-time-social-security-reform/. Prior, Reagan had frequently condemned Social Security as a big government-Socialist power grab par excellence.

[21] Gutmann and Thompson, *The Spirit of Compromise*, 34.

[22] Joseph H. Carens, "Compromises in Politics," *Nomos* 21 (1979): 127–128.

("positive-sum policy")[23] and to be transparent about their "real" objectives. Sometimes, personal friendships can emerge out of compromise, making future compromises easier to strike – for instance, between Orin Hatch and Kennedy and between McCain and Joe Biden. More modestly, compromise can help political competitors recognize that they share a commitment to the country and liberal democracy. As O'Neill's son, Thomas, notes:

My father fought tirelessly to see that Reagan's policies did not run roughshod over the disenfranchised. The president fought too, pushing back against spending he believed was out of control, and a social system he thought created dependency.

On occasion, these dueling philosophies brought both men to the mat – to the point where neither would back down ... But such unyielding standoffs were, in fact, rare. What both men deplored more than the other's political philosophy was stalemate and a country that was so polarized by ideology and party politics that it could not move forward.

Now, my father and Reagan weren't close friends. Famously, after 6 p.m. on quite a few work days, they would sit down for drinks at the White House. But it wasn't the drinks or the conversation that allowed American government to work. Instead, it was a stubborn refusal to not allow fundraisers, activists, party platforms or ideological chasms to stand between them and actions – tempered and improved by compromise – that kept this country moving.[24]

There is a danger, however, that principled pragmatists will become self-serving or *unprincipled* pragmatists who compromise, not to further justice or the common good but primarily to perpetuate the status quo, their own individual positions, and their collective position as a "class."[25] Notoriously, in 1877, in order to win the disputed 1876 election, Republican Rutherford Hayes won the support of Southern Democratic officials by agreeing to remove federal troops from the South, effectively ending Reconstruction. Principled pragmatists might not even necessarily become complacent out of malice or selfishness per se; they might become complacent out of a relatively innocuous desire to help one another out as friends.

Accordingly, some liberal democratic political actors should strive to be *principled purists* who more stubbornly refuse to readily compromise and tend to proclaim more extreme positions out of a sense of justice so as to keep pragmatists honest. As Franklin Delano Roosevelt remarked to a reform delegation, "Okay, you've convinced me. Now go out and bring pressure on me!"[26] Indeed, it was such pressure from Roosevelt's left – some of which was undeni-

---

[23] Matthew Yglesias, "Positive-Sum Policy vs Zero-Sum Politics," Think Progress, May 20, 2010, https://archive.thinkprogress.org/positive-sum-policy-vs-zero-sum-politics-270234a8391c/.

[24] Thomas P. O'Neill, "Frenemies: A Love Story," *The New York Times*, October 5, 2012, https://campaignstops.blogs.nytimes.com/2012/10/05/frenemies-a-love-story/.

[25] Grant, *Hypocrisy and Integrity*, 89.

[26] Suzanne Dovi, "Guilt and the Problem of Dirty Hands," *Constellations* 12(1) (2005): 136.

ably toxic[27] – that compelled him to fully turn his back on the laissez-faire economic approach he had espoused during his first presidential campaign and to enact his "Second New Deal." Unlike the "First New Deal," which focused on banking reforms and government jobs programs, the Second addressed economic inequality through tax increases on the rich and the establishment of Social Security.[28] In addition, by assuming more extreme positions, purists can also expand the range of political possibilities – what pragmatists can realistically achieve. As Suzanne Dovi remarks (discussing the problem of dirty hands), "Guilt-ridden political actors with dirty hands look more 'reasonable' and gain political leverage by contrasting their own views to those of absolutists."[29]

In other words, a division of labour between principled pragmatists and principled purists is needed to cultivate a sense of political trust. By behaving in different ways, principled pragmatists and principled purists can ensure that they will treat one another as adversaries to be defeated rather than as enemies to be destroyed, and that the trust they share will actually contribute to the common good.

Maintaining this productive tension between principled pragmatists and principled purists can prove tricky, for principled purists' denunciations of apparent hypocrisy – which surely would be warmly received by many citizens at large – constrain the degree to which principled pragmatists can compromise. Indeed, purists often end up encouraging citizens at large to equate integrity with consistency and to believe that inconsistencies and half-measures are inherently indicative of a *lack* of principle. Accordingly, principled pragmatists sometimes feel compelled to refrain from compromising or to repudiate their past compromises in a bid to demonstrate that they are principled – that they are not "sell-outs."[30]

There are, however, ways to mitigate this challenge. One is to encourage principled pragmatists and principled purists alike to recognize their common devotion to the country – to acknowledge that they both aim to advance the

---

[27] Here, I refer to the authoritarian-tinged left populism of Huey Long.

[28] Lest we think that the Social Security Act was not a compromise, let us remember that Roosevelt had to give up the dream of universal health care in order to secure its passage. Likewise, contrary to his own Committee on Economic Security, Roosevelt insisted that the management of unemployment insurance be left to the states and that old-age pensions be financed largely through regressive payroll taxes, knowing that including proposals to create a federal bureaucracy to manage unemployment insurance and underwriting pensions with Treasury funds would have jeopardized the Act's passage. See David M. Kennedy, "Compromise 4: Whittling Down the New Deal," *American Heritage*, 2010, 60(2), www.americanheritage.com/comprom ise-4-whittling-down-new-deal.

[29] Dovi, "The Problem of Dirty Hands," 136.

[30] It is a separate issue whether principled pragmatists do so convincingly. They frequently do not, further aggravating the problem.

public interest of the country, albeit in different ways.[31] Another is for principled pragmatists and principled purists to remember that in order to remain principled – to refrain from compromising or from resisting compromise for self-serving or self-righteous purposes – it is necessary either to appreciate the need for the other "type" or to incorporate a "touch" of the other type into their own approaches to politics.

For instance, principled pragmatists can appreciate the need for principled purists to operate alongside them, while principled purists can remember that refusing to *readily* compromise is not the same as refusing to *ever* compromise. (Indeed, the refusal to ever compromise likely makes one an *unprincipled* purist rather than a principled purist. When the purist only ever agrees to support proposals with which he or she *completely* agrees, he or she makes it difficult for *any* degree of progress to be achieved, and exposes himself or herself as moralistic rather than as justice-oriented.) Neither sort of recognition is farfetched. As we have seen, principled pragmatists like Roosevelt recognize the need for purists. Likewise, even purist Bernie Sanders recognizes the need for some compromise and coordination with pragmatists. During the 2010 Affordable Care Act negotiations, when the inclusion of a "public option" became implausible, Sanders agreed to support the bill in exchange for $11 billion in funding for community health clinics. Similarly, during the 2010 Tax Relief Act, Sanders filibustered the bill in protest of its extension of the "Bush tax cuts," but told then Democratic majority leader Harry Reid privately that he (Sanders) would not torpedo the compromise.[32]

Principled purists can also strive to be more nuanced in their condemnations of hypocrisy and inconsistency. Surely, it is necessary for principled purists to condemn the inconsistencies of unprincipled pragmatists. After all, unprincipled pragmatists compromise and act inconsistently to further their own interests. However, when the political system does not seem to be producing adequate results, rather than accuse individual principled pragmatists who might be closely identified with the system of acting in bad faith, it is more constructive for principled purists to focus their sharp criticisms on the system as a whole.

For example, during the 2008 Democratic National Convention, Obama (who, granted, is not a principled purist) certainly criticized his Republican opponent, renowned pragmatist McCain, for having questionable political judgement and even for being out of touch. Obama remarked, "I don't believe that Senator McCain doesn't care about what is going on in the lives of Americans; I just think he doesn't know. Why else would he define middle-

---

[31] On this score, liberal nationalism (or constitutional patriotism, in certain contexts) can help. So too can "translucent veils," which I discuss in Chapter 9.

[32] Sam Brodey and Sam Stein, "What Bernie Sanders Really Got Done in His 29 Years in Congress," *Daily Beast*, March 2, 2020, www.thedailybeast.com/what-bernie-sanders-really-got-done-in-his-29-years-in-congress.

class as someone making under five million dollars a year?" However, Obama went out of his way to express his underlying respect for McCain and focused on articulating a general critique of the system, rather than on demonizing McCain personally as uniquely responsible for the system's failures: "When Washington doesn't work, all its promises seem empty ... in this election, the greatest risk we can take is to try the same, old politics with the same, old players and expect a different result ... the change we need doesn't come from Washington. Change comes to Washington."[33]

Following this example, principled purists can pressure principled pragmatists to maintain an eye toward the common good *all the while* affording principled pragmatists the space necessary to perform the compromises required to pursue these objectives. As Judith Shklar, who otherwise encourages us to stop worrying so much about hypocrisy, notes:

> The only voice that damns hypocrisy to some purpose is one that laments that the society in which we live does not live up to its declared principles, promises, and possibilities. This outraged jeremiad is the mark of a moralistic rather than a moral society, perhaps; but it is not without effect, because this type of antihypocrite does at least have a sense of what is wrong, rather than only an urge to spread the blame.[34]

DIFFERENT CIRCUMSTANCES, DIFFERENT RESPONSES

A division of labour between principled pragmatists and principled purists can cultivate the desired sort of trust in the formal political sphere. Yet is this division of labour always plausible? Moreover, is it always appropriate to try to cultivate trust? I submit that the answer to both of these questions is no: this division of labour is not always plausible, and it is sometimes necessary to embrace contestation. However, I also stipulate that the purpose of such contestation should be to restore conditions where trust building can begin once again.

We can begin to see why this is all the case by considering the preconditions of this division of labour: what must already be in place for this division of labour to work? Well, most obviously, there has to be a somewhat balanced distribution of principled pragmatists among mainstream political vehicles, for

---

[33] Barack Obama, *We Are the Change We Seek: The Speeches of Barack Obama*, ed. E. J. Dionne Jr. and Joy-Ann Reid (New York: Bloomsbury, 2017), 70–87. Earlier, I noted that Obama's promises to radically change how politics works might have fueled discontent and cynicism on the left when it became apparent that he did not change how politics worked, yet acted as if politics had already changed. We can now refine this critique: the problem was not that he attacked how "Washington works," but that he actually tried to govern as if Washington had already changed – to "lead by example." In other words, the problem was that Obama was not hypocritical enough.

[34] Judith Shklar, *Ordinary Vices* (Cambridge, MA: The Belknap Press of Harvard University Press, 1984), 86.

the principled pragmatists of a given political party can only perform compromises when there are actually members of other parties with whom they can compromise. If most principled pragmatists belong to one side of the aisle – or if principled pragmatists feel pressured to not act upon their pragmatic inclinations, perhaps because unprincipled purists dominate their parties or because many of their supporters vehemently oppose compromise – then it will be difficult to strike compromises.[35]

Even more fundamental than a balanced distribution of principled pragmatists across mainstream parties, in order for this division of labour to work, some basic degree of political trust must already exist. After all, an unbalanced distribution indicates that substantial distrust persists; to be a principled pragmatist is to believe that one's opponents are not so heinous as to be unworthy of compromise. The fact that one side lacks principled pragmatists indicates that that side (rightfully or wrongfully) deems the other untrustworthy. Likewise, the absence of principled pragmatists on all sides indicates that mutual hostility reigns supreme. So, whether the division of labour in question can work depends in large part on whether some basic degree of trust already exists.

Now, it is *possible* for this division of labour to get off the ground and running in conditions of broad distrust; principled pragmatists can still try to compromise and cultivate trust. For example, in 2013, a group of Democratic and Republican senators known as the "Gang of Eight" reached a deal on immigration reform that passed the Senate with a strong bipartisan majority.[36] These compromises are possible because the parties involved deem them politically advantageous, despite the persistence of broad distrust; to compromise is not to be a martyr.[37] Indeed, the Gang of Eight included Marco Rubio, who likely participated to burnish his legislative credentials prior to his 2016 run for president.[38]

---

[35] More than undermine trust, this inability to form compromises risks trying the patience of those principled pragmatists who would prefer to strike deals. Irritated pragmatists might quit politics altogether. For example, Republican Senator Rob Portman cited partisan gridlock as a major reason for why he chose not to run for re-election in 2022. Alternatively, irritated pragmatists might gravitate toward a more uncompromising posture. Indeed, as I note earlier, the Democratic Left – and perhaps the Democratic Party as a whole – became more resistant to compromise over the course of Obama's tenure because they felt that there were hardly any Republicans willing to reciprocate. (Republican refusals to compromise were motivated partly by the fact that Republican voters were, toward the front end of Obama's term, much more resistant to compromise than Democratic voters. See Jeffrey M. Jones, "Democrats, Republicans Differ in Views of Compromise in D.C.," Pew Research Center, November 10, 2010, https://news.gallup.com/poll/144359/democrats-republicans-differ-views-compromise.aspx.)

[36] The bill, however, did not proceed in the Republican-controlled House.

[37] Stated differently, given that those compromises are a function of salutary hypocrisy, we have good reason to believe that they are more plausible than unilateral demonstrations of sincerity (discussed earlier).

[38] After anti-immigrant and far-right sentiments gained a stranglehold of the Republican Party, however, Rubio repudiated his support for immigration reform.

Yet such attempts to compromise are further hindered by the fact that the political sphere does not only contain committed liberal democrats; it also contains *enemies* of liberal democracy – autocrats. Autocrats typically do not proclaim themselves autocratic; as we shall see in the following section, they often rhetorically profess a commitment to democracy. However, they do not think that a politics of permanent campaigning is problematic. Instead, they reject the legitimacy of disagreement and *yearn* for a politics modelled on warfare. So, in a bid to gain influence and corrode liberal democracy, autocrats will do all they can to prevent principled pragmatists from compromising and cultivating trust. Indeed, autocrats will aim to turn liberal democrats against each other.

Now, just because distrust exists among liberal democrats does not mean that autocrats will necessarily succeed in assuming control. For example, in 2017, even though trust did not exactly exist among French conservatives (Les Républicains), liberals (La République En Marche!), and social democrats (the Socialist Party), they were able to form a "cordon sanitaire" – as they had done in 2002[39] – against Marine le Pen's National Front because they shared more distrust toward the National Front than toward one another. Several prominent Républicains urged their supporters to support En Marche's Emmanuel Macron in the run-off, with candidate François Fillon citing the National Front's extremism as a threat to French political principles: "The National Front ... has a history known for its violence, its intolerance. Its economic and social program would lead France to bankruptcy ... I assure you: extremists can only bring misery and division to France ... My dream for my children is that they should be able to live in a free, fraternal country that is proud of its values ..."[40] (Undoubtedly, it helped that the National Front was its own party, rather than a faction within Les Républicains. It also helped that the run-off admitted only two parties, eliminating the risk of spoiler effects from third parties.)[41] So, it is possible for liberal democrats to overcome their mutual distrust and fend off autocratic threats. Indeed, such consolidations can help clarify the basic commitments liberal democrats share, and might even serve as catalysts for future cooperation and trust.

Sometimes, however, autocratic efforts to aggravate the distrust that exists among liberal democrats *do* succeed. In such circumstances, *unholy alliances*

---

[39] In 2002, the Socialist Party supported Jacques Chirac of Les Républicains over the National Front's Jean-Marie le Pen in the run-off.

[40] "Francois Fillon Concession Speech," CSPAN, April 23, 2017, www.c-span.org/video/?427327-4/francois-fillon-concession-speech.

[41] Even so, fewer than half of Fillon supporters (48 percent) supported Macron in the second round, with 20 percent supporting Marine le Pen and 18 percent marking their ballots blank (Jocelyn Evans and Gilles Ivaldi, *The French Presidential Elections: A Political Reformation?* (Cham: Palgrave Macmillan, 2018), 190). A different question is whether conservative political actors would have been able to partake in the cordon sanitaire had more conservatives among the general citizenry opposed such coordination.

are formed between autocrats and some liberal democrats; those liberal democrats effectively become *former* liberal democrats.[42] These unholy alliances then typically proceed to do liberal democracy harm.

The most prominent recent example of this can be found in the United States, where the far right, led by Donald Trump, took over the Republican Party. During the 2016 Republican Presidential Primary, Trump actually received little support among Republican lawmakers.[43] Fearing that Trump would launch a third-party bid should he fail to secure the nomination, Republican National Committee chair Reince Priebus urged Republican candidates to "pledge" that they would support the eventual nominee. Likewise, several prominent Republicans (e.g., Nikki Haley)[44] denounced Trump's statements on immigration and minorities as un-American, demagogic, and divisive. One member of the Gang of Eight, Lindsey Graham, even dramatically compared the choice between Trump and Ted Cruz (the eventual runner-up) to the choice between getting shot and consuming poison.[45]

Yet once Trump secured the nomination, most fell in line.[46] Only a small group of "Never Trumpers" (typically, neoconservative intellectuals) openly defected to the Democrats, and only a handful of other Republicans either quietly did the same (e.g., George H. W. Bush) or left the presidential portion of their ballots blank (e.g., George W. Bush). Indeed, through the 2020 U.S. General Election, despite their private awareness that Trump has damaged American democracy,[47] most mainstream Republicans stuck by Trump. Only 1 Republican senator (Mitt Romney) out of 52 voted to convict Trump during his (Trump's) first impeachment trial for attempting to blackmail the Ukrainian

---

[42] Note that such alliances can be formed with both the far right and the far left. In what follows, I primarily discuss unholy alliances involving the far right because the far right threat is currently more pressing. This is not always the case.

[43] According to 538's "The Endorsement Primary" tracker, which assigns presidential candidates 1 point for each congressional representative endorsement, 5 points for each senatorial endorsement, and 10 points for each gubernatorial endorsement, Trump placed fourth among Republican candidates, behind Marco Rubio, Ted Cruz, and John Kasich. See Aaron Bycoffe, "The 2016 Endorsement Primary," FiveThirtyEight, June 7, 2016, https://projects.fivethirtyeight .com/2016-endorsement-primary/.

[44] Daniella Diaz, "Nikki Haley: Anyone but Donald Trump," *CNN*, February 17, 2016, www.cnn .com/2016/02/17/politics/nikki-haley-donald-trump-south-carolina/index.html.

[45] Seung Min Kim and Connor O'Brien, "Graham: Choice between Trump, Cruz like 'being shot or poisoned,'" *Politico*, January 21, 2016, https://www.politico.com/story/2016/01/lindsey-graham-trump-cruz-choice-218069.

[46] Note that some of them did temporary suspend their support when a private recording of Trump boasting about his tendency to grope women was leaked. See Rachel Wellford, "Here's the List of GOP Responses to Trump's Vulgar Comments about Groping Women," *PBS News Hour*, October 7, 2016, www.pbs.org/newshour/politics/headline-republicans-react-trump-comments-objectifying-women.

[47] Eric Lutz, "Carl Bernstein Tweets Out His Republican Burn Book," *Vanity Fair*, November 23, 2020, www.vanityfair.com/news/2020/11/carl-bernstein-tweets-republican-trump-critics.

government into helping him win the 2020 Election. Some (notably, Graham and Haley) dramatically reversed their public stances and embraced Trump's rhetoric in a bid to curry favour with Trump and position themselves as inheritors of Trump's legacy, should they run for president in 2024. Meanwhile, others more reluctantly maintained their alliances with Trump in order to advance traditional Republican priorities. As Peter Baker and Susan Glasser write about Cold War warrior James Baker, "Though the myriad ethical scandals surrounding Trump were head-spinning, Baker kept telling himself it was worth it to get conservative judges, tax cuts and deregulation."[48] So deep this transformation of the Republican Party has been, some studies now indicate that the Republican Party has more in common with ruling far right parties in Hungary, India, Poland, and Turkey than with its traditional sister conservative parties in Canada, Australia, and Western Europe.[49]

In short, the division of labour between principled pragmatists and principled purists is a way to cultivate trust among political actors (liberal democrats in particular), yet whether this division of labour can work depends in large part on whether some degree of trust already exists. In the absence of such basic trust, principled pragmatists will find it difficult to compromise and cultivate trust. More than that, autocrats will find it easier to turn liberal democrats against each other, form unholy alliances with some (former) liberal democrats, and corrode liberal democracy. Certainly, if such unholy alliances have not yet been formed, principled pragmatists should try to beat the odds and compromise – but what should happen if those alliances do emerge? Is trust building desirable in such circumstances? Should liberal democrats who stand outside those unholy alliances – the *defenders* of liberal democracy – still try to compromise?

CONTESTATION IN THE NAME OF FUTURE TRUST

I submit that the defenders of liberal democracy should not. Rather than seek reconciliation, they should embrace contestation and discern the most effective strategies to defeat those unholy alliances – preferably, resoundingly.[50] This

---

[48] Peter Baker and Susan Glasser, *The Man Who Ran Washington: The Life and Times of James A. Baker III* (New York: Penguin Random House, 2020), 579.

[49] Anna Luehrmann, Juraj Medzihorsky, Garry Hinde, and Staffan I. Lindberg, "New Global Data on Political Parties: V-Party," V-Dem Institute, October 26, 2020, www.v-dem.net/media/filer_public/b6/55/b65553f85-5c5d-45ec-be63-a48a2abe3f62/briefing_paper_9.pdf.

[50] Such strategies might involve coopting some of their opponents' policies. For example, it might be necessary to make some concessions on immigration despite the fact that those policies might have first been conceived by nativists. Almost certainly, the goal of such policies would be to gain the trust of some supporters of those autocratic political forces – or at least to seem somewhat trustworthy to them. In other words, in these circumstances, the defenders of liberal democracy ought to fight against the opponents of liberal democracy, but not with the supporters of those opponents. For research that supports such an approach in some contexts, see Frederik Hjorth and Martin Vinaes Larsen, "When Does Accommodation Work? Electoral Effects of

might seem like a surprising recommendation, for it seems to concede that politics is defined by warfare rather than by something like fellowship. However, the failure to secure such victories risks consolidating the status of autocrats as mainstream political actors and normalizing de facto (or actual) warfare as "politics as usual."

A major challenge here concerns political judgment: how can the defenders of liberal democracy know exactly when an unholy alliance has been formed, or when autocratic forces have taken over a mainstream political vehicle? Now, there is good reason to believe that not all alliances necessitate such emergencies. For example, following the 2017 New Zealand General Election, Jacinda Ardern's Labour Party forged a coalition with the far right New Zealand First Party. Yet the coalition posed no threat to liberal democracy. Ardern was able to maintain firm control of the coalition's agenda and promptly ended the coalition after winning a majority government in the 2020 General Election.

Still, we can say that liberal democrats should keep in mind that unlike during the 1930s and 1940s, autocrats today will tend not to attempt to supplant liberal democracy with its mirror opposite – totalitarianism or unadulterated authoritarianism. Rather, autocrats will tend to try to transform liberal democracy into what empirical scholars have called "illiberal democracy"[51] or "competitive authoritarianism."[52] These alternatives to liberal democracy typically maintain the shell of liberal democracy. They keep elections intact, allow opposition parties to compete for executive power, permit the press to operate above ground, and have a nominal justice system. However, elections are unfree and unfair: fraud runs rampant, voter lists are manipulated, and opposition activists, voters, and poll watchers are intimidated. Opposition members, their supporters, and the press are routinely harassed, arrested, or even attacked, while the judiciary, independent arbiters, and the civil service are politicized. So, as a rule of thumb, if the defenders of liberal democracy see their opponents working toward such a regime, then they (the defenders of liberal democracy) must set their efforts to cultivate trust aside.

As we have seen, however, liberal democracy cannot sustain itself if warfare becomes permanent – and temporary victories on behalf of liberal democracy can indeed further aggravate the institutionalized enmity problem. Therefore, it is vital that liberal democrats remember that the purpose of such contestation is not victory per se, but rather the destruction of those unholy alliances. That is, the objective is to make these alliances politically costly – to make former liberal

Mainstream Left Position-Taking on Immigration," *British Journal of Political Science* (2020): 1–9. For research opposing such an approach, see Tarik Abou-Chadi, Denis Cohen, and Werner Krause, "Does Accommodation Work? Mainstream party Strategies and the Success of Radical Right Parties," Unpublished Manuscript.
[51] Fareed Zakaria, "The Rise of Illiberal Democracy," *Foreign Affairs* 76(6) (1997): 22–43.
[52] Steven Levitsky and Lucan A. Way, *Competitive Authoritarianism: Hybrid Regimes after the Cold War* (Cambridge: Cambridge University Press, 2010).

democrats think twice about whether they ought to continue alongside the forces of autocracy, and reconsider whether they (former liberal democrats) ought to instead try to win by catering to the liberal democratic mainstream. So, in the event that the defenders of liberal democracy do manage to secure victory, they should aim to entice former liberal democrats to re-enter the liberal democratic fold and – cautiously – try to begin re-establishing trust; this will involve some compromise. If former liberal democrats do not reciprocate, however, and decide to remain in their unholy alliances, then it is necessary to try to disincentivize participation in those alliances once again.

Undoubtedly, it will be difficult, in the aftermath of such confrontations, to perform grand "integrative compromises"[53] that provide great benefits to both sides. After all, a lack of trust characterizes these situations; the individualistic orientation prevails. So, unless the spectre of immanent disaster looms in the horizon, during which case even enemies are compelled to agree to big compromises which they would ordinarily reject,[54] the most that the defenders of liberal democracy can reasonably hope for are "distributive compromises" which provide only small benefits to both sides.[55] Still, these smaller compromises are better than nothing. To rebuild trust – to rebuild conditions where liberal democrats of different partisan stripes can compromise and where the division of labour between principled pragmatists and principled purists is plausible once again – liberal democrats must start somewhere.

To see how this would all play out concretely, consider again the United States. Having made Trump the first incumbent president to lose re-election in almost 30 years, Biden and Democratic Congressional Leadership rightfully tried to strike compromises with (former) mainstream conservative Republicans – not just those like Romney who have been steadfast critics of Trump, but also those who (however cowardly) harboured anti-Trump sentiments in private only. After all, there were signs that the mainstream conservative alliance with the far right was beginning to fray. Following the Democratic sweep of the Georgia senate seat run-off elections – and, more importantly, the Trump-inspired storming of the U.S. Capitol during congressional certification proceedings of the Electoral College – some mainstream conservative Republicans publicly broke away from Trump. Seven Republican senators voted to convict Trump during his second impeachment trial, while others – including Mitch McConnell, the Republican leader in the Senate – condemned Trump rhetorically, even though they voted to acquit Trump on (allegedly) procedural grounds. This seemed to indicate that mainstream conservative Republicans had begun to view Trump and his flank as either political liabilities or genuinely autocratic.

---

[53] Carens, "Compromises in Politics," 127.
[54] Such compromises were struck during the 2007–2008 Global Financial Crisis and the 2019 coronavirus pandemic.
[55] Carens, "Compromises in Politics," 127.

Regrettably, however, many mainstream Republican politicians soon reversed course. Within a month, McConnell announced that he would "absolutely" support Trump should Trump be the 2024 Republican nominee for president,[56] and several former conservative critics of Trump expressed their sympathy or support not just for Trump's efforts to delegitimize the 2020 election, but also for the insurrectionists who had stormed the US Capitol.[57] Yes, some conservatives – notably, House Republican Conference Chair Liz Cheney – stood firm in their condemnation of Trump. However, they soon found themselves attacked by their Republican "colleagues" and supporters, and Cheney was swiftly stripped of her leadership position.

It is thereby apparent, at the time of writing, that most mainstream Republicans have not abandoned their unholy alliance with the far right.[58] In light of my analysis, we can say that even though Biden and the Democrats should try to compromise with those mainstream Republicans who have denounced Trump and entice them further away from Trumpian politics, the Democrats must maintain a confrontational posture toward the rest of the Republican Party. It is necessary to prove once again that Trumpian politics is a bad political strategy.[59]

TABLING OUR DISCUSSION OF THE LIMITS OF SALUTARY HYPOCRISY

We shall return to how liberal democratic political actors should contribute to a culture of trust in Chapter 8. There, I note that even though formal politics is a sphere of activity with a distinctive normative character, non-political intuitions are nonetheless prone to inform how citizens at large judge political actors. Yes,

[56] Paul Leblanc, "McConnell Says He'll 'Absolutely' Support Trump in 2024 if He's the GOP Nominee," CNN Politics, February 25, 2021, www.cnn.com/2021/02/25/politics/mitch-mcconnell-donald-trump-2024/index.html.

[57] For a particularly sad example of such a reversal, see Tom Nichols, "The Moral Collapse of J.D. Vance," *The Atlantic*, July 24, 2021, www.theatlantic.com/ideas/archive/2021/07/moral-collapse-jd-vance/619428/. Concurrently, several Republican-controlled state legislatures also sought to aggressively curtail voting rights, probably to disqualify minority voters who tend to vote Democratic. See Anthony Zurcher, "Voting Rights: How the Battle Is Unfolding across the US," BBC News, July 13, 2021, www.bbc.com/news/world-us-canada-56287375.

[58] By contrast, the Canadian Conservative Party has largely eschewed nativist politics and instead focused on winning the support of socially conservative immigrants. It does so because it recognizes that it would be punished politically for engaging in nativist politics. See Darrell Bricked and John Ibbitson, *The Big Shift: The Seismic Change in Canadian Politics, Business, and Culture and What It Means for Our Future* (Toronto: HarperCollins, 2014), 21ff and Joshua Gordon, Sanjay Jeram, and Clifton van der Linden, "The Two Solidtudes of Canadian Nativism: Explaining the Absence of a Competitive Anti-immigration Party in Canada," *Nations and Nationalism* 26(2) (2019): 902–922.

[59] I recognize that this can prove difficult, not only because the 2021–2022 Senate is split 50–50 but also because midterm elections tend to favour the party that does not control the White House.

hypocrisy in politics might be inevitable and useful, but people nonetheless tend to dislike hypocrisy, including salutary forms of hypocrisy. So, even though the practice of salutary hypocrisy can produce trust among political actors, it can generate *distrust* between political actors and citizens at large. On this basis, I will argue that it is necessary for liberal democratic political actors to either moderate their salutary hypocrisy – even if doing so entails that they forgo some opportunities to strike compromises and to cultivate trust among themselves – or justify their apparent hypocrisy in the appropriate manners.

Still, we now have an idea of what it takes to overcome the institutionalized enmity problem. I have argued that such trust can emerge through a division of labour between principled pragmatists and principled purists. Practicing forms of salutary hypocrisy, principled pragmatists can perform compromises and produce trust, while principled purists can more stubbornly refuse to readily compromise so as to keep those principled pragmatists honest. Yet I also argued that in contexts where some mainstream liberal democratic political actors have forged unholy alliances with autocrats (and have thus become former liberal democrats), it is necessary for the defenders of liberal democracy to discern the most effective strategies and tactics to defeat those alliances. The purpose of such contestation, however, is not to win per se, but rather to disincentivize further participation in those alliances – to restore conditions where it is appropriate to cultivate trust once again. So, I concluded that the defenders of liberal democracy should cautiously reach out to their former liberal democratic counterparts and aim to re-establish trust, should they (the defenders of liberal democracy) win.

Let us now turn our attention to the problem of trust among citizens at large. How can citizens at large overcome the social domination problem?

7

Talking, Shouting Back, and Listening Better

In this chapter, I show how trust can emerge among citizens at large. As we saw in Chapter 5, citizens who trust one another believe that their fellow citizens largely do not wish to have special, unequal privileges of citizenship as a result of their various differences. In order for this trust to emerge, citizens must overcome the social domination problem, the tendency for undue social hierarchies to indeed make the notion of equal citizenship promised by liberal democracy seem like a farce. Sometimes, these hierarchies are sustained by base passions like cruelty, prejudice, and subconscious insecurities. Often, however, those hierarchies are perpetuated unwittingly by the well-intentioned or disinterested everyday actions and norms of law-abiding citizens. In what follows, I aim to answer the question of how citizens – in particular, the underprivileged and the oppressed – can come to believe that their fellow citizens do largely take the persistence of undue social hierarchies seriously and do wish to treat the underprivileged and the oppressed in manners befitting their equal citizenship.

I note that some members of privileged and dominant groups – people whom I call "proud oppressors" and "harder complicit oppressors" – relish their social statuses and will likely never be persuaded to support efforts to redress social hierarchies. Still, I maintain that undue social hierarchies can be identified and rectified in manners that facilitate, rather than hinder, trust production. I argue that a division of labour among the underprivileged, the oppressed, and their allies is needed between two distinct types of practices – "talking" and "shouting back." Through talking, the underprivileged, the oppressed, and their allies can potentially rectify injustices while cultivating trust with the privileged and the dominant – in particular, with what I call "unwitting, well-intentioned oppressors" and "softer complicit oppressors." However, these interactions can only serve this function if the privileged and the dominant are willing to talk as well – and the privileged and the dominant frequently do not. Therefore, in order to force the privileged and the dominant to pay attention to those claims of injustice, to talk, and to stop asserting their dominance by, yes, shouting, the underprivileged, the oppressed, and their allies must also sometimes angrily force those injustices "on to the agenda" by shouting back.

As part of this discussion, I clarify the relationship between the underprivileged and the oppressed on the one hand and their allies on the other hand. I argue that allies should strive to fulfill a mediating role of sorts by *listening well*. Listening well manifests itself in two ways. First, in addition to standing up for the underprivileged and the oppressed when necessary, allies who listen well can convey to the underprivileged and the oppressed – particularly in contexts where many fellow citizens do not seem to afford the underprivileged and the oppressed adequate recognition – that there are in fact members of privileged and dominant groups who do take the persistence of injustices seriously. Second, allies who listen well can provide a softer touch and assure unwitting oppressors and softer complicit oppressors that they (oppressors) are not merely being condemned as bad people. In these manners, allies can persuade the underprivileged and the oppressed that progress within the liberal democratic framework is possible, and dissuade unwitting oppressors and softer oppressors from moving into political alignment with proud oppressors and harder complicit oppressors.

In what follows, I first engage with Danielle Allen's *Talking to Strangers* and its critics. Through this conversation, I derive the general motivating principle of this chapter, that the promotion of the desired sort of trust involves a division of labour among the oppressed, the underprivileged, and their allies between talking and shouting back. Second, I articulate the mediating roles allies ought to assume. Third, I describe what it takes to cultivate trust between the underprivileged, the oppressed, and their allies on the one hand and unwitting, well-intentioned oppressors and softer complicit oppressors on the other hand – to *persuade* those oppressors into becoming supporters, rather than opponents, of the general effort to redress injustices. I argue that these different groups of citizens can cultivate trust by adhering to *and*, vitally, continuously revising the social conventions of good manners. Ideally, talking would instead take the form of open, transparent discourse about the differences, disagreements, and injustices that exist. However, I show that these conversations can only take place on a limited basis and in special forums, such as in carefully curated workplace diversity workshops. So, we should view these more transparent conversations as special interventions to make it easier to sustain the balance between shouting back and less vigorous forms of talking.

THE NEED FOR SHOUTING BACK

Allen advances an understanding of political friendship that seeks to help citizens navigate their differences and disagreements in manners that honour their political equality. On her account, when citizens are political friends, the losers of majority rule are motivated to consent to the basic liberal democratic order. This is because when citizens understand their social relations in terms of political friendship, *pleonexia* transforms into *equity*. *Pleonexia* means "'wanting more than' – more than someone else, more than what one deserves, more than is consistent with concord."[1] Under *pleonexia*, people pursue their interests without a concern for how those pursuits affect others. In contrast, under equity, people – as friends – treat the good of others as part of their own interests.[2] They autonomously consent to limits on their own agency within the context of the relationship – to receive smaller shares than they otherwise would receive. So, when citizens understand their social relations in terms of political friendship, even though they might not know one another or share any emotional bonds, they nonetheless develop the habits required to treat one another equitably.[3] Specifically, they are motivated to *share power* – to not only compensate one another with money or be willing to lose out in some public decisions, but also to make themselves *vulnerable* to one another and to ask one another for favours.

What this means, according to Allen, is that political friends are committed to ensuring that no citizen perform disproportionate sacrifices for the sake of everyone else. In particular, the privileged become willing to voluntarily perform sacrifices so as to alleviate their underprivileged and oppressed counterparts of the burden and pain of having to assume most or all of the sacrifices entailed by citizenship. That is, under political friendship, the privileged become committed to forgo their positions of dominance, as well as the material, psychological, and social benefits entailed by that dominance. According to Allen, such voluntary assumptions of sacrifice "open[] a covenant . . . [whereby all citizens] who benefit from a sacrifice see themselves as recipients of a gift that they must not only honor but also reciprocate."[4] This makes it less likely that majority rule will further cement entrenched majorities and minorities, and that minorities will deem it necessary to combat injustices violently. After all, when majority decisions fail to "incorporate the reasonable interests of those who have voted against those decisions . . . minorities . . . have no reason to remain members of a democratic polity."[5]

In other words, political friendship is oriented toward an equitable distribution of sacrifice, and such a distribution alleviates the underprivileged and the oppressed of the "strange form of psychological pressure" that "democracy puts [them] under" – the fact that democracy "build[s] them up as sovereign and then regularly undermin[es] each citizen's experience of sovereignty."[6] Under political friendship, *all* citizens feel *some* meaningful degree of

---

[1] Danielle S. Allen, *Talking to Strangers: Anxieties of Citizenship since* Brown v. Board of Education (Chicago: University of Chicago Press, 2004), 126.
[2] Allen, *Talking to Strangers*, 132–134.   [3] Allen, *Talking to Strangers*, xxi.
[4] Allen, *Talking to Strangers*, 111.   [5] Allen, *Talking to Strangers*, xix.
[6] Allen, *Talking to Strangers*, 27.

sovereignty. A culture of trust can thereby emerge where citizens who have differences and disagreements "act as if they were friends,"[7] work toward rectifying undue social hierarchies, and judge one another as "valu[ing] the continuation of [their] relationship."[8]

Allen characterizes political friendship as a metaphor of citizenship generally, but it is clear that she hopes that this understanding of citizenship can encourage the privileged and the dominant in particular to help rectify undue social hierarchies. This focus on the privileged and the dominant is well merited. Pointing to the famous 1957 photo of an angry white mob shouting at Elizabeth Eckford in front of Central High School, Little Rock,[9] Allen notes that the privileged and the dominant have long sought to *assert* their dominance. Likewise, it is, at least prima facie, problematic to ask the underprivileged and the oppressed to: (1) do the heavy lifting in the general effort to rectify undue social hierarchies *and* (2) maintain faith in the system. So, Allen's contention is that reconceptualizing citizenship in terms of political friendship can make it easier for the privileged and the dominant to forgo their habits of dominance, and to stop forcing the underprivileged and the oppressed to develop habits of acquiescence.[10] In short, when the privileged and the dominant act like political friends, they no longer *shout*, but rather *talk* and *listen*.

There is good reason to believe that this effort to reconceptualize citizenship can have an effect on some members of privileged and dominant groups. Indeed, from the Civil Rights Movement of the 1950s and 1960s and the fight for labour rights during the Progressive Era to their parallel struggles today, the underprivileged and the oppressed have been supported by justice-conscious members of privileged and dominant groups: *allies*. So, it is conceivable that the metaphor of political friendship can convert some members of privileged and dominant groups into allies, and help them be better allies.

Yet it is unclear whether there are any mechanisms in Allen's framework, other than the power of language[11] and the practice of political friendship by

---

[7] Allen, *Talking to Strangers*, 156.   [8] Allen, *Talking to Strangers*, 189.
[9] Allen, *Talking to Strangers*, 3ff.   [10] Allen, *Talking to Strangers*, 13.
[11] There is evidence that language shapes how we think and, by implication, how we behave. We apply these narratives and metaphors to our everyday experiences – sometimes consciously, but, more typically, *unconsciously* and *reflexively*. For example, in one study, Lera Boroditsky and Paul Thibodeau find that the metaphors with which research participants considered the problem of crime deeply impacted what sorts of crime policies they supported. Presented with the same set of statistics, participants who were told that crime is like a beast ravaging through a city were more inclined to support tough law-and-order solutions (e.g., more police, more prisons, harsher sentences), whereas participants who were told that crime is like a virus were more inclined to support structural reforms to make the community immune to the virus (e.g., better schools, poverty reduction, rehabilitation). Participants stuck with their respective conclusions even when presented with alternative policy options and, importantly, did not think that their reasoning was affected by the metaphor with which they were presented at the beginning of the study. What this indicates, Boroditsky and Thibodeau conclude, is that metaphors help complex and abstract issues seem more familiar, and that even a simple word that appeals to a particular

the underprivileged, the oppressed, and their allies, to motivate less justice-oriented members of privileged and dominant groups to forgo their habits of dominance – to stop shouting, let alone proactively work toward rectifying structural injustices. If this is the case, then does Allen's political friendship not reveal itself to be somewhat of a hope, that the privileged and the dominant will voluntarily sacrifice their power out of the goodness of their hearts?[12] What if they oppose social and political pluralism on a basic level, and what if they feel threatened by claims of injustice? Indeed, even if they oppose injustices on a level of principle and stop shouting, might they not engage in "motivated ignorance" and continue to listen poorly? They might "seek out, selectively attend to, and disproportionately weigh evidence that supports ... an understanding of [themselves] as [] good [people] ... [so that they can] at the same time enjoy[] the benefits of complicity in practices that violate those principles [of equity]."[13] Worse still, since political friendship seems to elevate the sacrifices and "peaceful acquiescence" of the oppressed and the underprivileged to the level of "political exemplarity,"[14] political friendship seems to delegitimize the radical and violent acts of resistance that are often required to make visible the anger and pain experienced by the oppressed and the underprivileged – to compel the privileged and the dominant to actually listen,[15] or at least to make it harder for them to claim that they are not actively trying to not listen.

As a result, the identification and rectification of injustices which Allen's metaphor of political friendship is intended to facilitate seems to relapse into a form of enlightened benevolence on the part of the privileged and the dominant. Moreover, any actual "conversations" that do occur will take place between the privileged and the dominant on the one hand and those select members of oppressed and underprivileged groups who have managed to slip into the socio-economic circles of the privileged and the dominant via "merit" on the other hand – those whose presence might very well be used to paper over the persistence of undue social hierarchies.[16]

In other words, Allen's framework appears to have an initiation problem. Her brand of political friendship aims to counteract civic aggression by

---

metaphor can invoke a whole framework about how to consider a given issue. See Lera Boroditsky and Paul H. Thibodeau, "Metaphors We Think With: The Role of Metaphor in Reasoning," *PLoS ONE* 6(2) (2011): e16782, doi:10.1371/journal.pone.0016782; George Lakoff, *The Political Mind: Why You Can't Understand 21st Century Politics with an 18th-Century Brain* (New York: Viking, 2008); George Lakoff and Mark Johnson, *Metaphors We Live By* (Chicago: The University of Chicago Press, 2003).

[12] Juliet Hooker, "Black Lives Matter and the Paradoxes of U.S. Black Politics: From Democratic Sacrifice to Democratic Repair," *Political Theory* 44(4) (2016): 458.

[13] Clarissa Rile Hayward, "Disruption: What Is It Good For?," *The Journal of Politics* 82(2) (2020): 454.

[14] Hooker, "BLM," 450.   [15] Hooker, "BLM," 464.

[16] Anne Lawton, "The Meritocracy Myth and the Illusion of Equal Employment Opportunity," *Minnesota Law Review*, 85(2) (2000): 587–661.

facilitating a collaborative effort to rectify injustices, but seems to lack adequate mechanisms to kick-start that collaboration. If this is the case, then Allen's political friendship risks becoming the sort of "ideal theory" that Charles Mills condemns – one that, by virtue of being more of a way of thinking than an actual practice, prevents people from perceiving, recognizing, and/or understanding systemic injustices.[17]

What this critique suggests is that more aggressive forms of disruption are required to compel the privileged and the dominant to stop ignoring injustices and oppressing. In order to compel the privileged and the dominant to stop shouting and to listen better – or, at least, in order to make it more difficult for them to claim ignorance – it is necessary to force them to recognize that it is unacceptable in a liberal democracy for there to exist "different etiquette[s] of citizenship: dominance on the one hand and acquiescence on the other."[18] In short, talking back often does not suffice; it is necessary to *shout back*. Along these lines, Juliet Hooker argues that "perhaps we should instead consider instances of 'rioting' as a form of democratic redress."[19]

To this point, Clarissa Hayward observes that, according to Gallup polling, Americans have only taken racial injustices seriously when African Americans have engaged in civic disruption – sometimes aggressive disruption. The only times when more than 10 percent of Americans have named racial injustice among the most important issues facing the country have been during the Civil Rights Era, the 1992 L. A. Riots following the murder of Rodney King, and the Black Lives Matter Era, beginning in 2014 with the murders of Eric Garner and Michael Brown. This suggests that uncompromising forms of disruption that threaten violence and, in extreme circumstances, can turn into actual violence are more effective than talking as ways to compel the privileged and the dominant to either stop shouting or to listen better. Moreover, this suggests that such disruption should be encouraged, *even if* it does not succeed in "winning hearts and minds," because it is such "withdrawals of cooperation" that *alter the agenda* and *force* the privileged and the dominant to pay attention.[20]

THE NEED FOR TALKING

As we saw in Chapters 1 and 2, however, even though liberal democracy might not accommodate efforts to rectify injustices as well as it should, insofar as we believe that liberal democracy secures important goods and is worth preserving, it is dangerous to embrace a politics where aggression simply meets more aggression. After all, even though shouting back might compel the privileged and the dominant to back down and acknowledge the political equality of the

<hr>

[17] Charles Mills, "'Ideal Theory' as Ideology," *Hypatia* 20(3) (2005): 165–184.
[18] Allen, *Talking to Strangers*, 13.   [19] Hooker, "BLM," 464.
[20] Hayward, "Disruption," 449ff.

underprivileged and the oppressed, shouting back does not guarantee that the privileged and the dominant will listen better and stop shouting. That is, even though shouting back can make it harder for the privileged and the dominant to *ignore* the claims of the underprivileged and the oppressed (or to claim ignorance), the privileged and the dominant might still choose not to listen. Indeed, the privileged and the dominant might shout even harder. So, even though aggressive disruption can help set the agenda, unintended consequences might follow should the effort to rectify injustices consist primarily (or solely) of aggressive disruption. Listening and talking do not necessarily follow from shouting back.

For example, Omar Wasow finds that while non-violent protests during the Civil Rights Movement shifted public opinion in favour of the movement (particularly when these protests were met by state or vigilante repression), protester-initiated violence shifted public discourse away from the rectification of racial injustice toward restoring social control. The former sort of protests increased the presidential Democratic vote share in proximate counties by 1.6–2.5 percent, whereas the latter sorts of violence fuelled a 1.5–7.9 percent shift among whites toward Richard Nixon's "law and order" Republicans in the 1968 General Election.[21]

Likewise, as we saw in Chapter 4, even though right populist movements and parties do draw support from those who harbour "out-group" racial-ethnic prejudices – from those whom we can call "proud oppressors" – these movements and parties have grown in recent years because they have managed to secure the sympathies of culturally conservative members of the racial-ethnic majority or plurality. These cultural conservatives lack out-group prejudices but nonetheless identify (to varying degrees) with – and are proud of – their race or ethnicity.[22] Some of these cultural conservatives are complicit in domination; we can call them "complicit oppressors." Those who are "merely" thankful for their privileges and status can be described as "softer" complicit oppressors, while those who worry about what might happen to those privileges if out-group members gain more power can be described as "harder" complicit oppressors.[23] (Indeed, the latter do not seem so far removed from proud oppressors.) Yet we can describe those who hold these attitudes more mildly as "unwitting, well-intentioned oppressors." Unwitting oppressors genuinely oppose prejudice on the level of principle, but also underestimate the degree to

---

[21] Omar Wasow, "Agenda Seeding: How 1960s Black Protests Moved Elites, Public Opinion and Voting," *American Political Science Review* 114(3) (2020): 638–659.

[22] Eric Kaufmann, *White Shift: Populism, Immigration, and the Future of White Majorities* (New York: Abrams Press, 2019); Ashley Jardina, *White Identity Politics* (Cambridge: Cambridge University Press, 2019).

[23] Indeed, they often oppose policies that they perceive as undermining their racial status, even if those policies would demonstrably improve their lives and prevent death. See Jonathan M. Metzl, *Dying of Whiteness: How the Politics of Racial Resentment Is Killing America's Heartland* (New York: Basic Books, 2020).

which injustices are systemic and not necessarily perpetuated purposefully. They might also harbour some implicit or unconscious biases, and underestimate the degree to which their racial-ethnic identities contribute to the oppression of others.

Often, softer complicit oppressors and unwitting oppressors are moved (somewhat ironically) to align politically with proud oppressors because they resent being shouted at. They might have reservations about white supremacists, proud racists, and the like, but they also dislike being condemned as "bad people" simply for having culturally conservative inclinations. They feel that the underprivileged, the oppressed, and the allies of the underprivileged and the oppressed do not give them a chance to respond and to express their disagreements or reservations – that it is the underprivileged, the oppressed, and their allies who are the bad listeners. Indeed, these different sorts of oppressors sometimes come to believe as a result that it is *they* who are being unjustly treated – that they are being denied their right to free speech, as well as their right to celebrate their identity "just like everyone else."

In short, even though aggressive disruption is necessary to force instances and patterns of injustice onto the agenda, and even though such disruption can inspire some members of privileged and dominant groups and demographics to support efforts to rectify injustice, aggressive disruption (particularly when it turns into actual violence) can also motivate both complicit oppressors and unwitting oppressors to align politically with those who do have out-group prejudices, rather than with the disruptors. Aggressive disruption, coupled with the backlash it often inspires, can therefore lead to a cascade of more and more civic strife. Shouting back can lead to more shouting, more shouting back, and so forth. So, an approach to justice that consists solely of shouting back is both dangerous and counterproductive.

These limitations of shouting back go to suggest that even though Allen's framework has an initiation problem, we should not hastily reject that framework wholesale. Instead, we should recognize that Allen's ideal – the pursuit of *both* equity and trust – presupposes behaviour that seemingly contradicts the ideal. That is, talking can only form part of a broader ecology of democratic practices. Collectively, this ecology must (1) provide the underprivileged, the oppressed, and their allies with the space required to engage in sometimes aggressive civic disruption; *and* (2) prevent unwitting oppressors and perhaps softer complicit oppressors from siding with the proud oppressors and actively fighting efforts to rectify injustices.

A DIVISION OF LABOUR BETWEEN TALKING AND SHOUTING BACK

The underprivileged, the oppressed, and their allies therefore ought to pursue a division of labour between the practices of "talking" and "shouting back."

Talking involves practices (discussed in later sections of this chapter) that can help persuade unwitting oppressors and softer complicit oppressors to join the coalition for greater justice and, in time, come to share in trust with the underprivileged and the oppressed. Such activities can help counteract the possibility of backlash against efforts to rectify injustices and make the results of those efforts more enduring. Certainly, talking will likely leave proud oppressors and harder complicit oppressors unmoved. However, these activities can reduce the degree to which unwitting oppressors and softer complicit oppressors will feel like they are being unfairly accused of being bad people. If unwitting oppressors and softer complicit oppressors feel more at ease, then they will be more inclined to take claims of injustice seriously and less inclined to align politically with proud oppressors and harder complicit oppressors.[24]

Now, talking might sometimes involve civic disruption. However, these particular forms of civic disruption typically eschew violence and are explicitly inclusive, meaning that they are designed to attract sympathy and support from members of privileged and dominant groups. The most publicly celebrated elements of the Civil Rights Movement – Martin Luther King Jr.'s non-violent protests and acts of civil disobedience – exemplify such civic disruption.

Meanwhile, shouting back can help to set the stage for talking – to set the agenda. Certainly, shouting back is not necessarily "irrational" or "merely" passionate. Those who shout back often do so because their analyses of the particular situations at hand lead them to deem shouting back necessary, and they often make arguments *through* shouting back. However, shouting back involves more absolutist forms of civic disruption. Exemplified by the early activism of Malcolm X, these forms of civic disruption typically lack the element of inclusion just discussed, and they threaten violence and disorder. Indeed, in extreme circumstances, such as during riots, aggressive civic

---

[24] George Goehl, director of People's Action (a multiracial, low-income, and working class people's organization), reports that his organization had considerable success persuading rural and small-town voters to re-examine their views and change their support from Trump to Biden. Rather than engage in "verbal leafleting," the organization aimed to "have a real conversation":

> We don't try to directly persuade people to change their minds on a candidate or an issue. Rather, we create intimacy, in the faith that people have an ability to reexamine their politics, and their long-term worldview, if given the right context ... When the voter realized that Judith wasn't trying to 'force Biden down his throat,' he opened up about his anxieties. (George Goehl, "How We Got Trump Voters to Change Their Minds," The Atlantic, October 26, 2020, www.theatlantic.com/ideas/archive/2020/10/how-we-got-voters-to-change-their-mind/616851/)

Joshua L. Kalla and David E. Broockman, "Reducing Exclusionary Attitudes through Interpersonal Conversation: Evidence from Three Field Experiments," *American Political Science Review* 114(2) (2020): 410–425 and Joshua L. Kalla and David E. Broockman, "The Minimal Persuasive Effects of Campaign Contact in General Elections: Evidence from 49 Field Experiments," *American Political Science Review* 114(2) (2018): 144–166 find that such an approach is 102 times more effective than traditional electioneering at persuading voters to change their votes and at "facilitat[ing] durable reductions in exclusionary attitudes."

disruption can turn into actual violence. For reasons discussed previously, it is dangerous for the effort to rectify injustices to consist solely of shouting back. However, shouting back is sometimes necessary to compel the privileged and the dominant to either pay attention to injustices or relinquish the practice of motivated ignorance. (If the privileged and the dominant are not moved to do so, then shouting back can at least deprive them of the ability to plausibly plead ignorance.) So, shouting back mitigates against the danger that talking will serve to merely put a smile on domination.[25]

Now, it is sometimes appropriate to speak of "talkers" and "shouters" – of those who primarily talk and those who primarily shout. Talkers might tend to be comparatively optimistic about the possibility of progress and reconciliation, and shouters, more pessimistic. Indeed, it is unlikely that the likes of Malcolm X could have shouted so effectively had they bought into the notions that the American project was worth salvaging, that reconciliation with whites was worthwhile, and that the arc of history is long but bends toward justice. Talkers will also likely disavow violence as a matter of principle in ways that shouters will never do. However, this need not mean that talkers are therefore more utopian and oblivious to the resistance that efforts to rectify injustices will encounter. For example, Malcolm X was more pessimistic than Martin Luther King Jr., yet King was undoubtedly realistic about the depth of the racial problem in America and about how difficult it would be to achieve social justice. So, the difference between talkers and shouters is less about the content of their diagnoses of various social problems than about temperament and their philosophies about how change can come about.

There are some advantages for the underprivileged, the oppressed, and their allies to organize themselves in this manner. Chiefly, if the talkers among them accept that a division of moral labour and of moral responsibility exists between themselves and shouters, then the fact that shouters reliably shout makes it easier for talkers to focus on talking.[26] However, it is more typical that people sometimes talk and sometimes shout. For example, the average person of colour might typically go about his or her daily life, going to work and engaging in the trust-building interactions that I delineate in later sections of this chapter, but forcefully demand accountability for police brutality during the aftermath of police shootings or strangulations. So, it is more apt to describe shouting back and talking as two distinct yet ultimately mutually

---

[25] Peter Gelderloos, *The Failure of Nonviolence: From the Arab Spring to Occupy* (Seattle: Left Bank Books, 2013) similarly calls for a "diversity of tactics." However, as an anarchist, Gelderloos endorses a diversity of tactics out of frustration over the alleged ineffectiveness of what I call talking. In contrast, I advocate for my division of labour from a more moderate perspective.

[26] Andrew Sabl, *Ruling Passions: Political Offices and Democratic Ethics* (Princeton: Princeton University Press, 2002), 44.

dependent set of practices that the underprivileged, the oppressed, and their allies can employ to redress undue social hierarchies within the liberal democratic framework.

Regardless, what is clear is that the underprivileged, the oppressed, and their allies should recognize that shouting back is often necessary to help set the agenda – to force the privileged and the dominant to start listening or to stop trying to not listen. Indeed, there is good reason to believe that much of the gains of the Civil Rights Era were secured through this dual-track effort to combat racial oppression, not through talking alone. As Ta-Nehisi Coates observes,

The Civil Rights Bill of 1964 is inseparable from the threat of riots. The housing bill of 1968 – the most proactive civil-rights legislation on the books – is a direct response to the riots that swept American cities after King was killed. Violence, lingering on the outside, often backed nonviolence during the civil-rights movement. "We could go into meetings and say, 'Well, either deal with us or you will have Malcolm X coming into here,'" said SNCC organizer Gloria Richardson. "They would get just hysterical. The police chief would say, 'Oh no!'"[27]

Providing those who shout back with this leeway can be difficult. After all, the threat of violence implied by shouting back can turn into actual violence, and actual violence can spiral out of control. For example, those who shout might, in a frenzy, end up vandalizing private residences or small businesses.[28] It is necessary to denounce such extreme instances of violence, not only because they are wrong but also because it is important to not appear to condone these actions. These actions threaten the distinction between the public sphere and the most intimate of spaces, and (in the case of small businesses) target people who might feel economic insecurity and find it difficult to rebuild post-vandalism. So, even the appearance of toleration or tacit approval of such actions can inspire backlash and destroy the possibility of conversation. (It is especially important for those who engage in *some* talking and *some* shouting to condemn these activities, for the failure to do so will make it harder for these people to shake off their apparent approval of those extreme actions when they do try to talk.)

Not all acts of violence, however, are created equal. Nonlethal acts of violence like rioting and vandalism can be directed against state or large corporate entities; these entities can easily absorb the costs required to repair damages. For example, during the 2020 protests against anti-black racism following the murder of George Floyd, some protestors vandalized the CNN

---

[27] Ta-Nehisi Coates, "Barack Obama, Ferguson, and the Evidence of Things Unsaid," *The Atlantic*, November 26, 2014, www.theatlantic.com/politics/archive/2014/11/barack-obama-fer guson-and-the-evidence-of-things-unsaid/383212/.

[28] Needless to say, assassination and murder are never justified.

headquarters in Atlanta. These actions helped to keep the issue of racial injustice on the agenda, and the costs involved with repairing the headquarters certainly did not jeopardize CNN's viability. So, even if bystanders feel compelled to criticize such instances of shouting-turned-violent, bystanders should qualify those critiques with the understanding that these aggressive disruptions potentially make their own justice-oriented, trust-building interactions possible.

Still, there are ways in which those who shout back can make it easier for others to stick by them, particularly when they (those who shout back) deem it necessary to turn to violence. One approach is to observe a principle of proportionality, analogous to the same principle in Just War Theory. They should care to shout at the appropriate agents. More than that, if they deem it necessary to appeal to violence, they should calibrate the size of their riots and/ or the amount of public property they vandalize according to the degree of harm they have suffered.[29] They can also articulate clearly why they are moved to shout and/or engage in such violence. Such considerations help show that they are acting with cause – that they are not merely trying to "pick fights" and cause disruptions for the sake of causing disruption – and therefore make it easier for others to stand by them.

Even though the 2019 protests against the Hong Kong government are not exactly analogous to the rectification of social hierarchies – the Hong Kong protestors decried incipient government tyranny, not oppressive social inequalities – the relationship between moderate and radical opponents of the government illustrates this principle neatly. Moderate protesters worried that radical protesters' riots and acts of vandalism would alienate unaligned Hong Kongers, as well as some moderates. However, the radicals largely made their escalations of violence seem reactive – like responses to increasing government heavy-handedness. The 2019 local elections, widely seen as a referendum on the protests, indicated that moderate Hong Kongers were not disaffected by the radicals' violence.[30] Similarly, then, those who shout back make it easier for others to stand by them when they care to make their aggressive disruptive activities seem like proportional responses to attempts by the privileged and the dominant to consolidate relations of injustice. The more brazen those attempts by the privileged and the dominant are, the more leeway those who shout have to pursue aggressive forms of disruption.

---

[29] I roughly follow Avia Pasternak, "Political Rioting: A Moral Assessment," *Philosophy and Public Affairs*, 46(4) (2018): 384–418.

[30] Francis Lee, "Solidarity in the Anti-Extradition Bill movement in Hong Kong," *Critical Asian Studies* 52(1) (2020): 18–32. Note that the Carrie Lam Administration's response to these protests – broadly deemed incompetent by both pro-Beijing and pro-democracy forces – has prompted the central Chinese government to adopt a more strident posture against the pro-democracy movement.

THE ROLE OF ALLIES: LISTENING WELL

Before we consider how unwitting oppressors and softer complicit oppressors can be persuaded to more readily support efforts to rectify undue hierarchies and come to share in trust with their less privileged and more oppressed counterparts, let us pause to elaborate on the relationship between the under-privileged and the oppressed on the one hand and their allies on the other. As we have seen, allies are those members of privileged and dominant groups who are committed to do their part to identify and rectify injustices, or at least to support those efforts. Allies have a responsibility to help rectify injustices. After all, allies benefit from those injustices. The question, then, is how allies ought to go about fulfilling this responsibility.

One possibility is that allies should take the lead in rectifying injustices. However, there is good reason to believe that they should not. The primary reason is that they themselves do not experience first-hand the burdens of those injustices.[31] So, there is a danger that allies will either erroneously assume that the experiences of the underprivileged and the oppressed are less dissimilar to their own than might in fact be the case,[32] or presume that the experiences of the underprivileged and the oppressed are more monolithic than they might actually be.[33] As a result, there is a danger that unless allies attentively listen to the underprivileged and the oppressed, allies will underestimate the degree to which structural change is necessary. Indeed, only until recently, white Democrats were prone to believe (75 to 25 percent) that Black Americans should "work their way up ... without special favors."[34] White Democrats' attitudes on race have since shifted, yet white Democrats are still wary of firm policies to address racial inequalities. White Democrats are far less supportive of strong policies on residential and school integration, let alone slavery reparations.[35]

---

[31] Some argue that the beneficiaries of those injustices do suffer from a sort of sickness insofar as they fear the lack of control that comes with redressing those injustices (e.g., John A. Powell, "Othering and Belonging: An Embodied Spiritual Practice," *Deep Times*, August 29, 2017, https://journal.workthatreconnects.org/2017/08/29/othering-and-belonging-expanding-the-circle-of-human-concern/.). However, such burdens are different in kind than those experienced by the underprivileged and the oppressed.

[32] As we shall see, much of the problem has to do with the unreliability of empathy.

[33] For instance, allies might not appreciate how African Americans might tend to interpret their experiences of racial hierarchy differently than how Hispanic Americans might tend to interpret their experiences of ethnic hierarchy. Likewise, allies might fail to recognize the diversity of viewpoints that exist within those other groups.

[34] Matthew Yglesias, "The Great Awokening," Vox, April 1, 2019, www.vox.com/2019/3/22/18259865/great-awokening-white-liberals-race-polling-trump-2020.

[35] See Meredith Conroy and Jerry Bacon Jr., "White Democrats Are Wary of Big Ideas to Address Racial Inequality," FiveThirtyEight, July 14, 2020, https://fivethirtyeight.com/features/white-democrats-are-wary-of-big-ideas-to-address-racial-inequality/. Alternatively, allies can end up combatting injustices dogmatically by seeking to silence unwitting oppressors and softer compli-cit oppressors, not just proud oppressors and harder complicit oppressors. According to critics of so-called cancel culture, "social justice warriors" aim to "cancel" or shame those who say even

How, then, should allies act? Certainly, they should not stand idly by when they observe aggressive assertions of dominance or condescending behaviour. For example, white allies should put their bodies between racial-ethnic minorities and the police in cases where police brutality seems imminent, just as male allies should stand with their female counterparts when they (male allies) witness other men acting dismissively. In addition, however, allies should strive to play a sort of mediating role by *listening well*.

Listening well entails two things. First, it entails that allies afford the underprivileged and the oppressed recognition. I have argued that conversations between the underprivileged, the oppressed, and their allies on the one hand and unwitting oppressors and softer complicit oppressors on the other hand are key to cultivating trust while redressing injustices. So, the goal is a culture where both sides talk and – crucially – listen to each other. However, up unto this point, I have focused on how the underprivileged and the oppressed, as well as their allies, ought to go about talking, implying that they must strive to listen to the privileged and the dominant. Who, then, should listen to the underprivileged and the oppressed? Sure, in the *goal* I have outlined, unwitting oppressors and softer complicit oppressors do talk and listen to the underprivileged and the oppressed, but the presupposition of my vision (as I have articulated it thus far) is that unwitting oppressors and softer complicit oppressors currently do not listen – at least, not well enough. So, it seems that this vision places special burdens on the underprivileged and the oppressed: *they* are the ones who have to lead the effort to redress injustices, *they* are the ones who have to reach out to the privileged and the oppressed, and *they* (the underprivileged and the oppressed) are the ones who have to do all the listening, at least at first.

I confess that a tragic imbalance does exist in my vision. However, the point I would like to make now is that allies can alleviate some of this imbalance. Specifically, by listening well to the underprivileged and the oppressed, allies

---

one (allegedly) sexist, racially insensitive, homophobic, or transphobic thing into losing their jobs or issuing public apologies; and dogmatic activists tend to interpret dissenting opinions – the refusal to issue such apologies immediately – as signs of bigotry. There is some evidence that the existence of a cancel culture is exaggerated, and that cancel culture is "a catch-all for when people in power face consequences for their actions or receive any type of criticism, something that they're not used to (Sarah Hagi, "Cancel Culture Is Not Real – At Least Not in the Way You Think," *Time*, November 21, 2019, https://time.com/5735403/cancel-culture-is-not-real/)." Needless to say, such dogmatic activism is problematic when it does occur. Not only does such behaviour make practitioners seem absolutist; it also allows proud oppressors – ideological sexists, racists, homophobes, and the like – to claim the high ground as the self-anointed defenders of free speech, and transforms their prejudices into defenses of free speech. Cancel culture, in short, distracts from constructive efforts to combat injustice: those who wish to redress injustice are forced to waste time, energy, and resources distinguishing themselves from social justice warriors. *Moreover*, dogmatic activists sometimes also criticize members of oppressed groups who offer dissenting or more moderate perspectives for "not getting it" or for being "afraid to speak up by themselves." So, such dogmatism can reveal itself to be paternalistic and, ironically, a form of dominance.

can convey to the underprivileged and the oppressed that they (allies) take the perspectives and experiences of the underprivileged and the oppressed seriously. Listening well here involves committing oneself to develop more nuanced understandings of the diverse experiences of the underprivileged and the oppressed. (Preferably, listening well takes place in the context of actual conversations. However, it can also take place indirectly through research – reading, watching films or documentaries, and the like.)[36] When allies listen well, they do not necessarily automatically *defer* to the various judgments of their underprivileged and oppressed counterparts.[37] However, allies do give the perspectives of the underprivileged and the oppressed more weight when forming their own political judgments. In this manner, allies – for example, white, feminist men – can help minorities and women feel that there are at least some fellow citizens who take the persistence of undue social hierarchies seriously, and that it is worth reaching out to fellow citizens, rather than merely fight.[38]

Second, listening well entails that allies refrain from condemning unwitting oppressors and softer complicit oppressors at first blush. For one thing, assuming this posture can help allies better discern *who* among the privileged and the dominant is an unwitting or softer complicit oppressor, and who is a proud or harder complicit oppressor. After all, appearances can deceive, so only through listening can allies determine who is what.

For another, by listening well to unwitting oppressors and softer complicit oppressors, allies give those oppressors the space to express their (oppressors') own perspectives and anxieties; allies demonstrate that they (allies) are more interested in realizing a state of affairs defined by greater political equality than in shaming others or in displaying their (allies') own moral superiority. Indeed, such interactions can help reveal instances of intersectionality – cases where

---

[36] Note that this implies that allies should refrain from avoiding these conversations. There is evidence that some would-be allies ironically (and problematically) do try to avoid having such conversations, lest they say or do anything that might be taken as racist. See John F. Dovidio, Samuel L. Gaertner, and Adam R. Pearson, "Aversive Racism and Contemporary Bias" in *The Cambridge Handbook of the Psychology of Prejudice*, ed. Chris G. Sibley and Fiona Kate Barlow (Cambridge: Cambridge University Press, 2016), 267–294.

[37] Avery Kolers argues that allies should defer to the underprivileged and the oppressed: "in solidarity we act as others direct or would direct – in effect, we act as their understudy or their surrogate" (Avery Kolers, *A Moral Theory of Solidarity* (Oxford: Oxford University Press, 2016), 7).

[38] Mary F. Scudder, *Beyond Empathy and Inclusion: The Challenge of Listening in Democratic Deliberation* (Oxford: Oxford University Press, 2020), 6). I agree with Scudder that it is necessary to listen to proud oppressors *some* of the time. However, for my present aims, I submit that the primary purpose of listening to proud oppressors is to distinguish between them and softer sorts of oppressors, rather than to "fairly consider" the input of proud oppressors.

someone is at once dominant and oppressed. For example, through such interactions, white professional class allies of racial-ethnic minorities can discern that their white working class interlocutors harbour both racial anxieties and economic anxieties. Accordingly, white professional class allies can work toward acknowledging those economic anxieties and support efforts to redress those anxieties,[39] even if they must oppose the racial ones. In this manner, allies can coax unwitting oppressors and softer complicit oppressors into a less defensive posture. As a result of this softer touch, unwitting oppressors and softer complicit oppressors will be more inclined to receive claims of injustice.

In short, by listening well, allies can help the underprivileged and the oppressed feel some meaningful degree of recognition, and keep faith in the liberal democratic framework. Likewise, allies can help encourage unwitting oppressors and softer complicit oppressors to listen better and to talk. In these manners, allies can (1) persuade the underprivileged and the oppressed that liberal democracy will not inevitably serve to entrench domination, and that the privileged and the dominant are not necessarily irredeemable; and (2) dissuade unwitting oppressors and softer complicit oppressors from aligning politically with proud oppressors and harder complicit oppressors.

THE PERSUASION OF UNWITTING OPPRESSORS: VARIOUS FORMS OF TALKING

How can trust emerge between the underprivileged, the oppressed, and their allies on the one hand and unwitting oppressors and softer complicit oppressors on the other hand?[40] How can unwitting oppressors and softer complicit oppressors be persuaded to support the efforts of the underprivileged, the oppressed, and their allies to rectify undue social hierarchies? Put differently, what forms should the practice of talking assume? (In this section, for simplicity's sake, I shall refer to the underprivileged, the oppressed, and their allies as talkers. Even if they might shout in some cases, in the context of the interactions I describe, they do "talk" and thus can be described as occupying the "role" of talkers. I shall also refer primarily to unwitting oppressors, even though what I have to say applies to soft complicit oppressors as well.)

---

[39] This might involve supporting higher taxes on the upper middle class – that is, themselves.

[40] Proud oppressors are likely more intransigent, so it is unlikely that they will be participants in these trust-producing activities. Even here, however, conversion is possible. George Wallace, the governor of Georgia who famously proclaimed, "Segregation now, segregation forever!," ultimately renounced his strident racism and appointed a (then-) record number of African Americans to his cabinet during his final term. (This is not to say that Wallace's apparent late-life conversion absolves his past bigotry.)

Empathy?

It might seem at first glance that the key to producing trust is to encourage unwitting oppressors to practice empathy. For example, white Americans can imagine what it would be like to live without white privilege. The advantage of this course of action is that it is scalable. Although personal familiarity with specific members of underprivileged and oppressed groups can make it easier to practice "imaginative perspective taking," personal familiarity is not required for this to happen. So, the empathetic, unwitting oppressor need not cross any social cleavages to come to identify and support the rectification of injustices.

It turns out, however, that empathy is an unreliable way to identify, let alone rectify, injustices, for the imperfect practice of empathy leads people to believe that others think and feel just as they do. Empathy can dissuade people from listening to one another and from developing accurate understandings of others' experiences, as well as of the history of the injustices in question.[41] In the United States, where neighbourhood segregation persists, Americans vastly underestimate the degree to which race-based economic inequalities persist. They believe that for every $100 the average white American has, the average Black American has $80 – when in fact the average Black American has less than $10.[42] So, empathy is not a reliable way to realize the sort of trust we are seeking.

Transparent Discourse?

If empathy from a distance cannot reliably facilitate the joint identification and rectification of injustices, then perhaps actual conversations between talkers and unwitting oppressors can? Specifically, in the vein of Allen's political friendship, perhaps talkers and unwitting oppressors can cultivate trust by demonstrating to one another their sincerity?[43] They can reveal their moral maxims to one another to demonstrate an attempt to adhere to a rule of law approach to politics, and they can address one another as equal judges or as listeners worthy of respect. Unwitting oppressors can demonstrate that they do oppose discrimination in good faith, while talkers can explain how unwitting oppressors' actions, as well as the basic structure of society, do still perpetuate injustices. Meanwhile, unwitting oppressors can reveal their anxieties – for instance, that their sense of collective identity is under threat. Certainly, these disclosures can serve as opportunities for talkers to explain why unwitting

---

[41] Mary F. Scudder, "Beyond Empathy: Strategies and Ideals of Democratic Deliberation," *Polity* 48(4) (2016): 524–550.

[42] Michael W. Kraus, Ivuoma N. Onyeador, Natalie M. Daumeyer, Julian M. Rucker, and Jennifer A. Richeson, "The Misperception of Racial Economic Inequality," *Perspectives on Psychological Science* 14(6) (2019): 899–921.

[43] Allen, *Talking to Strangers*, 140ff.

oppressors' collective identity might perpetuate injustice. However, these disclosures can also prompt talkers to express how their subordinate statuses cause them to feel similar anxieties. In this manner, talkers and unwitting oppressors can rectify injustices together, even if they do not agree completely about what constitutes injustice. Trust can thereby emerge and persist, despite the fact that there might be some "bad apples" who champion injustice and/or threaten to "poison the well."

This proposed course of action is attractive because it allows talkers and unwitting oppressors alike to actually express themselves to each other. When differently situated citizens talk to one another in these manners, they do not jump to conclusions about one another as they are in danger of doing were they to only practice empathy. So, mutual understanding can potentially emerge. Famously, after the fall of apartheid, the South African government, led by Nelson Mandela, set up the Truth and Reconciliation Commission (TRC). Victims were able to give testimony about the human rights violations and systemic injustices that had occurred under apartheid, and some perpetrators of those abuses were allowed to seek amnesty, provided that they fully disclosed their crimes.[44] While the TRC certainly had its limitations – and while vast inequities in South Africa persist – observers have largely deemed the TRC successful at diffusing racial distrust. Accordingly, in response to the 2021 storming of the US Capitol (discussed in Chapter 6), Allen urges Americans to engage in similar conversations, formally and informally:

> To slap the simple label of white supremacy on the Capitol rioters is to take the easy way out. Extremists led the charge, yes. But why were so many others with them? Why do so many who voted for Trump still think the election was stolen? Not only disinformation is at work; so is people's real sense of loss of agency and control over the lives of their families and communities. Some of this loss is a result of the effects of globalization; some arises from our cultural fights over gender, sexuality and religion.
>
> Understanding people as they understand themselves gives us a chance to pursue a shared social truth. We can begin the process of moral sorting – of trying to identify which views are out of bounds (white supremacy), and which have recognizable validity as one option among many on contested terrain (traditional family structures). Our renovated social truth should combine recognition of people's hunger for personal empowerment with an embrace of deep pluralism.[45]

TRC's, however, are only plausible when there is widespread acknowledgment that severe injustices have occurred, and that there is a need for collective atonement. Indeed, whereas this was the case in South Africa following the

---

[44] Desmond Tutu. *Encyclopaedia Britannica*, s.v. "Truth and Reconciliation Commission, South Africa." Chicago: Encyclopedia Britannica, 2019. www.britannica.com/topic/Truth-and-Reconciliation-Commission-South-Africa (accessed August 5, 2021).

[45] Danielle Allen, "The Four Kinds of Truth America Needs to Pursue Reconciliation," *New York Times*, January 21, 2020, www.washingtonpost.com/opinions/2021/01/21/four-kinds-truth-america-needs-pursue-reconciliation/.

collapse of apartheid, this has distinctly *not* been the case in the United States following the attempted insurrection; American attitudes toward the event have polarized along partisan lines.[46]

The question thus emerges: where can citizens engage in such transparent discourse during less extraordinary times? Herein lies the difficulty: such transparent discourse depends on several demanding preconditions. First, to reiterate, such conversations often can only facilitate the joint rectification of injustices if the practices of shouting back succeed in forcing those injustices onto the agenda. If shouting back fails to do so, then these conversations will obfuscate the persistence of injustices in a sea of *apparent* friendliness, for unwitting oppressors and even some talkers might fail to even realize that many injustices did not make it onto the agenda. Second, setting the need for shouting back aside, even if both unwitting oppressors and talkers have good intentions, why would they interact in such friendly manners? Given their differences, would their interactions not be fraught with tension – akin to a clash of civilizations in microform? So, not only do these conversations depend on shouters to set the agenda; these conversations can only take place in special, favourable environments.

Now, we have some idea about what such environments might look like. Let me highlight two. First, due to wide variation in how they are conducted, workplace diversity workshops can seem rather hit-and-miss, with some workshops yielding seemingly profound changes in their participants, and others, inspiring phony progress and backlash – increased stereotyping, resentment among "non-target" groups over the perceived unfairness of providing special resources to "target" groups, and tokenism.[47]

Some researchers, however, have found that there are ways to structure these workshops so that they can, with reasonable reliability, facilitate the sorts of conversations we are currently considering. For example, one study finds that much hinges on how diversity workshops are presented. If leaders merely try to promote the idea, in the manner of a cheerleader or a preacher, that "diversity is good," then participants will not take these workshops seriously; and if they do voice support for greater inclusiveness, they will not put much effort in following through on that support. However, if leaders instead promote the idea that "diversity is good, but also really hard," then it becomes more likely that participants will be receptive to the claim that inclusion is important, as well as more likely that they will actually try to help improve workplace diversity. So, the "thesis" of these workshops becomes more credible when leaders

---

[46] "Declining Share of Republicans Say It Is Important to Prosecute Jan. 6 Rioters," *Pew Research Center*, September 28, 2021, www.pewresearch.org/politics/2021/09/28/declining-share-of-republicans-say-it-is-important-to-prosecute-jan-6-rioters/.

[47] Lisa Leslie, "What Makes a Workplace Diversity Program Successful?," *Greater Good Magazine*, January 21, 2020, https://greatergood.berkeley.edu/article/item/what_makes_a_workplace_diversity_program_successful.

present diversity as having both upsides and downsides, not just upsides.[48] Another study investigating diversity workshops in academia finds that presenting participants with

common terminology and ways to promote the development of an inclusive and diverse academic workforce ... [can result in] a statistically significant improvement in attendee knowledge of correctly identifying definitions of "implicit bias," "status levelling," "color-blind racial attitudes," "tokenism," and "failure to differentiate ... [as well as] in self-perceptions regarding the importance of improving diversity and recognizing biases and stereotypes in graduate education, knowing what to say when interacting with people from different cultures, and the ability to acknowledge bias when mentoring students from [underrepresented] groups.[49]

Likewise, despite my earlier critique of empathy, some studies have found that encouraging participants to adopt the perspective of minorities – even by "writing a few sentences imagining the distinct challenges a marginalized minority might face" – can help encourage participants to develop more inclusive social attitudes.[50] So, diversity workshops can potentially facilitate the sorts of conversations we are currently considering, *if* they both provide participants with conceptual tools to engage in discourse about these challenging issues and grant unwitting oppressors opportunities to voice their own anxieties:

In one session that I led with school secretaries, we worked through their confusion and frustration related to all the diverse languages being spoken in the school offices and, in some cases, their feelings of anger and resentment about the demographic changes that had taken place in "their" schools. Asked what they learned from the session, participants commented, "I saw the frustration people can have, especially if they are from another country." "We all basically have the same feelings about family, pride in our culture, and the importance of getting along." "I learned from white people that they can also sometimes feel like a minority."[51]

---

[48] Leslie, "Workplace Diversity"; Mike Allen, "Meta-analysis Comparing the Persuasiveness of One-Sided and Two-Sided Messages," *Western Journal of Speech Communication* 55(4) (1991): 390–404.

[49] Lisa M. Harrison-Bernard, Allison C. Augustus-Wallace, Flavia M. Souza-Smith, Fern Tsien, Gregory P. Casey, and Tina P. Gunaldo, "Knowledge Gains in a Professional Development Workshop on Diversity, Equity, inclusion, and implicit bias in academia," *Advances in Physiology Education* 44(3) (2020): 286–294.

[50] Alex Lindsey, Eden King, Ashley Membere, and Ho Kwan Cheung, "Two Types of Diversity Training That Really Work," *Harvard Business Review*, July 28, 2017, https://hbr.org/2017/07/two-types-of-diversity-training-that-really-work; Lisa M. Leslie, Coleen Flaherty Manchester, and Patricia C. Dahm, "Why and When Does the Gender Gap Reverse? Diversity Goals and the Pay Premium for High Potential Women," *Academy of Management Journal* 60(2) (2017): 402–432; Andrew R. Todd, Galen V. Bodenhausen, and Adam D. Galilnsky, "Perspective Taking Combats the Denial of Intergroup Discrimination," *Journal of Experimental Social Psychology* 48(3) (2012): 738–745.

[51] Gary R. Howard, "As Diversity Grows, So Must We," *Education Leadership* 64(6) (2007): 16–22.

Second, some researchers have found that "minipublics" are forums where citizens who have differences and disagreements can demonstrate to themselves that they are capable of meaningful cooperation. A minipublic is "a deliberative forum typically consisting of 20–500 participants, focused on a particular issue, selected as a reasonably representative sampling of the public affected by the issue, and convened for a period of time sufficient for participants to form considered opinions and judgments."[52] Minipublics incorporate "screens against conflicts of interest to provide checks against particularistic motivations that undermine a minipublic's attentiveness to the interests of the public from which it is selected," and organizers can purposefully ensure that the composition of participants is reasonably representative of the citizenry at large. In addition, like juries, minipublics ensure that participants are deliberatively competent – that they gain salient knowledge. For instance, the Government of British Columbia set up a citizens' assembly (the BCCA) in 2004 to study electoral reform. Composed of 160 randomly selected citizens, the assembly deliberated for 10 months. It learned about electoral systems, conducted public hearings, and endorsed a specific reform that was then considered in a referendum. Importantly, although the referendum fell short of the legislated supermajority of 60 percent (it garnered 57.7 percent support), the more voters knew about the assembly, the more likely they were to vote "yes," for they felt that it consisted of "people like us."

This suggests two things. First, minipublics can help citizens demonstrate to themselves that they are capable of deliberating across difference.[53] Experiments support this inference. One Finnish experiment had citizens deliberate immigration. Participants began as moderately to extremely hostile toward immigrants; by the end, they were more tolerant.[54] So, under the appropriate circumstances, trust across social cleavages can be the *result* of deliberation – not the *precondition*. Second, as awareness of these "trusted information proxies"[55] grows, observers will increasingly view participants as proxies for themselves and experience similar attitudinal shifts: "Such deliberation can promote recognition, mutual understanding, social learning, and even solidarity across deep ... religious, national, racial and ethnic divides."[56]

---

[52] Michael K. Mackenzie and Mark Warren, "Two Trust-Based Uses of Minipublics in Democratic Systems," in *Deliberative Systems*, ed. John Parkinson and Jane Mansbridge (Cambridge: Cambridge University Press, 2012), 95ff.

[53] Robert C. Luskin, Ian O'Flynn, James S. Fishkin, and David Russell, "Deliberating across Deep Divides," *Political Studies* 62(1) (2014): 116–135.

[54] Kimmo Grönlund, Herne Kaisa, and Maija Setälä, "Does Enclave Deliberation Polarize Opinions?," *Political Behavior* 37(4) (2015): 995–1020.

[55] Mark E. Warren and John Gastil, "Can Deliberative Minipublics Address the Cognitive Challenges of Democratic Citizenship?," *The Journal of Politics* 77(2): 562–574.

[56] Nicole Curato, John S. Dryzek, Selen A. Ercan, Carolyn M. Hendriks, and Simon Niemeyer, "Twelve Key Findings in Deliberative Democracy Research," *Daedalus* 146(3) (2017): 28–38.

Even proponents of minipublics concede, however, that minipublics are "highly artificial constructions, and are themselves costly of time, attention, money, and sometimes political capital for the organizer."[57] Participants must suspend their ordinary lives for extended periods of time in order to participate in minipublics like the BCCA. Moreover, the fact that organizers in some minipublics can carefully craft the composition of participants to be reasonably representative of the citizenry at large means that minipublics cannot be everyday occurrences. It is costly to ensure that all geographic regions are represented (e.g., it is necessary to fund participants' transportation and housing costs), and ordinary citizens (let alone the underprivileged and the oppressed) cannot afford to regularly take leaves of absences from their jobs. So, the more frequently minipublics occur, the less representative they will be – and the more likely they will be dominated by the privileged and the dominant, or *politicos*.

Similarly, diversity workshops involve employees and stakeholders – yet many workplaces and schools are not representative, and those that are are often internally segregated. The privileged and the dominant tend to occupy higher status positions, and the underprivileged and oppressed, lower status ones.[58] Moreover, not all these organizations conduct such workshops. So, even though these forums can facilitate discussions about injustice, it is unlikely that these forums can become fixtures in the fabric of society.

Accordingly, it is best to view these transparent discussions as potentially useful interventions – special sites for the cultivation of trust among participants. These positive effects can potentially "spill over" into the broader public. Observers or acquaintances of participants can learn from these conversations and shift their views accordingly (or experience shifts in attitudes). However, these discussions, by virtue of being special, cannot be the primary sources of trust between talkers and unwitting oppressors.

The Practice and Revision of Good Manners?

We have good reason to believe, then, that the primary source of trust between talkers and unwitting oppressors, beyond the basic sense of solidarity promised by liberal nationalism, must be the practice – and importantly, revision – of good manners. This is because adherence to the conventional forms of good manners is less demanding – and, thus, less dependent on the curation of special or artificial conditions – than the open exploration of difference, disagreement, and injustice.

There is disagreement about what the practice of good manners ought to communicate. Today, we typically understand good manners to convey mutual

---

[57] Mackenzie and Warren, "Minipublics in Democratic Systems," 116.

[58] Matthew Hall, John Iceland, and Youngmin Yi, "Racial Separation at Home and Work: Segregation in Residential and Workplace Settings," *Population Research and Policy Review* 38(4) (2019): 671–694.

respect – in Kantian language, the commitment to treat others as having dignity and unconditional value[59] – or, at least, the *effort* to convey respect.[60] As Karen Stohr notes, "I may not be able to summon up the gratitude that I should be feeling, but I can at least say the right words and act as I should."[61]

Teresa Bejan, however, argues that good manners – or rather, the notion of *civility* – initially emerged not as a way to cultivate mutual respect, but rather as a way to promote toleration in the face of disagreement. So, conceptions of civility that equate it with mutual respect miss the point: they "necessarily move the discussion to an aspirational realm of ideal theory in which the kinds of problems civility is needed to address *do not even arise*,"[62] and actually do not address the problem of deep disagreement. Accordingly, Bejan resuscitates Roger Williams's notion of *mere* civility. Under mere civility, citizens might disdain one another – and they likely know that they do disdain one another – yet they are nonetheless committed to keep the peace and to find a path forward together: "The virtue of mere civility lay in its ability to coexist with and even communicate our contempt for others' most fundamental commitments while continuing the conversation."[63] In other words, mere civility is what we turn to when we cannot conjure respect.

I maintain that, in the liberal democratic context, good manners should embody mutual respect to the greatest extent possible. The chief reason is that liberal democracy *promises* its citizens political equality; it promises citizens normative goods that are more expansive than mere co-existence. Indeed, according to many, contemporary liberal democracy promises more expansive notions of equality as well – at a minimum, equal respect. So, even though mere civility can plausibly serve as a sort of stop-gap should all else fail, it is unclear whether mere civility can sustain itself in the long-run if people believe that disrespect bubbles beneath the surface: people would then be at risk of perceiving a contradiction between the promise or *expectation* of equal respect on the one hand and the reality that civility is a sort of masquerade on the other hand. Not only would people then be more tempted to not adhere to the conventions of (mere) civility; they might also dismiss those conventions – and perhaps the very *concept* of good manners or civility – as irredeemably reactionary. Indeed, we see something similar at play in regards to how many justice-oriented citizens are losing faith in liberal democracy. With several academic disciplines honing in on the contradictions of the Enlightenment (the era that arguably

---

[59] Karen Stohr, *On Manners* (New York: Routledge, 2012), 23ff.

[60] In prior eras, where societies were far more stratified formally, the conventions of good manners served to codify those social distinctions. See Ruth W. Grant, *Hypocrisy and Integrity: Machiavelli, Rousseau, and the Ethics of Politics* (Chicago: The University of Chicago Press, 1997), 33.

[61] Stohr, *On Manners*, 83.

[62] Teresa M. Bejan, *Mere Civility: Disagreement and the Limits of Toleration* (Cambridge, MA: Harvard University Press, 2017), 161.

[63] Bejan, *Mere Civility*, 159.

gave birth to liberal democracy), more and more students believe that liberal democracy only offers a hollow sense of equality and might even be inherently *unequal* – racist, colonialist, and heteronormative.[64] Therefore, my contention is that people should be encouraged to practice good manners in an effort to demonstrate mutual respect, and that only so can good manners contribute to a lasting sense of trust between talkers and unwitting oppressors.[65]

There are at least two challenges here. First, manners do involve an element of deception or opacity. Even when one does conform to the conventional forms of good manners in an effort to bridge the gap between what one should be like and what one is really like, one still conceals one's "true" thoughts and attitudes – who one "really is." So, there will – inevitably – always be some uncertainty in the act of judging whether others practice good manners for the purposes of conveying respect or purely for the purposes of expediency.

Second, even if good manners *ought* to express mutual respect, they can still serve to consolidate undue social hierarchies. This is most obviously the case when the social conventions of good manners do not actually embody respect. Indeed, given that social conventions typically reflect the moral intuitions that are shared by "the mainstream" of society – dominant members of society in particular – "good" manners might serve an ideological function. The practice of good manners might not just keep the underprivileged and the oppressed down, but also convince them that those undue social hierarchies are in fact just, or at least, simply "how things are." For example, King points out in *A Letter from Birmingham Jail* that the conventions of "good" manners in 1950s America, whereby Black women were never called "Mrs." and where Black adult men were frequently called "Boy," were underpinned by racist moral principles and helped to perpetuate racist social relations and institutions.[66]

The social conventions of good manners, however, can genuinely express respect yet *still* serve to consolidate undue hierarchies. For one thing, the practice of good manners can dissuade the dominant and the oppressed from investigating whether deeper structural problems persist. The appearance that unwitting oppressors are attempting in good faith to demonstrate respect can tempt talkers into focusing on strengthening the sense of reciprocity which might have emerged, rather than on addressing deeper structural issues.[67] For

---

[64] Yascha Mounk, *The People vs. Democracy: Why Your Freedom Is in Danger & How to Save It* (Cambridge, MA: Harvard University Press, 2018), 248ff.

[65] In Chapter 9, I will discuss the associational types where such interactions are most plausible.

[66] Martin Luther King Jr., "Letter from a Birmingham Jail [King Jr.]," African Studies Center University of Pennsylvania, April 16, 1963, www.africa.upenn.edu/Articles_Gen/Letter_Birmingham.html.

[67] Bernard E. Harcourt, "The Politics of Incivility," *Arizona Law Review* 54 (2012): 345–373 and Linda M. G. Zerilli, "Against Civility: A Feminist Perspective" in *Civility, Legality, and Justice in America*, ed. Austin Sarat (Cambridge: Cambridge University Press, 2014), 107–131 accuse

example, unwitting oppressors might care to say "please" and abstain from cutting lines.[68] While such courtesies are far cries from the racist conventions of the 1950s, they can distract unwitting oppressors from rectifying structural features of society that provide them undue social privileges and material advantages.

For another, implicit and historical biases can make it more difficult for the members of some demographics to *appear* to be treating others with respect. For example, during disagreements, a man might appear to treat his interlocutors calmly and respectfully while speaking forcefully, while his female counterparts (especially if she is Black) might come across as ill-tempered and disrespectful, despite adopting the same tone.[69] So, by adhering to the conventions of good manners, not only can unwitting oppressors delude themselves into believing that they are doing everything they can to help rectify injustices; they can also find it difficult to recognize that it is often harder for their underprivileged and oppressed counterparts to appear to practice good manners. The "merely forceful" man who genuinely believes himself to be acting respectfully can end up feeling exacerbated by the fact that his "angry" female counterpart does not seem to reciprocate or acknowledge his "good-faith" efforts.

Of course, as we have seen, similar difficulties bedevil efforts to openly and transparently discuss difference, disagreement, and injustice. However, the dangers are more pressing here, for the practice of good manners already involves a layer of opacity: the practice of good manners can conceal not just who people "really are" but also their differences and social hierarchies.

Still, hope lies in the fact that the social conventions of good manners are not immutable. They can evolve as citizens' moral intuitions evolve. So, the moral intuitions that underpin the content of good manners can change – and the conventions that constitute good manners can change accordingly. For example, although racial injustices continue to plague the United States, the conventions of "good" manners of the 1950s described by King, along with the racist moral vision they embodied, have long been discredited and, for the most part, have been supplanted by those of equal respect. Likewise, people can come to better understand that it is harder for the members of some demographics to *appear* to behave respectfully than the members of others. Indeed, there is more awareness now than 50 years ago that women are often

civility of codifying the subordinate status of those who allegedly need special protection. I discuss toward the end of this section how to counteract this danger.

[68] Stohr, *On Manners*, 28ff.

[69] For a famous illustration of such a double-standard, see Anna Kessel, "Serena Williams again Bears Brunt of Double Standards in Tennis," *The Guardian*, September 9, 2018, www.theguardian.com/sport/2018/sep/09/serena-williams-again-bears-brunt-double-standards-tennis.

condemned as "angry," whereas men are praised as "forceful" for behaving in the same manners. (Evidently, much more progress still needs to be made on this front.)[70]

Likewise, even if the practice of (the desired sort of) good manners might divert attention from deeper structural injustices, this does not necessarily need to be the case. As recent mass protests against racist police brutality indicate, the supremacy of the social conventions of equal respect has not stopped forceful attempts to shine a light on the persistence of structural injustices. So, good manners can potentially serve as a source of trust or basic good will, but are not so rigid as to necessarily stymie attempts to rectify injustices.

Even so, role-based constitutional fellowship has other elements that can help prevent good manners from stymieing the rectification of injustices. Most obvious are the contributions of shouting back. Yet the practices of talking – indeed, of good manners themselves – can also help on this score. Namely, when one practices good manners, one does not have to give unwitting oppressors a free pass on problematic behaviour. The practice of good manners does not require that one maintain a smile and nod when unwitting oppressors say offensive things. Talkers can firmly express their concerns and feelings of being slighted. A Black woman need not hide her aggravation when a white man repeatedly interrupts her or makes racially insensitive jokes. She can call him out for his rudeness, and just because she does so does not make her rude. Civility, in other words, does not entail peaceful acquiescence.

UNCOMPLACENT GRADUALISM

A rather fragile balancing act, in short, is needed to overcome the social domination problem and cultivate trust among citizens at large. This balancing act consists of the practice and revision of good manners among talkers and unwitting oppressors (as well as softer complicit oppressors) on the one hand, and the aggressive disruptions of shouters on the other. Open, transparent discussions among talkers and unwitting oppressors (and softer complicit oppressors) about the differences, disagreements, and injustices that exist between them can take place on a limited basis in special forums as useful interventions to make it easier to sustain that balance.

The question remains: what sorts of practices can help produce trust *between* the formal political sphere and the general citizenry? Let us turn our attention to this question next.

---

[70] Eric Thomas, "Kavanaugh Gave a Messy, Angry Performance That Would Never Be Allowed from a Woman," *Elle*, September 27, 2018, www.elle.com/culture/career-politics/a23496358/kavanaugh-angry-opening-statement/.

8

Justifying (and Constraining) Salutary Hypocrisy

We now have an understanding of how trust can emerge, under role-based constitutional fellowship, in the formal political sphere and in the general citizenry. Yet how can trust emerge *between* these two spheres of activity? How can citizens at large come to believe that political actors largely do try to further the public good? In this chapter, I aim to answer this question by addressing the representative cynicism problem. This problem refers to the tendency for citizens at large to believe that political actors are largely in it for themselves, individually and as a class. While citizens at large should be encouraged to maintain healthy skepticism[1] – after all, liberal democracy was arguably born out of a fear of the corrupting tendencies of power – liberal democracy is vulnerable to the growing influence of autocrats when citizens are excessively skeptical. So, liberal democratic political actors ought to counteract and avoid further aggravating the political cynicism of citizens at large.

In what follows, picking up from my discussion of salutary hypocrisy in Chapter 6, I first elucidate the predicament at hand. As we have seen, proponents of salutary hypocrisy are right to insist that formal politics is its own sphere of activity with its own normative dynamics, and that trust production here is more plausible if pursued through salutary hypocrisy than demonstrations of sincerity. I show, however, that this perspective misjudges the depth of people's distrust of hypocrisy and the potential for even salutary forms of hypocrisy to cause distrust. That is, proponents of salutary hypocrisy do not fully appreciate the degree to which non-political intuitions are prone to inform how citizens judge political actors – and the degree to which those intuitions inform the

---

[1] Patti Lenard calls such skepticism *mistrust*, rather than distrust. For Lenard, mistrust helps citizens remain vigilant and is compatible with trust, whereas distrust opposes trust and corrodes democracy. See Patti Tamara Lenard, "Trust Your Compatriots, but Count Your Change: The Roles of Trust, Mistrust and Distrust in Democracy," *Political Studies* 56(2) (2007): 312–332.

normative dynamics of the formal political sphere and constrain how political actors might act. In other words, I show that the formal political sphere is distinctive but not autonomous.

Accordingly, I argue that liberal democratic political actors (principled pragmatists in particular) must either (1) limit the degree to which they practice salutary hypocrisy or (2) justify their apparent hypocrisy in the appropriate manners. Given that the first course of action jeopardizes the possibility of trust among liberal democratic political actors *and* might politicize and further enflame social cleavages, I outline guidelines for (1) how these political actors can go about justifying their apparent hypocrisy and (2) how they can avoid needlessly aggravating citizens' political cynicism *without* putting themselves (political actors) at a competitive disadvantage. Liberal democratic political actors can refrain from excessively demonizing one another, explain why they might have compromised (but only after the fact and with care), and avoid promulgating fantastical understandings of politics. I also note that citizens at large can prepare themselves to return these good faith efforts by reflecting on how they too act hypocritically in their own lives – for instance, in business, in the job market, and even at school. Citizens will more likely do this preparatory work if political actors act in the manners I outline.

THE LIMITS OF SALUTARY HYPOCRISY

In Chapter 6, I argued that proponents of salutary hypocrisy are right to insist upon the distinctiveness of the formal political sphere. On their account, politics-as-usual is defined by relationships of dependence among people with conflicting interests: political actors must cooperate to attain what they need and want, yet they must also compete and are prone to distrust one another. As a result, they are bound to misrepresent their characters – to act hypocritically – both to get what they want alongside others when their interests overlap and to defeat one another when their interests conflict. Accordingly, political actors should not develop trust by practicing a politics of sincerity. Rather, they should appeal to the *right sorts* of hypocrisy. By doing this, they can compete and cooperate simultaneously more successfully, and come to share in *quasi-trust* – not unlike how people who dislike one another can come to enjoy peaceful and commodious social relations by adhering to the conventional forms of good manners. On this basis, I argued that principled pragmatists can, acting as salutary hypocrites, cultivate a sense of reciprocity and trust by performing compromises. By striking compromises, political actors agree to get less than they might otherwise want to get, and they might "break promises" they had previously made to their supporters and/or constituents. Yet in doing so, political actors demonstrate to one another that they are committed to finding a way forward together, despite their differences and disagreements.

The point I would like to make now, however, is that even if politics is indeed a sphere of activity with its own distinctive normative character, non-political intuitions are prone to inform how citizens judge political actors. That is, even though hypocrisy might be inevitable and useful in politics, people still generally dislike hypocrisy and tend to associate "principle" and "sincerity" with consistency – "purity." There is a reason why political actors frequently aim to expose their rivals' double standards, even though they themselves also act inconsistently – and even though their constituents and supporters also often act and think inconsistently. As one example, Timothy Collins recounts an incident at a 2015 Democratic Presidential Primary debate, when Hillary Clinton criticized Republicans for espousing small government in the context of economic policy while practicing big government in the context of women's health: "raucous applause followed … Hypocrisy of political attitudes grabbed the audience's attention as an attack … they may not have registered that they were probably also logically inconsistent."[2] Therefore, even if hypocrisy can help generate (quasi-)trust among *practitioners* of salutary hypocrisy, it can lead *observers* to distrust those practitioners of hypocrisy.

In addition, even though salutary hypocrisy can facilitate short-term cooperation, the proliferation of (salutary) hypocrisy can undermine people's trust in outward appearances generally. As Amy Gais notes, "while political correctness thwarts the public declaration of prejudice, it might also cultivate a culture of distrust because we never know for certain if we are interacting with friend or foe, especially after it has been exposed as mere pretense."[3] Indeed, even though good manners (salutary social hypocrisy) can facilitate civil public relations among non-friends, non-friends often only practice good manners when they feel that they are more likely to be potential friends than potential enemies – that good manners express basic respect or an effort to express basic respect and are not mere pretense. As societies with deep social or political cleavages show, when different groups of non-friends (e.g., supporters of opposing political parties) feel that they are likely enemies, they become more inclined to express their sincere disdain for one another than to practice good manners,[4] and more likely to do "whatever it takes" to pursue their respective goals, even if doing so harms others. Empirical research indicates that in the United States, citizens sort themselves into mutually hostile "'teams' of partisans" and that they increasingly believe that "winning justifies any tactics" – cheating, lying, personal attacks on candidates and families, stealing elections,

---

[2] Timothy P. Collins, *Hypocrisy in American Political Attitudes: A Defense of Attitudinal Incongruence* (Cham: Palgrave Macmillan, 2018), 7.

[3] Amy Gais, "The Politics of Hypocrisy: Baruch Spinoza and Pierre Bayle on Hypocritical Conformity," *Political Theory* 48(5) (2019): 20.

[4] Note that such displays of sincere disdain are more frequent online than in person. See "Civility in America 2019: Solutions for Tomorrow," Weber Shandwick, June 26, 2019, www .webershandwick.com/wp-content/uploads/2019/06/CivilityInAmerica2019SolutionsforTomorrow .pdf.

voter suppression, physical assault on intimidation, destroying signs, filibuster abuse, and the like.[5]

What this goes to suggest is that even though the formal political sphere is distinctive, it is not autonomous. The normative dynamics of the non-political affect the normative dynamics of the political. That is, the non-political constrains what political actors can do; political actors must take non-political intuitions and moral intuitions into account when forming their political judgments.[6] A politics of salutary hypocrisy seems to end up depending on one of two things: (1) the ability of salutary hypocrites to skilfully hide their hypocrisy so as to *seem* sincere; or (2) the unlikely event that citizens at large will get over their revulsion toward political hypocrisy.

To this point, David Runciman draws a distinction between "honest hypocrites" and "sincere liars." Honest hypocrites like Hillary Clinton, Al Gore, and Gordon Brown try not to lie. However, they struggle to seem trustworthy, for it is apparent to observers that they have consciously "donned a mask." The distrust generated by this apparent inauthenticity is compounded when they try to cautiously "sidestep" around the truth, rather than lie outright. Honest hypocrites then come across not only as inauthentic, but also as trying to hide something. In contrast, skilful liars who *seem* sincere like Bill Clinton, Tony Blair, and Donald Trump might also "don masks," but they do so without seeming like they have done so.[7] So, even though sincere liars are less committed to the truth than honest hypocrites, sincere liars are judged to be more trustworthy – or, at least, more "authentic" and beguiling.[8]

The juxtaposition of hypocrisy against worse vices can counteract some of the distrust people feel toward hypocrisy. For example, citizens in a society that

---

[5] See Patrick R. Miller and Pamela Johnston Conover, "Red and Blue States of Mind: Partisan Hostility and Voting in the United States," *Political Research Quarterly* 68(2) (2015): 225–239.

[6] As another example, according to Bernard Williams, given the distinctive normative dynamics of the political sphere, withholding the truth is not conducive and is perhaps unbecoming of personal friendships, yet government secrecy is often justified to safeguard national security (Bernard Williams, *In the Beginning Was the Deed: Realism and Moralism in Political Argument*, ed. Geoffrey Hawthorn (Princeton: Princeton University Press, 2005), 157–159.). It is evident, however, that given its opacity, government secrecy is a source of public cynicism toward government – particularly when the government is revealed to have secretly conducted untoward activities, such as mass warrantless surveillance, torture, and even the fabrication of evidence to go to war. So, it is not enough for political actors to merely proclaim that government secrecy is not analogous to personal secrecy. In order to avoid fueling public cynicism toward government, political actors must account for people's distrust of secrecy when crafting government secrecy laws. Indeed, when people broadly distrust government, it might be necessary for those laws to allow for more transparency than might be ideal, if one were to judge those laws solely on the basis of national security concerns.

[7] In Trump's case, it might be more accurate to say that he dons a mask that is so crude that it seems like he has "no filter" and that he "tells it like it is."

[8] David Runciman, *Political Hypocrisy: The Mask of Power from Hobbes to Orwell and Beyond* (Princeton: Princeton University Press, 2008), 228–229.

is not excessively polarized might be willing to tolerate the hypocrisy of political actors, for those citizens – out of a sense of basic unity – might recognize that the alternative is a politics (and perhaps society) defined by open and honest, mutual hostility. Seemingly heeding Judith Shklar's advice that we stop worrying so much about hypocrisy because it is a relatively benign vice compared to cruelty,[9] many who felt betrayed by Obama's pragmatism looked back nostalgically as they observed his successor's cruelty. Hypocrisy also does not seem so bad when it yields good results. During the Great Depression, Franklin Roosevelt criticized Herbert Hoover for not balancing the budget, but ran huge deficits once he became president. Some accused Roosevelt of "flip-flopping"; more praised him for saving the United States from economic depression.

Still, a politics of salutary hypocrisy remains fragile. For one thing, it seems to rely on the persistence of worse vices to help maintain perspective. For another, the failure of salutary hypocrisy to secure results can inspire backlash. According to some, this explains today's populist moment.[10] During the 1990s, the center-left coopted the center-right's "neoliberal" economic platform. For a time, the left tolerated this "triangulation" because it seemed to generate prosperity, as well as electoral victories. However, the left lost faith when triangulation stopped securing those benefits. Thus emerged an antagonistic politics where "the people" understands itself to be the victim of "the [centrist] establishment," which (according to the left) acts hypocritically not to secure progress but to enrich itself and its real constituents – international finance. In short, given that the political sphere is not autonomous, even though hypocrisy can facilitate cooperation among some, that cooperation can breed suspicion among others, and the failure of salutary hypocrisy to secure good results can lead to its rejection.

COUNTERACTING CYNICISM

This all suggests one of two things. First, it suggests that in order to counteract citizens' political cynicism, liberal democratic political actors – principled pragmatists specifically – must limit the degree to which they engage in salutary hypocrisy and act more like consistent purists. The problem with this course of action, however, is that it jeopardizes the possibility of compromise and trust among themselves. More than that, as I alluded to earlier in regards to the United States, such obstinance can aggravate the distrust that might exist among citizens at large. With fewer political competitors willing to cooperate, the social cleavages which exist between different groups of citizens risk becoming further politicized – leaving citizens more prone to view partisan competition as a proxy for their social differences, and more apt to understand their

---

[9] Judith Shklar, *Ordinary Vices* (Cambridge, MA: The Belknap Press of Harvard University Press, 1984).
[10] Chantal Mouffe, *For a Left Populism* (New York: Verso, 2018).

differences in the same zero-sum terms that they often interpret partisan politics.

Second, the paradox of salutary hypocrisy suggests that principled pragmatists must care to justify their apparent hypocrisy and that they must take steps to avoid needlessly aggravating citizens' cynicism – this is the preferred course of action. Of course, pulling this balancing act off successfully will be challenging. Nonetheless, there are certain guidelines that principled pragmatists, as well as principled purists, can adhere to in order to mitigate citizens' cynicism. Importantly, adhering to these guidelines does not condemn oneself to political irrelevance.

Refrain from Excessively Demonizing Opponents

Now, some dramatization is inevitable and welcome, particularly during campaigns. It can help voters see what is at stake more clearly, as well as catalyze political participation. For example, it is clarifying for a free-marketeer who understands a largely unregulated free market to be an expression of foundational American principles to construe activist governments as un-American, just as it is clarifying for a progressive who identifies more with the labour movement to decry the dismantling of unions as compromising the foundations of the middle class. However, political competitors who share a commitment to liberal democracy should refrain from reflexively accusing one another of having heinous motives. Progressives should not, in the absence of adequate evidence, accuse free-marketeers of purposefully trying to suck the lower and middle classes dry,[11] just as free-marketeers should not construe progressives as seeking to bankrupt the country. Such attacks do not merely clarify differences; they violate the ideal of political pluralism. Along these lines, principled purists should also avoid condemning principled pragmatists as self-serving pragmatists simply for compromising, settling for half-measures, or, even, shifting their positions to reflect shifts in the composition of their electorates. Instead, principled purists should discriminate between principled and unprincipled pragmatists, reserving their accusations of bad faith for the latter.[12]

Failure to entertain such subtleties fuels cynicism. First, with liberal democratic political actors accusing one another of unpardonable sins, citizens might just take them at their word. Second, when political actors undermine political pluralism, they risk polarizing the general citizenry and undermining confidence in liberal democracy. The United States is so polarized – and Americans,

---

[11] For an example of such excessive demonization, see BarackObamadotcom, "Obama for America TV Ad: 'Firms,'" YouTube video, 0.32, July 14, 2012, www.youtube.com/watch?v= Ud3mMjoAZZk.

[12] Admittedly, discriminating between principled and self-serving pragmatists in some cases will prove difficult.

increasingly unable to accept the legitimacy of elections[13] – in part because political actors have demonized one another and because their supporters cannot fathom how others can support such heinous political actors and causes. Not only has this made it difficult for political actors to practice the sorts of salutary hypocrisy on which liberal democratic politics depends; it has also made it more difficult to form liberal democratic fronts when such fronts are required to fend off liberal democracy's insurgent enemies. Put differently, the lack of trust among liberal democratic political actors is not the only impediment to the formation of liberal democratic fronts; so too is a citizenry that has been encouraged by partisans to assume the worst of both political opponents and those opponents' supporters.

The failed efforts of the "Never Trump" movement to stop a Trump presidency illustrate these dangers neatly. Largely consisting of neoconservative intellectuals and strategists (many of whom were alumni of John McCain's 2008 presidential campaign), these Republicans attempted to convince Republican voters to either abstain from voting for Trump or to vote for Clinton. However, 90 percent of Republicans voted for Trump.[14] The reasons for this are myriad, but surely part of Never Trumpers' failure can be attributed to the fact that they spent the preceding 30 years stoking what some have called negative partisanship, waging abstract yet potent culture wars for short-term partisan gain.[15] In particular, they paid lip service to far right cultural themes (e.g., on race, immigration),[16] underestimating the potential for far right forces to take over the party,[17] and demagogued Democrats as out-of-touch, "coastal elites" who aimed to impose "San Francisco values" – post-modernism, non-traditionalism, collectivism, multiculturalism, and moral relativism[18] – onto the

[13] Jon Cohen and Nathaniel Persily, "Americans Are Losing Faith in Democracy – And in Each Other," *The Washington Post*, October 14, 2016, www.washingtonpost.com/opinions/americans-are-losing-faith-in-democracy–and-in-each-other/2016/10/14/b35234ea-90c6-11e6-9c52-0b10449e33c4_story.html.

[14] "An Examination of the 2016 Electorate, Based on Validated Voters," Pew Research Center, August 9, 2018, www.people-press.org/2018/08/09/an-examination-of-the-2016-electorate-based-on-validated-voters/.

[15] As Julia Azari, "Weak Parties and Strong Partisanship Are a Bad Combination," Vox, November 3, 2015, www.vox.com/mischiefs-of-faction/2016/11/3/13512362/weak-parties-strong-partisanship-bad-combination explains, "The more abstract party identification is, the more resentment can foster against people whom you do not know or encounter, whose lives you have not considered, but who seem like useful targets for your frustration."

[16] Some scholars interpret the entire modern Republican Party platform – anti-tax, pro-gun, and anti-health care reform – as "white backlash conservatism." See Jonathan M. Metzl, *Dying of Whiteness: How the Politics of Racial Resentment Is Killing America's Heartland* (New York: Basic Books, 2020), 6.

[17] Perhaps most symbolic of this phenomenon was McCain's selection of Sarah Palin as his running-mate. Many observers now view Palin's candidacy for vice president as a precursor to Trump's candidacy for president eight years later.

[18] George Lakoff, *Moral Politics: How Liberals and Conservatives Think*, 2nd ed. (Chicago: The University of Chicago Press, 2002), 171.

rest of the country.[19] Part of this included a "thirty-year War on Hillary."[20] Beginning with how they distorted Clinton's comments during the 1992 Democratic Presidential Primary on how she "could have stayed home and baked cookies and had teas but ... decided [instead] to fulfill my profession" into a denunciation of all traditional, stay-at-home mothers, Never Trumpers transformed Clinton into the personification of those out-of-touch values – the "demon-of-all-demons."[21]

The catch here is that there were probably "grains of truth" embedded in these caricatures. The Democratic Party *did* steadily shift its base of support away from the working class toward the professional class (whose interests and values are often opposed to the working class's),[22] and some of those professionals – driven by a meritocratic ethos – do have a tendency to view themselves as more deserving than others and to dismiss supporters of Reagan, Bush II, and Trump as "stupid" or "uneducated." Aspects of Clinton's personality also likely made her uniquely vulnerable to Republican attacks.[23] However, the point I would like to make here is that the Never Trumpers' past behaviour undermined their abilities to encourage defection and to rally support for Clinton, whom they considered wrongheaded but ultimately "a patriot."[24] Never Trumper Rick Wilson puts it vividly:

[Clinton] got so brittle over the years because she got beat the [expletive] out of her ... so the genuine person was really hard to drag it out of her. She was always very defensive. You could see the gears in her head ... So that made it even easier to turn her into this creature, this harridan, this Machiavellian shrew ... So when you got to the point of absurdity – "Hillary Clinton is the center of a global child pedophilia ring based in a Pizza restaurant" – there were people in the Republican party who were like, "Of course

---

[19] As Never Trumper Rick Wilson notes, "For the GOP, the culture clash between hard progressives and most of America is a prime opportunity. They listen closely to it. They stoke it. They exploit it. It doesn't matter if this is right or wrong, or if progressives huff of and say, 'Well, Middle America is too stupid to understand monetary theory or that there are 740 genders anyway.' The scaring-the-[expletive]-out-of-Middle-America system exists to trap progs like hogs in a baited field." (Rick Wilson, *Running against the Devil: A Plot to Save America from Trump – and Democrats from Themselves* (New York: Crown Forum, 2020), 97.)

[20] Wilson, *Running against the Devil*, 93.   [21] Lakoff, *Moral Politics*, 171.

[22] Thomas Frank, *Listen Liberal or What Ever Happened to the Party of the People?* (New York: Metropolitan Books, 2016).

[23] Clinton's inner circle and sympathizers readily acknowledge "the gap" between her warm and attentive private character on the one hand and her more cautious and sometimes defensive public persona on the other hand. See Ezra Klein, "Understanding Hillary: Why the Clinton America Sees Isn't the Clinton Colleagues Know," Vox, July 11, 2016, www.vox.com/a/hillary-clinton-interview/the-gap-listener-leadership-quality. Clinton also seemingly "embodies" the meritocratic ethos, at least in terms of how she emphasizes the shattering of "glass ceilings" over the shoring up of "floors." See Frank, *Listen Liberal*, 217ff.

[24] David Frum, "The Conservative Case for Voting for Clinton," *Atlantic*, November 2, 2016, www.theatlantic.com/politics/archive/2016/11/dont-gamble-on-trump/506207/.

she was, because that stands to reason. She's part of George Soros's international lizard-person cabal!" They believe this lurid craziness because they've been prepped for it for so many years.[25]

As of December 2016, 46 percent of Trump voters either believed that Clinton was connected to such a ring or were not sure one way or the other.[26]

The difficulty with the practice of self-restraint, which is required to prevent such cynicism, of course, is that it must take place amidst formal competition. Yet this challenge is not insurmountable. For one thing, even though the opponents of political pluralism might exploit unilateral moderation, moderation does not necessitate strategic disadvantage. Even democratic realists acknowledge that "address[ing] their arguments to the entire political community, thereby making themselves at least minimally accountable to all groups ... rather than firing up one's base by demonizing the enemy may come with costs, but it may also have benefits."[27] Empirical research indicates that in close congressional races, extremists nominees decrease their party's share of turnout, skewing the electorate toward their opponents.[28]

For another, there are cultural features that can help political actors resist these pressures. One feature, which I discussed in Chapter 4 and will return to in Chapter 9, is a sense of bounded solidarity: it is more likely that political competitors will restrain themselves if they recognize one another as fellow patriots. Another is a citizenry that is unwilling to tolerate such hyperbole and that does not reward wedge politics. For example, even though Stephen Harper's Conservative Party did take negative campaigning to new heights in Canada and won successive elections as a result,[29] many voters grew tired of Harper's aggressive partisanship and ended up supporting the "Sunny Ways" of Justin Trudeau's Liberal Party during the 2015 Federal Election. More broadly, the relative lack of animosity between whites and non-whites (at least in English Canada) motivates the Conservative Party – unlike the Republican

---

[25] Rick Wilson and Melissa Caen, "Rick Wilson: Saving America from Trump (and Democrats from Themselves)," filmed January 22, 2020 at the Commonwealth Club of San Francisco at the Marines Memorial, video, 41:00, www.youtube.com/watch?v=tg9lCl8nMdY.

[26] Tom Jensen, "Trump Remains Unpopular; Voters Prefer Obama on SCOTUS Pick," Public Policy Polling, December 9, 2016, www.publicpolicypolling.com/polls/trump-remains-unpopular-voters-prefer-obama-on-scotus-pick/.

[27] Samuel Bagg and Isak Tranvik, "An Adversarial Ethics for Campaigns and Elections," *Perspectives on Politics* 17(4) (2019): 10–11.

[28] Andrew B. Hall and Daniel M. Thompson, "Who Punishes Extremist Nominees? Candidate Ideology Turning Out the Base in US Elections," *American Political Science Review* 112(3) (2018): 509–524.

[29] John Doyle, "Farewell Stephen Harper, Master of Attack Ads," *Globe and Mail*, August 29, 2016, www.theglobeandmail.com/arts/television/john-doyle-farewell-stephen-harper-master-of-attack-ads/article31591082/.

Party – to chase minority votes, rather than construe their opponents' support for diversity as evidence of a lack of patriotism.[30]

Therefore, the existence of a culture of trust among citizens is even more vital than the existence of trust among political actors. Even if such a culture does not necessarily forestall the development of political enmity, it can, at least, motivate political competitors to moderate their partisan attacks,[31] and deprive them of some of the tools they would otherwise use to engage in negative partisanship. If such trust is lacking – as it is in the United States – then citizens will encourage political actors to become increasingly hyperbolic, engage in negative partisanship, and stoke social divisions (racial-ethnic divisions in particular). It will, then, become increasingly difficult for political actors to compromise and treat one another with civility without jeopardizing their standing with their respective supporters.

Explain Why One Compromised ... after the Fact and With Care

Principled pragmatists can also embrace the fact that compromises are "internally contradictory ... [and] [un]satisfying if judged from the perspective of any single principle ..."[32] They can explain what they gained in exchange for sacrificing some of their supporters' and/or constituents' interests and that they did not compromise to merely further their own interests. Electronic town halls can facilitate such conversations. One study finds that a congressperson, conducting two-hour electronic town halls every week with randomly selected constituents, can talk to 25 percent of his or her constituents in six years. Ninety-five percent of participants have found these meetings "very valuable to democracy."[33]

---

[30] This is not to say that Canada is free of social divisions. The 2019 Federal Election revealed considerable divisions, particularly between East and West and between English and French.

[31] Daniel Diermeier and Christopher Li, "Partisan Affect and Elite Polarization," *American Political Science Review* 113(1) (2019): 277–281 demonstrate that affective polarization among citizens at large incentivizes parties to become more polarized themselves and to bias their policies toward affective partisans – even if citizens are not that polarized on actual policy.

[32] Amy Gutmann and Dennis Thompson, *The Spirit of Compromise: Why Governing Demands It and Campaigning Undermines It* (Princeton: Princeton University Press, 2012), 37.

[33] See Michael A. Neblo, Kevin M. Esterling, and David M. J. Lazer, *Politics with the People: Building a Directly Representative Democracy* (Cambridge: Cambridge University Press, 2018). Some might object that such trust will make it easier for incumbents to get re-elected. However, this is not necessarily a bad thing. Even though there is certainly a risk that well-established incumbents will "lose touch" with their constituents, it is also easier for them to compromise. As Amy Gutmann and Dennis Thompson note about a related topic, term limits, "the mutual respect necessary for compromise depends on collegial relationships that take time to cultivate. The frequent turnover caused by term limits reduces the opportunities for trust-building interactions and disrupts those that do happen to develop" (Gutmann and Thompson, *The Spirit of Compromise*, 178).

Incidentally, this reveals that the practice of principled hypocrisy actually depends on some degree of transparency. In order to demonstrate that they strike compromises in order to further justice and the common interest, not merely to further their own self-interests, principled pragmatists must demonstrate that their compromises do indeed further justice and the common interest. This is rather counterintuitive; on one level, such disclosures seem to render hypocrisy no longer hypocrisy. However, this need reflects the fact that non-political intuitions have a tendency to filter into the political sphere. Even if the normative dynamics of the political sphere demand hypocrisy, given citizens' broad distrust of hypocrisy, principled pragmatists must demonstrate that their hypocrisy is indeed principled and salutary.

Evidently, one problem with such disclosures is that no minimally competent politician will describe himself or herself as having acted purely for selfish reasons. Still, there is at least one potential upside to these disclosures. Political actors understand justice and the common interest in different ways, so their justifications will help reveal the principles they stand for – or their lack of fixed principled commitments. Their constituents can then judge them accordingly.

Still, there are limits to how transparent principled pragmatists should be. First, there is good reason to believe that they should not be upfront about their willingness to compromise, for some opaqueness is required to pursue justice amidst competition. After all, campaigns are zero-sum affairs, and political actors must strive to strengthen their post-campaign bargaining positions. Too much disclosure can prevent them from fulfilling the responsibility they have to their supporters to increase the likelihood that they will achieve the policies they value. For example, a recurrent critique of Obama's presidency from his left emphasized his tendency to pre-emptively compromise in a bid to seem reasonable. According to this critique, even if Obama would have ultimately compromised, he should have either entered negotiations with more extreme proposals or *seemed* less eager to compromise. Had he done so, the compromises he did strike would have been more balanced. By seeming too eager, Obama allowed Republicans to continually "move the goalposts" and dictate the terms of negotiation.[34]

Second, although a political actor can help dispel the perception that he or she is purely selfish by disclosing his or her principles or priorities, such disclosures can hamper coalition building. This is because those disclosures can give critics of those principles or priorities more to complain about. For example, Republican Alan Simpson certainly revealed his convictions when he characterized Social Security as "a milk cow with 310 million tits!"[35] Yet this

---

[34] Luke Savage, "Centrists Aren't Political Realists. Leftists Are," Jacobin, November 21, 2019, https://jacobinmag.com/2019/11/realism-pragmatism-barack-obama-centrist-democrats-green-new-deal-medicare-for-all.

[35] Stephanie Condon, "Alan Simpson: Social Security Is Like a 'Milk Cow with 310 Million Tits!,'" *CBS News*, August 25, 2010, www.cbsnews.com/news/alan-simpson-social-security-is-like-a-milk-cow-with-310-million-tits/.

comment did not do him any favours: it encouraged defenders of Social Security to interpret the Simpson-Bowles Commission on deficit reduction as a plot to destroy Social Security. Likewise, Obama's support for agreements that included cuts to entitlements encouraged many of his supporters, as well as some Democratic congressional leaders, to believe that he was hostile toward those core Democratic priorities, or that he did not prioritize protecting entitlements.[36]

What this indicates is that even if the practice of principled hypocrisy does rely on some transparency, there are practical limits to how much principled pragmatists can showcase their pragmatism. Before negotiations, pragmatists must appear more "purist" than they actually are. Following negotiations, they must justify their compromises in the right way. So, rather than merely emphasize the need for "shared sacrifices" and insist that "people making a million dollars or more have to do something as well,"[37] Obama should have emphasized to a greater degree how the compromise would bring macroeconomic benefits *and*, counterintuitively, strengthen entitlement programs in the long run.

Refrain from Encouraging Fantastical Understandings of Politics

Inspiration is important in politics. It prevents citizens from becoming complacent, can fuel progress, and counteracts cynicism. However, there is a fine line between inspiration and fantasy. Now, fantastical proposals offered on the margins of political debate can be useful in outlining the extremes. However, liberal democratic political actors who have a realistic chance of holding power should avoid promoting platforms that they know cannot possibly be enacted, and they should refrain from construing anything that falls short of those platforms as an abject failure. Likewise, they should avoid promoting the idea that change can be made without compromise (legislative "wheeling and dealing") – or, conversely, the idea that the political system is so irremediably corrupt that only someone who is "pure" or "above politics" can have the strength and goodness to overcome the corrupt establishment.

Promulgating these fantasies can fuel cynicism in one of two ways. First, it can cause citizens to become even more cynical than they otherwise would have been, should those offering such visions of politics fail to enact the changes they promised. Second, as demonstrated by countries currently controlled by left and right populist movements – notably, Venezuela, Ecuador, Bolivia, Poland, and Hungary – it can result in citizens' embrace of autocratic forces who are willing to destroy the built-in inefficiencies of the liberal democratic system

[36] Eric Zuesse, "Obama's Entitlement Plan Was Four Years in the Making," Salon, April 11, 2013, www.salon.com/2013/04/11/obamas_entitlement_plan_was_four_years_in_the_making/.
[37] Zuesse, "Four Years in the Making."

(e.g., separations of powers, judicial oversight, the freedom of the press) in the name of getting things done for "the people."

On this score, Franklin Delano Roosevelt's public posture during the Great Depression is instructive. Facing the worst economic crisis in US history, he understood the importance of inspiration, proclaiming during his First Inaugural Address that "the only thing we have to fear is ... fear itself – nameless, unreasoning, unjustified terror which paralyzes needed efforts to convert retreat into advance." At the same time, however, he did not make promises that he could not have possibly kept. Likewise, he did not downplay just how difficult it would be to overcome the challenges the United States faced. Nor, conversely, did he, in the manner of a demagogue, construe the American political system as a wholly corrupt enterprise that he alone could overcome. Had he done so, and had his policies failed, Americans might have very well lost faith in the liberal democracy altogether, as did many people and peoples during this time period. Instead, he embraced the challenges that lay ahead:

The country needs and, unless I mistake its temper, the country demands bold, persistent experimentation. It is common sense to take a method and try it: If it fails, admit it frankly and try another. But above all, try something. The millions who are in want will not stand by silently forever while the things to satisfy their needs are within easy reach.[38]

Likewise, although Obama's soaring rhetoric during the 2008 campaign ("Hope and change") might have caused some, particularly on the left, to believe that Obama would pursue more radical change than he ultimately did pursue, he also aimed to "level" with Americans and his supporters about the challenges the United States faced. Facing the worst financial crisis since the Great Depression, as well as two costly wars, Obama did reiterate during his First Inaugural Address that it was necessary to aspire toward ambitious change. However, he also opened his speech by emphasizing that "the challenges we face are real. They are serious and they are many. They will not be met easily or in a short span of time. But know this America: They will be met." Moreover, he proclaimed:

What is required of us now is a new era of responsibility – a recognition on the part of every American that we have duties to our nation and the world; duties that we do not grudgingly accept, but rather seize gladly, firm in the knowledge that there is nothing so satisfying to the spirit, so defining of our character than giving our all to a difficult task.[39]

---

[38] Franklin D. Roosevelt, "Oglethorpe University Address: The New Deal, May 22, 1932," Pepperdine School of Public Policy, https://publicpolicy.pepperdine.edu/academics/research/fac ulty-research/new-deal/roosevelt-speeches/fro52232.htm.

[39] Barack Obama, *We Are the Change We Seek: The Speeches of Barack Obama*, ed. E. J. Dionne Jr. and Joy-Ann Reid (New York: Bloomsbury, 2017), 96–105.

Liberal democratic political actors would do well to follow Roosevelt's and Obama's lead: inspire, and do not be complacent, but also be frank about how formal politics is necessarily difficult. Even if most political actors act in good faith, liberal democratic politics is, typically (although not always), a slow boring of hard boards.[40]

* * *

As I have stressed, getting people to accept the fact of hypocrisy is difficult. Still, even though redressing the representative cynicism problem is largely the burden of political actors, there are things that citizens can do to prepare themselves to reciprocate good faith efforts by (liberal democratic) political actors to win their trust. Citizens can reflect on how they too act hypocritically – how they don masks to get hired, to close business deals, or even to get on teachers' good sides. After all, even though there exists a distinction between political and extra-political relations, quasi-political dynamics partly define extra-political relations: "there is a 'politics' of business, of relations between the sexes, et cetera."[41] Even if such reflection does not engender sympathy for political actors, it can help citizens appreciate the pressures political actors face and imagine how they (citizens) too might act hypocritically, were they to enter into the political arena. Such preparatory work, in short, can help citizens believe that political actors are often not especially heinous but are rather people who act as people do – except out in the open for everyone to see, amidst high stakes.

Evidently, though, citizens will not do this work if they already believe that political actors are indeed, for the most part, irredeemably heinous. Therefore, it is vital that liberal democratic political actors act in the manners I have outlined. The more political actors successfully show that they act hypocritically in service of the public good, the more citizens at large will be inclined to reciprocate. The less political actors succeed in showing their commitment to the public good, the less citizens will be inclined to reciprocate – and the more political actors will be in danger of seeming like they care about no one but themselves.

ONWARDS

We now have a good idea of how citizens can work through their differences and disagreements in ways that can contribute to a culture of trust, and how that emerging culture of trust can then make it easier for citizens to indeed work

---

[40] Max Weber, *The Vocation Lectures*, ed. David Owen and Tracy B. Strong (Indianapolis: Hackett, 2004).

[41] Ruth W. Grant, *Hypocrisy and Integrity: Machiavelli, Rousseau, and the Ethics of Politics* (Chicago: The University of Chicago Press, 1997), 23.

through their differences and disagreements. I have argued that the promotion of a culture of trust where citizens feel that their fellow citizens probably value the continuation of their civic relationship and are committed to supporting social and political arrangements that can allow them to continue that relationship – liberal democracy – demands role-based constitutional fellowship. Under role-based constitutional fellowship, citizens work toward overcoming three barriers to the production of trust – the institutionalized enmity problem in the formal political sphere, the social domination problem in the general citizenry, and the representative cynicism problem between the formal political sphere and the general citizenry – by observing a series of divisions of labour. First, to counteract the institutionalized enmity problem, a division of labour among political actors who are committed to liberal democracy is needed between principled pragmatists and principled purists. Second, to counteract the social domination problem, a division of labour is needed among the underprivileged, the oppressed, and their allies between the practices of shouting back and talking, with allies in particular also striving to listen well. Third, to counteract the representative cynicism problem, liberal democratic political actors should demonstrate that they act hypocritically for the sake of furthering the public good. They can do this by refraining from excessively demonizing one another, by explaining why they might have compromised (but only after the fact and with care), and by not promulgating fantastical understandings of politics. These actions can encourage citizens to both exhibit good will toward their representatives and prepare themselves to reciprocate good faith efforts by their representatives to win their trust.

Undoubtedly, the path I have proposed is a fragile one. There is no guarantee that the various balancing acts toward which role-based constitutional fellowship aspires – the balance between principled pragmatists and principled purists, the balance between confronting unholy alliances and enticing former liberal democrats to re-enter the liberal democratic fold, the balance between talking and shouting back, and the balance between disrupting the lives of unwitting oppressors and softer complicit oppressors and building trust with them – will be sustained. Still, I have shown that role-based constitutional fellowship is the best hope we have to deal with the challenges of difference and disagreement.

What sorts of political institutions and associations can make it easier for principled pragmatists to strike compromises and for talkers and unwitting oppressors (and softer complicit oppressors) to develop trust? What can make the initiation of role-based constitutional fellowship more likely? Let us now address these questions.

9

Facilitating Fellowship

Translucent Veils, Unlikely Associations, and Constraints on Campaigns

In order for liberal democracy to harness the benefits of difference and disagreement and avoid unduly squashing difference and disagreement, yet also prevent the expression of difference and disagreement from overheating and spiralling out of control, citizens must be encouraged to share in a sense of unity. This sense of unity should assume the form of a culture of trust where citizens believe that their fellow citizens probably value the continuation of their civic relationship and are committed to supporting social and political arrangements that can allow them to continue that relationship: liberal democracy. Under role-based constitutional fellowship, citizens can work toward realizing this culture of trust by redressing three problems. First, political actors who are committed to liberal democracy can counteract the institutionalized enmity problem by observing a division of labour between principled purists and principled pragmatists. Second, citizens at large – in particular, the underprivileged, the oppressed, and their allies – can counteract the social domination problem by observing a division of labour between shouting back and talking, with allies in particular also striving to listen well. Third, to counteract the representative cynicism problem, liberal democratic political actors can justify their apparent hypocrisy in the appropriate manners and avoid needlessly promoting fantastical understandings of politics. Doing so can encourage citizens at large to exhibit good will toward their representatives and to prepare themselves (citizens at large) to reciprocate good faith efforts by their representatives to win their trust.

Evidently, in order for these roles and practices to have their intended effects, political actors and citizens at large must choose – as agents – to act in these manners. I have argued that acting in these manners is not far-fetched, even in conditions of distrust. First, role-based constitutional fellowship takes advantage of what I call the "natural distribution of personality types." Some political actors are more disposed to be pragmatists, and others, purists – just as some citizens at large are more disposed to talk, and others, to shout back. Second, role-based constitutional fellowship does not demand that citizen-fellows "buy into" the entire apparatus of fellowship (at least, not initially). Third, while the less uncooperative and less disruptive sorts of roles and practices – for example, principled pragmatism and talking – do seem to hinge more on either a principled commitment to liberal democracy or a general sense that things are not so bad that the status quo must be completely overturned, role-based constitutional fellowship recognizes that it is not always appropriate to try to cultivate trust. Pragmatists are urged to embrace contestation when the mainstream consensus over the value of liberal democracy is wavering – to try to demonstrate that entering into (or staying in) unholy alliances with auto-cratic political actors is politically costly. Likewise, role-based constitutional fellowship makes space for those who are normally more inclined to talk to change course and shout back when necessary. So, there is good reason to believe that role-based constitutional fellowship is less beholden to the sorts of first-starter problems that often beleaguer theories of democratic reciprocity.

Yet are there ways to make the emergence of role-based constitutional fellow-ship more likely? In this chapter, I propose concrete measures to promote fellow-ship. First, reaching back to my discussion of liberal nationalism in Chapter 4, I note that bounded solidarity can help promote a preliminary culture of trust and support fellowship. Accordingly, I identify ways of imagining the nation that can nudge solidarity in an inclusive direction, and I urge liberal democrats to promote that inclusion cautiously and gradually so as to minimize backlash. Second, pivoting back to fellowship, I discuss trust production among political actors. I note that some institutional arrangements – namely Westminster systems – seem relatively effective at channelling competition and alleviating the need for fellow-ship. Most democracies, however, are not Westminster systems, and recent reforms in Westminster systems tend to push those systems toward proportional representation. Accordingly, I suggest reforms to proportional representation-based systems, as well as to the US presidential system, that can encourage political competitors to act like role-based constitutional fellows.

Third, I discuss trust production among citizens at large. In addition to democratic education arrangements that can help students develop the ability to negotiate difference and disagreement, I argue that the integrated workplace and less voluntary associations like neighbourhood associations are promising forums where citizens can develop trust. As part of this discussion, I cast doubt on the ability of voluntary civil societal associations to foster trust across difference and disagreement. By virtue of being voluntary, these associations are easy to exit, so they often end up being relatively homogeneous – places where citizens can *escape*, rather than encounter, difference and disagreement. Fourth, I demonstrate the need for some material redistribution to ensure that citizens feel that they are all in it together.

SUPPORTING FELLOWSHIP: INCLUSIVE BOUNDED SOLIDARITY

In Chapter 4, I argued that liberal nationalism (or, in some contexts, constitutional patriotism) cannot, by itself, adequately redress the potential perils of difference and disagreement. However, I did note that such bounded solidarity can help promote a *preliminary* culture of trust – however fragile that sense of basic unity might be. Indeed, empirical research suggests that Americans are more likely to see supporters of the opposing party as *fellow* Americans, rather than as enemies, when their sense of national identity is heightened.[1] So, there is good reason to believe that bounded solidarity can support role-based constitutional fellowship.

History provides us with many examples of how to promote bounded solidarity. The state can ensure that children learn about their country's history, cultural icons, and artistic-literary traditions in school, while public broadcasters, galleries, museums, and festivals can provide adults with similar experiences informally. Likewise, movie-makers can dramatize the achievements, crises, and persistent challenges of the country. Citizens can rally together in support of national sports teams, and parents can pass on national recipes to their children.

The trickier question concerns how bounded solidarity can be structured so that it is broadly socially inclusive. This is a vital question. After all, there is a long history of bounded solidarity serving to inhibit the identification and rectification of injustices. For instance, there is evidence that America's problematic record on racial and economic injustice is partly the result of Americans' patriotic or nationalistic sentiments. Poor Americans (77 percent) are more likely than working class (71 percent) and middle-class Americans (74 percent) to agree that America is better than most other countries. Likewise, poor Blacks (85 percent) are more likely than poor whites (78 percent) to agree to the same proposition. These beliefs are based on the belief, erroneous at best, that America is exceptional in the goods, freedom, and opportunity it provides.[2]

In Chapter 4, I showed that something like role-based constitutional fellowship is needed to help citizens work through their differences and disagreements, rather than merely tolerate those differences and disagreements. There are, however, additional ways of imagining the nation state, as well as certain policies, that can help ensure that bounded solidarity is inclusive.

Translucent Veils

Liberal democrats can care to describe the nation state in terms – metaphors and images – that encourage citizens to support social inclusion and efforts to

---

[1] Matthew W. Levendusky, "Americans Not Partisans: Can Priming American National Identity Reduce Affective Polarization," *The Journal of Politics* 80(1): 59–70.

[2] Francesco Duina, *Broke and Patriotic: Why Poor Americans Love Their Country* (Stanford: Stanford University Press, 2018), 8–9, 22.

redress undue social hierarchies. Ajume Wingo's notion of "political veils" can help us think through how this would work concretely. Similar to how real veils mediate one's perception of objects, political veils – symbols, myths, rituals, and traditions – mediate how citizens interpret their political experiences and collective identity.[3]

This proposition can seem to imply the worst sort of collective hypocrisy – an "opacity politics" where citizens are sold an illusory image of the polity that *forestalls* the identification of injustices through the deployment of "impenetrable veils … designed and employed in a way that resists efforts to see through those veils."[4] Alternatively, it can seem to imply an authoritarian politics of *as if*, where citizens recognize the regime's symbols as phony, yet uphold those symbols in public as if they do believe them to be true.[5] Yet first appearances can deceive. Veil politics does not necessarily imply opacity politics or a politics of as if. Rather, it suggests the use of "*translucent* veils." These veils distort not to hide "the truth," but to "enhance perception of the object by setting off its more attractive features." Translucent veils can, on a surface level, unite citizens while motivating those inspired by "the *hint*" of the "deep image" to look beneath the surface and interpret what it "really means."[6]

Translucent veils are therefore somewhat analogous to the "ideal portraits" of the nineteenth century. Typically depicting lone human figures, these portraits did not document individuals as they "really were," but rather rendered those individuals "representatives of certain ethnic character traits, or emotions."[7] At the same time, however, according to some art historians, ideal portraits idealized those ethnicities, character traits, and emotions in manners that encouraged discussion; ideal portraits were not conducive to ideological projects:

[W]hat they had to say differed markedly from the emerging discourse of political nationalism: as images that travelled the circuits of the art world, easily transferred from one national context to the next, they embodied the idea that ethnic difference was in the eye of the beholder. Hence, they implied what nationalists were eager to construe as eternal and organic was in fact flexible and shaped by contemporary discourse.[8]

The Declaration of Independence is such a veil. Drafted principally by Thomas Jefferson, the Declaration has played a central role in America's civic mythology, beginning with America's heroic account of its own birth. More

---

[3] Ajume H. Wingo, *Veil Politics in Liberal Democratic States* (Cambridge: Cambridge University Press, 2003), 4–5.

[4] Wingo, *Veil Politics*, 16–17.

[5] Lisa Wedeen, "Acting 'As If': Symbolic Politics and Social Control in Syria," *Society for Comparative Study of Society and History*, 40(3) (1998): 503–523.

[6] Wingo recognizes that those who look "beneath the surface" might become disenchanted.

[7] Nóra Veszprémi, "Ideals for Sale: 'Ideal Portraits' and the Display of National Identity in the Nineteenth-Century Austrian Empire," *Art History* 42(2) (2019): 275.

[8] Veszprémi, "Ideals for Sale," 276–277.

than that, it is crafted to invite re-interpretation. So, despite the fact that Jefferson himself was a slaveholder, the Declaration has not served to conserve America's slave-owning past. Nor has it been an empty platitude that people dismiss privately as a farce while hailing in public – something akin to the obviously false cult of personality that surrounded Hafiz al-Asad in Syria prior to the Civil War.[9] Instead, it has served as a resource that Abraham Lincoln mobilized to depict Gettysburg as a moment of rebirth during which America would begin to prioritize equality as a central value; and that Fredrick Douglass and (later) Martin Luther King Jr. used to "highlight[] a prima facie conflict between [America's] text ... and reality" and to "change the condition of African Americans."[10] So, the Declaration not only has helped to promote inclusion and rectify injustices but also has fashioned the pursuit of greater justice an expression of civic-national identity.

Of course, the Declaration is exceptional in its association with the "founding" of a country. However, veils need not be "foundational" to have practical power. For example, beginning in the 1960s, at the behest of political elites, English Canadian civic-national identity has changed profoundly. English Canadians in the 1960s understood their civic-national identity in ethnically laden terms; today, around two-thirds of them understand it in multicultural and multiethnic terms. This transformation, in part, has been facilitated by the deployment of the image of a "multicultural mosaic"; Canada, according to this image, is a mosaic portrait, and the portrait's constituent mosaics consist of different cultures. Interestingly, although the image of a mosaic implies that cultures should be encouraged to remain separate from one another and to not make any concessions to the majority culture, surveys indicate that more Canadians, by a two-to-one margin, prefer the practical implications of a *melting pot* – that minorities should assimilate, rather than remain separate from one another. Still, around two-thirds of Canadians believe that multiculturalism is good for Canada; and the younger Canadians are, the more likely they are to support the practical implications of the mosaic image.[11] So, it is reasonable for us to say that the image of a multicultural mosaic helped to shift how English Canadians understood their civic-national identity, even if they do not fully endorse all the practical implications of that image. Indicatively, despite the fact that Canadians have

---

[9] Syrians were required to act "as if" they believed that al-Asad was Syria's preeminent pharmacist, teacher, lawyer, and doctor, and that he had 99 percent support (Wedeen, "Acting 'As If,'" 506).

[10] Wingo, *Veil Politics*, 100–101.

[11] Whereas 83 percent of Canadians over 55 prefer the implications of the melting pot, 49 percent of Canadians aged 18–34 believe the same. See Philip Carl Salzman, "What Canadians Really Think of the 'Cultural Mosaic,'" Macdonald-Laurier Institute, October 24, 2016, www.macdonaldlaurier.ca/what-canadians-really-think-of-the-cultural-mosaic-philip-carl-salzman-for-inside-policy/.

assimilationist tendencies, the (self-congratulatory) juxtaposition of the "Canadian mosaic" against the "American melting pot" is an enduring Canadian myth.[12]

Caution and Gradualism

Although such metaphors and images are worth pursuing, it is also worth practicing caution. The attempt to make citizens' collective civic-national identity more inclusive too fast – or, more still, to challenge the basic notion of a common civic-national identity – can inspire the defenders of exclusivist understandings of the nation to challenge liberal democracy aggressively in an effort to oppose greater diversity.

Here, the case of English Canada is again instructive. Certainly, the transformation described above was aided by the existence of conditions unique to Canada. For instance, some argue that the decline of British immigration (coinciding with the decline of the British Empire) and of the political clout of Orangeism (a British-Protestant conservative movement) allowed "left modernists" to more easily push through a multiculturalist agenda and reshape Anglo-Canadian national identity.[13] Likewise, others emphasize how the mutual antagonism between Anglophone and Quebecois nativists fractured stronger anti-immigration and anti-diversity sentiments in rural-leaning areas, incentivizing the Conservative Party[14] to cater to "ethnic" voters in suburban Toronto and Vancouver instead.[15]

It is also the case, however, that rather than shame white Protestants into accepting diversity, policy makers took steps to assuage white Protestant anxieties. Most notably, lawmakers enacted a "points based" immigration system that explicitly favours "economically capable" or "highly skilled" immigrants over "lower-skilled immigrants." It also requires that immigrants wishing to sponsor a family member pledge financial support to that family member for 3–10 years, during which that family member cannot receive social assistance. (Periodic adjustments have been made to prevent any trend toward greater immigrant reliance on the welfare system.)[16] While such a bias arguably runs

---

[12] Howard Palmer, "Mosaic versus Melting Pot?: Immigration and Ethnicity in Canada and the United States," *International Journal* 31(3) (1976): 488–528; Ceri Peach, "The Mosaic versus the Melting Pot: Canada and the USA," *Scottish Geographical Journal* 121(1) (2005): 3–27.

[13] Eric Kaufmann, *White Shift: Populism, Immigration, and the Future of White Majorities* (New York: Abrams Press, 2019), 271ff.

[14] Daniel Westlake, "Following the Right: Left and Right Parties' Influence over Multiculturalism," *Canadian Journal of Political Science* 55 (2020): 171–188.

[15] Joshua Gordon, Sanjay Jeram, and Clifton van der Linden, "The Two Solitudes of Canadian Nativism: Explaining the Absence of a Competitive Anti-immigration Party in Canada," *Nations and Nationalism* 26(4) (2019): 1–21.

[16] There is some evidence that suggests that the system's ability to admit economically capable immigrants has waned somewhat and that new immigrants are more likely to require income support than their predecessors. See Ted McDonald, Elizabeth Ruddick, Arthur Swetman, and

afoul of principles of egalitarianism and global justice,[17] it has helped to reduce cultural conservative anxieties, shielding immigrants in general from the charge that they are mere "takers."[18] This has made it easier to gently nudge English Canadian civic-national identity in a more inclusive direction. This virtue of caution can be applied to other contexts.

FENDING OFF THE METAPHOR OF WARFARE AMONG POLITICAL ACTORS

How about role-based constitutional fellowship? What sorts of formal political institutions and associational arrangements can either facilitate or alleviate the need for fellowship? Let us consider the formal political sphere first.

Alleviating the Need for Trust among Competitors

Certain institutional frameworks are better at mitigating the need for trust among political actors than others. Frances McCall Rosenbluth and Ian Shapiro demonstrate that Westminster systems are better than rival electoral systems at channelling competition in manners that bolster citizens' trust in the *system*, albeit not their trust in political actors (or political actors' trust in one another). Whereas proportional representation (PR) and US presidential systems can, in different ways (as we shall see later in this section), make it difficult for voters to judge who is responsible for various decisions and make it easier for special interests and the political extremes to hijack decision-making processes, Westminster makes it relatively clear who should be held

---

Christopher Worsick, eds., *Canadian Immigration: Economic Evidence for a Dynamic Policy Environment* (Montreal: McGill-Queen's University Press, 2010) and Garnet Picot, Yuqian Lu, and Feng Hou, "Immigrant Low-Income Rates: The Role of Market Income and Government Transfers," *Perspectives* 75(1): 13–27.

[17] Likewise, 50 years later, during the 2015 Syrian Refugee Crisis, rather than have the state sponsor as many refugees as it could, Canadian policy "appeal[ed] specifically to the hospitality of ordinary Canadian families and depends on their willingness to sponsor individual refugees" (Michael Ignatieff, *The Ordinary Virtues: Moral Order in a Divided World* (Cambridge, MA: Harvard University Press, 2017), 217). Such a "one-to-one, family-to-family" policy can be interpreted as stingy. However, it helped dissuade Canadians from complaining that the government was prioritizing the needs of outsiders.

[18] Keith Banting, "Is There a Progressive's Dilemma in Canada? Immigration, Multiculturalism and the Welfare State," *Canadian Journal of Political Science*, 43(4) (2010): 797–820; Will Kymlicka, "Solidarity in Diverse Societies: Beyond Neoliberal Multiculturalism and Welfare Chauvinism," *Comparative Migration Studies*, 3(17) (2015): 1–19; Clem Brooks and Jeff Manza, *Why Welfare States Persist: The Importance of Public Opinion in Democracies* (Chicago: University of Chicago Press, 2007); Andrée Côté, Michèle Kérisit, and Marie-Louise Côté, *Sponsorship . . . for Better or Worse: The Impact of Sponsorship on the Equality Rights of Immigrant Women* (Ottawa: Status of Women Canada, 2001), http://vre2.upei.ca/govdocs/fedora/repository/govdocs%3A1346/PDF/PDF.

accountable. This is because the use of single member plurality districts (SMP) and first-past-the-post typically results in two large parties that alternate between government and opposition.[19] The official opposition is incentivized to call out the government's shortcomings. Meanwhile, when the governing party has a majority of seats, it does not need to compromise in order to form government and has the authority to enact its agenda[20] – and is judged accordingly. At the same time, when districts are large enough to be reasonably representative of the citizenry as a whole, parties are motivated to appeal to the interests of an electoral majority rather than to cater to narrow interest groups and activists. For instance, the main center-left party is incentivized to not scare away business; and the main center-right party, labour.[21] Accordingly, it is conceivable that under Westminster, citizens will come to trust the liberal democratic system, *despite* the fact that they might distrust political actors *and* despite the fact that political actors might engage in vigorous competition. The imperative to cultivate trust among political actors – to have political actors strike compromises – thus seems less urgent.

Still, beyond encouraging those who live under Westminster systems to appreciate Westminster's benefits, it is necessary to discern what sorts of institutional designs can facilitate fellowship among liberal democratic political actors. This is because actual governance, to varying degrees, inevitably depends on compromise and trust among political actors. For one thing, given the allure of the *principle* of PR and anti-elitism, recent reforms have tended to either make Westminster look more like PR[22] or shift decision-making power away from party leaders toward the "grassroots." These reforms have neutralized some of Westminster's advantages. They have made majority governments harder to attain, and they have made parties more responsive to activists and narrow interest groups.

For another, many electoral systems are not modelled on Westminster at all. Many incorporate at least some PR features. PR makes it difficult for any single party to ever form a majority by itself, thereby rendering coalition governments the norm. While parties sometimes signal in advance that they intend to enter into specific coalitions, parties more typically form coalitions via bargaining

---

[19] This tendency is known as Duverger's Law. Discounting the somewhat distorting effects of strong separatist regional or nationalist parties, Westminster sometimes manifests itself as a two-and-a-half party system – two large parties and one smaller party. This is the case in both the United Kingdom and Canada.

[20] This is not to say that majority governments lack constraints. For example, in many Westminster systems, laws are subject to judicial review.

[21] Frances McCall Rosenbluth and Ian Shapiro, *Responsible Parties: Saving Democracy from Itself* (New Haven: Yale University Press, 2018), 71–76.

[22] Famously, New Zealand replaced its Westminster system with a German-styled mixed-member plurality system in 1994.

post-election; citizens at large rarely actually choose who gets to govern. As a result, citizens must trust parties to strike bargains over who gets to govern. Not only are these arrangements never perfectly satisfactory to any of those parties' supporters from the standpoint of policy; these bargains also make it difficult for citizens at large to discern what those parties "actually stand for."[23] As G. Bingham Powell notes, "Given a diverse electorate and, hence, legislature, many governing or policy-making coalitions are possible. These could stray from the position of the median citizen ... [These] elite bargainers [have the freedom] to depart from voters' choice."[24]

Similarly, even though the US presidential system is based on SMP and first-past-the-post, its particular mix of separation of powers, checks and balances, federalism, and weak parties makes divided government commonplace. In addition, Americans have steadily "sorted" themselves into increasingly ideologically homogeneous communities over the past half-century,[25] and many congressional districts that might be ideologically representative or heterogeneous have been "gerrymandered" to be ideologically homogeneous so as to make it easier for the party in control of the given state to manufacture as many "safe seats" as possible. This incentivizes both parties and individual political actors to be more extreme, and the relative lack of party discipline and the significant influence of activists further aggravates this tendency.

Lest we simply wish for the fortuitous transformation of non-Westminster systems into Westminster systems and for perfection of flawed Westminster systems, we therefore must discern what sorts of institutional tweaks can encourage (liberal democratic) political actors to act like role-based constitutional fellows and/or make it easier to do so. If the given political system places compromise front and center, then we must strive to make the most of it.[26]

---

[23] For example, after having entered into several "grand coalitions" as the junior partner with the Christian Democratic Union, the German Social Democratic Party has steadily lost support, with some of its traditional voters questioning its leftist credentials.

[24] G. Bingham Powell, *Elections as Instruments of Democracy: Majoritarian and Proportional Visions* (New Haven: Yale University Press, 2000), 202–203.

[25] Bill Bishop, *The Big Sort: Why the Clustering of Like-Minded America Is Tearing Us Apart* (New York: Houghton Mifflin Books, 2008).

[26] It is worth noting that Westminster's advantages are somewhat neutralized in multinational states where separatist or sovereigntist sentiments run high. This is because Westminster's SMP system rewards geographic concentration; a separatist party might receive a low proportion of the total popular vote, yet win a large number of seats. Separatist parties are challenging because their explicit purpose is to end the continuation of their nation's relationship with the rest of the country. In multinational Westminster contexts (e.g., Canada, the United Kingdom), compromise and trust building are more vital than they would otherwise be in non-multinational Westminster contexts – among non-separatist parties (to pass legislation without the cooperation of separatist parties) or between separatist and non-separatist parties (to, perhaps, moderate separatist parties into merely *nationalist* parties that seek to advocate for their sub-state nation's interests more effectively, not to separate).

Counteracting the Permanent Campaign

The primary goal of any political institutional reforms should be to prevent politics from becoming (or continuing to be) a "permanent campaign." To reiterate: campaigns are vital components of any representative democracy. Campaigns are the most obvious forums where citizens at large can participate in popular sovereignty. Campaigns can clarify outstanding disagreements and help diagnose the political attitudes of the general citizenry.[27] However, campaigns are "contests ... with zero-sum outcomes, not opportunities for win-win solutions."[28] As a result, campaigns demand that political actors adopt an "uncompromising mindset" – that they maintain a posture of mutual distrust, condemn opponents for either acting hypocritically or pursuing objectionable agendas, and stand on principle.[29] Indeed, this posture is not just necessary for survival; it is also a normative requirement, for political actors have a responsibility to their followers to strengthen their post-campaign bargaining positions in a bid to achieve those substantive policies that they consider normatively valuable.

What this means is that it is dangerous for campaigns to not be appropriately circumscribed. For one thing, when the totality of democratic politics consists of campaigns, governing becomes increasingly difficult. Unless one party (or coalition) can secure an overwhelming majority, governing requires collaboration and compromise – actions at odds with the strategic and normative imperatives of campaigns. For another, when political actors are denied the space to collaborate and compromise – the space to discover positive-sum policies[30] – they cannot cultivate the sense of reciprocity required to counteract the mutual distrust they must assume during campaigns. That is, they are compelled to assume an "individualistic orientation" rather than a "problem-solving orientation";[31] they are moved to try to secure from one another as many concessions as possible, rather than to seek mutually satisfying solutions. More than that, they must purposefully further aggravate their mutual distrust: every decision must be made in consultation with the "war room." Permanent campaign seasons encourage political actors to compete not as adversaries to be defeated, with whom they might compromise and cooperate later, but rather as enemies to be destroyed. Politics threatens to become war itself, not an alternative to war – to the delight of liberal democracy's enemies. This is particularly

---

[27] Andrew Sabl, "Liberalism Beyond Markets," Niskanen Center, June 6, 2017, www.niskanencenter.org/liberalism-beyond-markets/.

[28] Amy Gutmann and Dennis Thompson, *The Spirit of Compromise: Why Governing Demands It and Campaigning Undermines It* (Princeton: Princeton University Press, 2012), 150.

[29] Gutmann and Thompson, *The Spirit of Compromise*, 64.

[30] Matthew Yglesias, "Positive-Sum Policy vs Zero-Sum Compromise," Think Progress, May 20, 2010, https://archive.thinkprogress.org/positive-sum-policy-vs-zero-sum-politics-270234a8391c/.

[31] Joseph H. Carens, "Compromises in Politics," *Nomos* 21 (1979): 127–128.

dangerous when political cleavages track the social cleavages of broader society, for then citizens at large are in danger of viewing their social relations in
terms of warfare as well.

It is therefore necessary to constrain campaigns – to strike a balance between
campaigns and governance. There are a number of ways to do this. Campaign
finance laws can be reformed to ensure that political actors do not need to
constantly solicit campaign funds and operate with an uncompromising mindset.[32] Spending limits on political advertising can also be imposed on political
actors and advocacy groups,[33] both during and outside of formal campaign
seasons.[34] In addition, although it is undemocratic for legislative or executive
terms to be too long, terms can be lengthened so that political actors do not
need to constantly spend their time operating as if they were campaigning. In
the US context, this means that presidential primary seasons should be
shortened, and the duration of House of Representatives terms lengthened.[35]
In contexts where at least some elements of PR are present, viability thresholds
should be raised to disempower smaller parties – which are often more extreme
and even autocratic – and to make it easier for mainstream parties to assemble
governing coalitions. This would help governments avoid having to rely on the
cooperation of those smaller parties to endure. PR-based systems can then
mimic the resilience of Westminster Britain, not the fragility of PR Weimar.[36]
(Admittedly, setting these thresholds too high can provoke accusations that big
parties are "rigging the game." A 5 percent threshold seems viable.)

Meanwhile, in Westminster contexts, while the dangers of permanent campaigning remain, it is important to retain and enhance the relative ability of the

---

[32] This suggests public campaign financing. Note that this argument in favour of public financing is
agnostic about whether the private financing of campaigns corrupts the democratic process.
Although there exists a widespread perception that private financing forces politicians to depend
on special interest donors, studies indicate that private contributions tend to chase winners
rather than make winners and that the impact of those contributions on public policy is
surprisingly muted. See Stephen Ansolabehere, John M. de Figueiredo, and James M. Snyder
Jr., "Why Is There So Little Money in U.S. Politics?," *Journal of Economic Perspectives* 17(1)
(2003): 105–130; Robert Hall and Allen Deardroff, "Lobbying as a Legislature Subsidy,"
American Political Science Review 100 (2006): 69–84; Barry Baimgartner, Jeffrey M. Berry,
Marie Hojnacki, David C. Kimball, and Beth L. Leech, *Lobby and Policy Change: Who Loses,
Who Wins, and Why* (Chicago: University of Chicago Press, 2009).

[33] There is good reason to believe, however, that spending limits should not be *too* low. Excessively
low spending limits can motivate political actors to develop excessively collegial relationships
with members of the press, undermining the press's ability to serve as a check on political actors.

[34] I recognize that in the US context, Supreme Court decisions like *Citizens United* v. *Federal
Election Commission* make such reforms difficult. These reforms are nonetheless necessary.

[35] This might involve eliminating midterm elections. A complicating factor in the US context is the
rigidity of its political system – of when elections must occur and how to remove dangerous
political actors from office.

[36] The former undermined Oswald Mosley's attempt to promote British fascism, whereas the latter
notoriously allowed itself to be taken over (and then dismantled) by the Nazis.

Westminster system to generate systemic trust in the absence of trust among political actors, as well as in the absence of trust in political actors. Therefore, majority governments are preferable to minority governments and coalition governments, and reforms in favour of greater proportional representation should be viewed with skepticism.[37]

DEMOCRATIC EDUCATION

Let us now consider the general citizenry. What sorts of arrangements can make it easier for citizens at large to identify and rectify injustices in manners that serve to bolster trust?

Some educational measures can help children learn how to work through their differences and disagreements. Most drastically, citizens on the cusp of adulthood can be obligated to spend a year-or-so participating in (funded) national or civilian service programs. Such programs can be structured so that citizens must reach across social cleavages to achieve common goals.

Likewise, students can be tasked with regularly making collective decisions as members of "classroom councils." In these councils, students discuss and vote on classroom rules and on their obligations as classroom members. For example, at the *Dolli Einstein Haus*, children are tasked with regularly deliberating and voting on a range of decisions, from what to have for breakfast to whose diaper should be changed by which care worker. *The Guardian* reports,

Once a week, each group at the nursery meets for a session at which there are two rounds of votes: one on the topping of the afternoon cake, and one on the Friday morning breakfast menu. The former is essentially a referendum, with the educators for example offering a choice between lemon and chocolate cake, while for the latter the children can nominate four meal options.

The options are drawn on pieces of paper which are placed in the middle of a circle of children, each of whom sits down on a cushion after listening to the sound of a quiet gong, facing outwards to allow an anonymous vote. When their names are called, the children take turns placing coloured pebbles, known as *Muckelsteine*, underneath their preferred option.

In both votes, the result is strictly first past the post and constitutionally binding. The nursery chef has to act out the will of the voters even if it seems disgusting or unhealthy – a principle which has tested the resolve of parents and educators alike. In the past, the Dolli Einstein Haus has served up pizza and stewed beef with beetroot for breakfast.

Bigger decisions, such as investment in new toys or rule changes in the playground, are made at a monthly children's council attended by pairs of boys and girls nominated as "passers on." At one recent such meeting, delegates took their leaders to task after Rodenwald made the unilateral decision to buy a pair of new tricycles.

---

[37] Note that the production of trust among liberal democratic political actors can further aggravate citizens' distrust of political actors. In Chapter 8, I discussed how to mitigate these dangers.

"It was such a good offer and we knew the kids liked tricycles, so I had just gone for it," she said. "But the children told us in no uncertain terms that we had not been authorised to make that decision."[38]

The stated goal of the nursery is to instil a certain ethos, that "[d]emocracy is not just about elections. For us, it is about people – or children – being taken seriously and learning to make decisions in a way that doesn't leave other people behind." Such democratic education measures cannot ease children into accepting social difference if the classrooms themselves lack social difference. Still, children can learn to abide by decisions that might impose some sort of cost or personal loss, and to disagree without feeling as though they are at war.

It becomes more difficult, however, to educate citizens who are adults. Accordingly, we must consider what sorts of associations can make it easier for them to engage in the trust-building interactions described in Chapter 7.

FACILITATING TRUST AMONG CITIZENS, ACROSS DIFFERENCE

One important variable to keep in mind as we embark on this investigation is that in order for the sort of culture of trust we seek to emerge, citizens must be able to participate in these trust-building interactions with a subset of the citizenry that can be described as reasonably representative of the citizenry as a whole – politically, religiously, racially, ethnically, perhaps even geographically. Less preferably (and more plausibly), citizens must at least be able to imagine themselves engaging in these interactions with reasonably representative subsets of the citizenry, perhaps by observing fellow citizens whom they consider similar to themselves engaging in such interactions. If this does not occur, then a culture of trust will not emerge. Rather, cultures of trust will emerge, potentially intensifying the problems associated with fragmentation and/or polarization.

Citizens at large typically find themselves in extra-political associations. There are two broad categories of extra-political associations: social associations and economic associations. Social associations are held together primarily by normative influence, persuasion, norms, and/or customs, rather than money or bureaucratic influence. Members interact with one another, not to pursue economic or political objectives but to reproduce identities, pursue common cultural objectives, or even simply have a good time. Many social associations – particularly those located in "civil society" – are voluntary: even though their criteria for membership might be based on nonvoluntary characteristics (e.g., race, ethnicity, perhaps religion), those associations rely on persuasion and normative influence – talk – to sustain themselves and tend to not

---

[38] Philip Oltermann, "Put to the Vote: German Nursery Where Children Make the Decisions," *The Guardian*, August 11, 2017, www.theguardian.com/world/2017/aug/11/german-nursery-children-make-decisions-vote-dolli-einstein-haus.

impose steep costs of exit.[39] Examples include religious groups, sports clubs, ethnic-cultural associations, arts groups, and, increasingly, on a more "virtual" and less concrete level, internet groups (e.g., forums, social media platforms, blogs). Other social associations are less voluntary – harder (albeit not impossible) to exit. These include public schools, neighbourhoods, and (to lesser extents) universities.

In contrast, economic associations are held together by money. This is not to say that these associations lack associational relations; discussion and persuasion do take place. Rather, it is to say that these associations are oriented toward the pursuit of common economic goals and are often organized by the consequences of market exchange.[40] Economic associations also tend to be less voluntary than civil societal associations. Even though people voluntarily choose whether to join firms or to accept job offers, there are pressures here that might compel them to stay. For instance, a worker might feel compelled to stay in a job that he or she would prefer to leave when no realistic alternatives are available. Examples of economic associations include firms, unions, business chambers, and consumer groups.

Red Herring: Civil Society

It might be tempting to think that the path forward lies in civil society. For example, echoing Alexis de Tocqueville's argument that face-to-face relations help foster the "orderly, temperate, moderate, careful, and self-controlled" habits of "self-interest properly understood,"[41] Robert Putnam argues that the development of "social capital" requires participation in voluntary associations that embody "horizontal relations of reciprocity and cooperation, not . . . vertical relations of authority and dependency [which often characterize economic and political associations]."[42] Trust can emerge between the CEO and the worker when they bowl in the same league or sing in the same choir. When a variety of racial, ethnic, cultural, economic, and political groups and categories are represented, these associations can do more than "bond" citizens together; they can also "bridge" different groups together.

There is good reason, however, to believe that these associations are, at best, imperfect forums to develop the sort of culture of trust we are seeking here, and that they are more useful as vehicles to empower the underprivileged and the

---

[39] Mark E. Warren, *Democracy and Association* (Princeton: Princeton University Press, 2001), 99.
[40] Warren, *D&A*, 76, 109.
[41] Alexis de Tocqueville, *Democracy in America*, ed. J. P. Mayer (New York: Harper Perennial Modern Classics, 2006), 527.
[42] Robert D. Putnam, *Making Democracy Work: Civic Traditions in Modern Italy* (Princeton: Princeton University Press, 1993), 88–89. In order to support his thesis, Putnam points to the divergent experiences of Northern and Southern Italy. He attributes the effective governance of the North and the corruption and ineffective governance of the South to the reserves of social capital in the former and the lack thereof in the latter.

oppressed – to ensure that those groups are heard and empowered. First, these associations are easy to exit. So, they tend *not* to be forums where citizens regularly encounter a diversity of perspectives. Since it is easier for dissenters to simply leave than to try to persuade their fellow group members to change,[43] these associations tend to be forums where people can *escape* difference and disagreement.

This is not necessarily a bad thing. In diverse working class communities like New York's Jackson Heights, groups that are organized by religion, ethnicity, and language provide minorities and immigrants with a sense of voice. These groups "represent those who do not have citizenship or language skills and might otherwise be voiceless: they fight unlawful deportations, report fraudulent landlords, and negotiate parades and public gatherings with the police. They also sponsor classes in the languages of the city, and these include computer skills, financial literacy, and rights education."[44] Still, these associations are forums where people can avoid interacting with people who challenge their identities or political convictions – not forums where they can practice (and revise) good manners, let alone engage in transparent discussions about the nature of injustice, across political and social cleavages. Indicatively, several studies suggest that voluntary associations tend to be characterized by internal homogeneity – racial or ethnic homogeneity, religious homogeneity, and even gendered homogeneity – and minority members tend to incur higher costs of membership than the majority.[45]

Second, since they are held together by normative influence, persuasion, customs, and norms, voluntary associations that are characterized by internal difference can find withstanding internal conflicts especially difficult. Mark Warren explains: "[T]hey will be fragile with respect to conflict resolution. Every utterance in purely social situations tends to communicate cognitive content as well as numerous signals and reassurances that reproduce the social relation. For this reason, disagreements on the cognitive level are more likely to

---

[43] Warren, *D&A*, 98–99.   [44] Ignatieff, *The Ordinary Virtues*, 37.

[45] Brad Christerson and Michael Emerson, "The Costs of Diversity in Religious Organizations: An In-Depth Case Study," *Sociology of Religion* 64(2) (2003): 163–181; Kevin D. Dougherty, "How Monochromatic Is Church Membership? Racial-Ethnic Diversity in Religious Community," *Sociology of Religion* 64(1) (2003): 65–85; Jason Kaufmann, *For the Common Good? American Civic Life in the Golden Age of Fraternity* (Oxford: Oxford University Press, 2002); Miller McPhearson and Lynn Smith-Lovin, "Women and Weak Ties: Differences by Sex in the Size of Voluntary Organizations," *Journal of Sociology* 87(4) (1982): 883–904; Miller McPhearson and Lynn Smith-Lovin, "Sex Segregation in Voluntary Associations," *American Sociological Review* 51(1) (1986): 61–79; Miller McPhearson, Lynn Smith-Lovin, and James M. Cook, "Birds of a Feather: Homophily in Social Networks," *Annual Review of Sociology* 27 (2001): 415–444; Thomas Rotolo, "A Time to Join, a Time to Quit: The Influence of Life Cycle Transitions on Voluntary Association Membership," *Social Forces* 78(3) (2000): 1133–1161; Michael A. Stoll, "Race, Neighborhood Poverty, and Participation in Voluntary Associations," *Sociological Forum* 16(3) (2001): 529–557.

spill over into the reproduction of social relations."[46] The more heterogeneous a given voluntary association is, the less likely that association can realistically serve as a forum where citizens explore their differences and disagreements seriously without disbanding. It is possible for white and Black Americans to be members of the same amateur basketball club, and, certainly, white athletes *ought* to listen to Black athletes. Yet there is a practical danger that such attempts by Black athletes to express their concerns will prompt some white athletes to shut down the conversation entirely, either out of hostility or (ironically) to preserve their self-image as egalitarian.[47]

Unsurprisingly, the most voluntary and norm-dependent sorts of associations – internet associations (if they can even be called associations) – tend to be either extremely homogeneous or fragile. They can provide opportunities for motivated individuals to "reach out" to those who are literally (i.e., geographically) and/or figuratively far away. However, internet associations are also easy to exit and – more importantly – do not allow participants to interact in person. Indeed, participants often don false identities or stay anonymous. As a result, particularly when it comes to politics, race relations, and the like, internet "discussions" often devolve into either "echo chambers" or shouting matches.[48]

Now, as with groups organized by minority religions, ethnicities, and languages, this can actually result in some good. As the worldwide protests against systemic racism and police brutality in the aftermath of George Floyd's murder illustrate, the internet can amplify the voices of the oppressed, shine a light on injustice, and compel the privileged and the dominant to stop ignoring those injustices: the internet can help the underprivileged, the oppressed, and their allies to shout back. However, in terms of facilitating the production of trust, the internet is less useful. When it comes to discussion, internet associations are more plausible as forums where people can discuss their hobbies or get advice on how to perform certain tasks (although even here, some participants find basic civility optional).

Economic Associations

Where, then, can citizens who have differences and disagreements engage in the desired interactions? Beyond the practice of good manners in shared public

---

[46] Warren, *D&A*, 112.

[47] Studies indicate that some white liberals who care about racial injustice avoid having conversations with Black people in order to pre-emptively avoid saying or doing anything that might be taken as racist. See John F. Dovidio, Samuel L. Gaertner, and Adam R. Pearson, "Aversive Racism and Contemporary Bias" in *The Cambridge Handbook of the Psychology of Prejudice*, ed. Chris G. Sibley and Fiona Kate Barlow (Cambridge: Cambridge University Press, 2016), 267–294.

[48] It does not help that internet companies profit from directing their users to resources that either glorify conflict or reinforce their pre-existing biases.

spaces, I submit that economic associations are more suitable vehicles for the practice of good manners and the production of trust. Given that these associations are both less voluntary and held together by the pursuit of common economic goals, not only is it harder for members of a given economic association to escape encounters of difference and disagreement by leaving; economic associations can also motivate members to work through some of their differences and disagreements while setting aside those differences and disagreements that do not pertain to their common economic objectives. Through these interactions, citizens can demonstrate to themselves that they are capable of cooperation and treating one another with respect.

Warren's juxtaposition of universities (a sort of social association, albeit less voluntary than those typically found in civil society) and corporations illustrates this point neatly. Universities frequently champion inclusion, yet they tend to find it difficult to deal with issues pertaining to race, ethnicity, and gender. First, given that universities champion discussion and persuasion, initiatives to confront race and gender issues can seem to threaten academic freedom. Second, these initiatives can come across as personal accusations of racism or sexism against faculty members. So, dissenting faculty members can be motivated to not speak out on these issues. In contrast, the resolution of such issues for corporations is instrumental, so people are more likely to find ways to overcome those controversies, rather than fixate on them. Moreover, whereas corporate employees and shareholders are united by a concrete common goal – profit – faculty members are united by something far vaguer: the pursuit of knowledge. Accordingly,

[i]n most cases, the mission of the firm (the production of commodities or services) is related only indirectly to the reproduction of identities of employees. Conflict over matters of race and gender can also be narrowly defined, limited to issues of competence, equity, and other matters directly related to the institution's market-determined mission. In this context, a dialogue about race – essential to reproducing associative relations within the firm – may be easier for members because it is limited in its ramifications ... the stakes lowered, and the significance not extended beyond the matters at hand.[49]

Economic associations can therefore help citizens become more comfortable with encounters of difference and disagreement; the successful negotiation of difference and disagreement *within* economic associations can help citizens feel more comfortable with encounters of difference and disagreement in broader society, which in turn can reduce the degree to which those differences and disagreements will serve as the bases of deep political cleavages.[50] This also suggests that even though economic associations tend to be more internally

---

[49] Warren, *D&A*, 113.
[50] This can facilitate economic cooperation. As I have noted, empirical research suggests that successful market cooperation is not the catalyst, but rather the result of a pre-existing, extra-economic culture of trust whose absence leads to "my-success-is-your-failure" competition.

diverse than neighbourhoods,[51] efforts should be made to make economic associations internally even more diverse. That way, their members can interact with subsets of the total citizenry that can more plausibly be described as representative of the whole. In particular, efforts should be made to redress the internal segregation that exists in workplaces – the fact that the privileged and the dominant tend to occupy higher status positions, and the underprivileged and oppressed, lower status ones.[52] The state can impose various quotas, and corporations can enact diversity programs (although, as I noted in Chapter 7, much depends on how those programs are structured). Ideally, corporations can also be reformed along "co-determinist" principles whereby corporate boards include representatives of a plurality of stakeholders – not just capital, but also labour and the broader community. However, in the absence of rough parity between the power of business and labour or the imminent threat of extreme class conflict, co-determinist reforms are less likely.[53]

Economic associations, however, cannot be the whole story. First, even though economic associations are *less* voluntary than civil societal associations, it is still possible to exit economic associations. Indeed, economic associations are more voluntary for those who have more resources than for others; the privileged can still find ways to escape encounters of difference and disagreement, if they are sufficiently motivated. Second, even though the practice of good manners can convey initial respect and help cultivate basic trust, workplaces (at least today) are typically hierarchical. So, there is more pressure for some people (e.g., employees) to practice good manners than others (e.g., managers, owners) – indeed, for minorities to practice good manners than whites, and for women to practice good manners than men.[54]

Third, economic associations encourage their members to sidestep those aspects of their differences and disagreements that do not present obstacles to the pursuit of their common objectives. That is, although economic associations are suitable as forums where citizens can practice good manners and work

---

[51] Again, note that the segregation of neighbourhoods is often partly the result of intentional racist policies. I shall address the need for pro-integration residential neighbourhood codes later in this chapter.

[52] Matthew Hall, John Iceland, and Youngmin Yi, "Racial Separation at Home and Work: Segregation in Residential and Workplace Settings," *Population Research and Policy Review* 38(4) (2019): 671–694.

[53] While co-determination has a long history, particularly in Northern and Central Europe, of facilitating cooperation between labour and employers, such arrangements often depend on *initial* and *continued* parity between labour and employers. Even in social democratic Sweden, in the absence of underlying trust between business and labour, as industrial jobs and the power of labour have declined, employers have begun to undermine both national- and industrial-level bargaining arrangements (Lucio Baccaro and Chris Howell, *Trajectories of Neoliberal Transformation: European Industrial Relations since the 1970s* (Cambridge: Cambridge University Press, 2017)).

[54] Needless to say, such workplace hierarchies often manifest themselves in deeply unjust and criminal manners – discrimination, verbal abuse, and sexual assault.

through *some* aspects of their differences and disagreements, these associations motivate their members to leave unaddressed other aspects of their differences and disagreements – dimensions that might contribute to the persistence of undue social hierarchies. In the absence of either the external disruptions caused by shouting back or other forums where citizens can engage in transparent discourse, the trust that emerges in economic associations can end up concealing important aspects of citizens' differences and disagreements and consolidating undue social hierarchies.

Minipublics, Diversity Workshops, and Less Voluntary Associations

Where can these transparent, frank conversations take place? In Chapter 8, I discussed how minipublics and workplace diversity workshops can serve as such forums on a limited basis. I refer the reader back to the subsection "Transparent Discourse?"

In addition, these conversations can potentially take place in less voluntary associations like public schools, neighbourhoods, and universities (to a lesser degree). It is hard, albeit not impossible, to exit these associations. So, members are more compelled to work through their differences and disagreements, rather than simply escape once they encounter difference and disagreement. At the same time, even though these social associations lack some resources, available to economic associations, to withstand internal conflict, they do operate in less explicitly adversarial terrain. As a result, they are more suitable forums for the sorts of transparent conversations required to explore citizens' differences and disagreements and to identify and rectify injustices.

For instance, even though universities themselves do sometimes find it difficult to negotiate internal race and gender controversies (particularly with the rise of dogmatic activism), they can encourage students to consider a variety of perspectives at a more theoretical level in classes. Universities can also sponsor public events that explore these issues; these events can be broadcasted online for wider viewing. While these events do not qualify as instances where people actually work through their differences and disagreements, they are forums, somewhat insulated from the pressures of politics, where people can be introduced to more facets of their differences and disagreements.

Meanwhile, members of neighbourhood associations or parent-teacher associations must address their differences and disagreements in order to arrive at collective solutions to salient problems – for instance, to improve neighbourhood safety, to cultivate positive learning environments, and to determine what values they wish to pass onto their children. This is not unlike how members of economic associations must negotiate their differences and disagreements to pursue common objectives. However, the collective action problems of these less voluntary associations involve more directly questions of identity and socialization. Solving these problems does not require members to agree

completely on these issues, but it does require them to reach a working understanding of how they agree or are similar, and how they disagree or are
different. This, in turn, requires them to go beyond the practice of good
manners: it requires them to address their racial, ethnic, cultural, religious,
economic, and/or even political differences. If this does not occur, then citizens
can only realize a tenuous peace where misunderstandings, grievances, and
animosities bubble underneath the surface.

The trouble with all of this is that the open interaction of these differences
and disagreements can be fraught with tension – akin to *clashes* of civilizations
in microform. However, just like how minipublics can insulate deliberators
from adversarial dynamics and considerations, these less voluntary associations
can employ strategies to diffuse these tensions. Specifically, these associations
can employ the sorts of diversity workshops that have taken place in some
workplaces. Again, see Chapter 8.

The prospect that less voluntary associations will, individually, provide their
members with opportunities to engage in these conversations with reasonably
representative subsets of the citizenry is improbable. However, operating *alongside* the aforementioned economic associations and minipublics, these less-
voluntary social associations can potentially allow citizens to engage in the
desired interactions and observe reasonably representative subsets of their
fellow citizens doing the same.

The Paradox of Liberal Democratic Freedom

Why, then, do I continue to insist that the cultivation of trust among citizens at
large must primarily consist of a balancing act between the practice of good
manners and the disruptions of shouting back? If less-voluntary associations
are widespread, then why can those transparent conversations only serve as
special interventions?

The answer lies in the fact that the liberal democratic commitment to
freedom prohibits the state from enacting aggressive measures to ensure that
these less voluntary associations are indeed somewhat representative of the
total citizenry. Many of these associations are not representative. In particular,
neighbourhoods tend to be more racially and ethnically segregated than workplaces. Certainly, neighbourhoods are, in part, segregated due to intentional
government policies and codes. So, motivated political actors can discourage
such segregation through pro-integration housing laws and regulations. Most
famously, in the aftermath of Martin Luther King Jr.'s assassination, Lyndon
Johnson signed the 1968 Fair Housing Act, prohibiting discrimination concern-
ing the sale, rental, and financing of housing on the basis of race, religion, and
national origin; and the 1974 Housing and Community Development Act made
it illegal to discriminate in housing matters on the basis of sex. Similarly, in
2015, the Obama Administration enacted a requirement that cities and

localities account for how they will use federal housing funds to reduce racial disparities, or face penalties should they fail to do so.[55]

Still, people can self-segregate if they have the motivation and the means to do so. As a result, neighbourhood associations are not ideal forums for citizens to explore those aspects of their differences and disagreements that they either cannot or are not inclined to explore in economic associations. Now, citizens who live "side by side" but not "together"[56] can still come to share in basic trust by practicing good manners in economic associations, as well as in shared informal public spaces more broadly. However, there is a danger that their differences and disagreements will remain suppressed and that the victims of injustice will accordingly view liberal democratic equality to be a hollow promise.

One solution to this problem is social engineering. For example, in order to promote a sense of ethnic equity, the Singaporean government mandates that all public housing blocks (where over 80 percent of Singaporeans live) reflect Singapore's ethnic composition. However, perhaps with the exception of universities or the workplace (where quotas can be imposed), such a remedy, which effectively amounts to forcing people to live where the government dictates, is strictly off limits. Although the liberal democratic state may require cities and localities to account for how they will use federal housing funds to reduce neighbourhood segregation, may revise zoning laws to permit more high-density housing in single family areas, and may prosecute racist landlords and lenders, it cannot stop those who have the resources to leave their neighbourhoods – to *flee* – from doing so. Such is the cost of freedom.

WE ARE ALL IN IT TOGETHER: CONSTRAINING MATERIAL INEQUALITY

Still, there are ways for the liberal democratic state to ensure that citizens' varying economic circumstances, at least, do not undermine the sense that they belong to the same polity. Material inequality is a problem for fellowship insofar as it prevents citizens of different economic standings from feeling like they are members of the same polity.[57] Consider the global "top 1 percent." The gains made by the global top 1 percent over the past half-century have far

---

[55] Julie Hirschfeld Davis and Binyamin Appelbaum, "Obama Unveils Stricter Rules against Segregation in Housing," *New York Times*, July 8, 2015, www.nytimes.com/2015/07/09/us/hud-issuing-new-rules-to-fight-segregation.html.

[56] Ignatieff, *The Ordinary Virtues*, 45.

[57] Note that on this score, the demands of distributive justice are distinct from the demands of role-based constitutional fellowship. Even if a certain level of inequality is permissible under the principles of distributive justice, that level of inequality can hinder role-based constitutional fellowship. Similarly, even if a certain level of inequality is impermissible under the principles of distributive justice, that level of inequality might not undermine role-based constitutional fellowship.

outpaced the gains made by everyone else. Global top 1 percenters largely interact exclusively among themselves, jet-setting to meet one another in a handful of global cities.

Such inequality undermines fellowship in at least two ways. First, such inequality makes it more difficult for global top 1 percenters to even interact with others, let alone grapple with difference and disagreement. Indeed, it is as if global top 1 percenters have set up their own parallel society. Second, such self-segregation can foster an ethos that contradicts the spirit of role-based constitutional fellowship. For example, today's global top 1 percent consists largely of new wealth. As Chrystia Freeland writes, global top 1 percenters tend to be "hardworking, highly educated, jet-setting meritocrats who feel they are the deserving winners of a tough, worldwide economic competition . . . and, as a result, have an ambivalent attitude towards those of us who haven't suc-ceeded quite so spectacularly."[58] Once upon a time, such a meritocratic ethos helped undermine entrenched, hereditary hierarchies; today, it makes it less likely that one will entertain objections that one's wealth might still be the product of injustice – and more likely that one will deny the obligations that one has to others. At most, one will develop a taste for philanthropy, through which one addresses social problems while consolidating one's own power.[59]

Although the problems that have resulted from the rise of the global top 1 percent illustrate this general principle most clearly, this principle does not only apply to the global top 1 percent. The professional class – roughly, those who find themselves in the top 20 percent of the income distribution in advanced liberal democracies – is also problematic on this front. Since the late 1970s, this class is the only other class that has enjoyed meaningful gains in income. Now, the fact that the professional class has enjoyed these gains is not necessarily a problem in and of itself; the professional class has not effectively set up its own parallel society. However, some of its actions have contributed to the emergence of a "glass floor" that prevents professional class children from falling downwards and (more importantly) other children from rising up. This glass floor is problematic because it limits the amount professionals interact with others, as well as the likelihood that professionals will consider claims of injustice seriously. After all, professionals too have meritocratic tendencies.

Certainly, professionals should not be condemned outright or reflexively. For one thing, as I alluded to in Chapter 7, professionals often qualify as "allies" in the effort to rectify undue racial-ethnic hierarchies. For another, there are choices that professionals make that are perfectly defensible, even if they do contribute to the emergence of the glass floor. For instance, professional class children disproportionally benefit from growing up in stable homes, being

---

[58] Chrystia Freeland, *Plutocrats: The Rise of the New Global Super-Rich and the Fall of Everyone Else* (New York: Penguin Books, 2012), 5.
[59] Rob Reich, *Just Giving: Why Philanthropy Is Failing Democracy and How It Can Do Better* (Princeton: Princeton University Press, 2018).

raised by married parents, living in safe neighbourhoods, and attending good schools.[60] It is unreasonable to criticize their parents for securing healthy environments for their children. It is more sensible to rectify the negative consequences of such trends by supporting non-professional class families, rather than by wrecking professional class families. In these instances, the needs of constitutional fellowship do not override the imperatives of the family.

Certain actions, however, ought to be condemned – specifically, those through which members of the professional class "rig" the market in their favour. Richard Reeves highlights three "opportunity hoarding mechanisms" in particular: exclusionary residential zoning laws, unfair university admission processes (including legacy admissions), and informally allocated (and often unpaid) internships.[61] The exploitation of these mechanisms is problematic because it exemplifies an unwillingness[62] to interact with other social classes, let alone do one's part to lessen the extent to which other citizens sacrifice disproportionately for the sake of the already privileged. Indeed, although professionals do not have the resources to set up their own parallel society, they often live in either gated communities or neighbourhoods – even whole cities – that are so expensive that their working class and poorer counterparts are priced out. From the standpoint of role-based constitutional fellowship, the inequality between the top 1 percent and the bottom 99 percent is not the only threat; so too is the inequality between the top 20 percent and the bottom 80 percent. These forms of inequality make it harder for citizens to feel that they are all in it together.

---

[60] Richard V. Reeves, *Dream Hoarders: How the American Upper Middle Class Is Leaving Everyone Else in the Dust, Why that Is a Problem, and What to Do about It* (Washington, DC: Brookings Institution Press, 2017), 9.

[61] Reeves, *Dream Hoarders*, 12.

[62] Perhaps it is more charitable to say that the exploitation of these mechanisms reflects an insufficient willingness to do one's part to ensure an equitable distribution of sacrifice. After all, some professionals welcome higher tax rates; this reflects some commitment to equity. The exploitation of opportunity hoarding mechanisms, in these cases, therefore represents an unwillingness to *go far enough* to fulfill that commitment.

Conclusion

The Question of Borders and the Problem of Enemies

Over the course of this book, I have advanced a vision of liberal democratic citizenship that I call "role-based constitutional fellowship." Role-based constitutional fellowship, I have argued, is a vital part of the infrastructure of liberal democracy.

Certainly, this vision is not the best of all conceivable worlds. Just because fellowship has been realized does not mean that perfect justice has been achieved (whatever that might look like), and fellowship itself assumes the form of a series of fragile balancing acts – between competition and compromise, between principle and purity, between contestation and reconciliation, between talking and shouting back, and between disrupting the lives of unwitting oppressors (and some complicit oppressors) and persuading them to become supporters of efforts to rectify injustice. More than that, even though fellowship does outline a path through which undue social hierarchies can be redressed, that path does place more burdens on the underprivileged and the oppressed than on their allies, let alone other members of privileged and dominant groups. Still, as I have shown, fellowship follows this path out of necessity.

Ultimately, role-based constitutional fellowship offers the most viable vision for liberal democracy to harness the benefits of difference and disagreement and avoid unduly squashing difference and disagreement, yet also sidestep the potential perils of difference and disagreement. The more citizens act like role-based constitutional fellows, the more they can share in a culture of trust whereby they shore up liberal democracy, make it harder for liberal democracy's enemies to grow in influence (or continue doing so), and, crucially, work toward identifying and rectifying undue social hierarchies – gradually, but surely.

To conclude, let me make some remarks on where I think this discussion leads.

FELLOWSHIP AND NON-CITIZENS

One line of inquiry that emerges concerns non-citizens: how should they be treated in a liberal democracy? Throughout this book, I have referred mainly to *citizens*. I did so in part because this is the standard custom in much contemporary democratic theory. However, I also did so because I took as the starting point of my theorizing the world as it is currently: a world of nation states, where people are largely citizens of one state (or perhaps two states) and non-citizens of most other states.

Accordingly, some of the arguments I advanced imply that citizens and non-citizens *do* ought to be treated differently under liberal democracy. For example, I argued that even though liberal democrats must seek to encourage inclusive understandings of the national community, they must be cautious about how to go about promoting actual diversity on the ground. (On this basis, I endorsed a moderate points-based immigration system that privileges "economically capable" immigrants, even if it does not promote homogeneity.) I also noted that it is important for liberal democrats to not seem like they are more interested in helping "outsiders" or "foreigners" than their fellow citizens – "insiders." On this basis, in a footnote, I deemed the Canadian government wise during the 2015 Syrian Refugee Crisis to pursue a somewhat stingy "one-to-one, family-to-family" sponsorship program, rather than a more generous state-sponsorship approach, even though Canada likely ran afoul of principles of global justice as a result.

The specific arguments for this differential treatment of citizens and non-citizens advanced here are primarily strategic. However, the broader question does arise as to how non-citizens – in particular, long-term residents – ought to be considered under liberal democracy. Should non-citizens share in a sort of fellowship with citizens – perhaps not role-based constitutional fellowship exactly, but something that does not condemn them to permanent guest status?[1] After all, as part of my critique of "mere" liberal nationalism, I argued that it is unacceptable to settle for understandings of the national community and of citizens' collective identity that treat racial-ethnic minorities with an ethic of hospitality. Should the same apply for long-term residents?

There are pressing practical issues that make it important to consider these questions. First, due to the principle of free movement, Europeans have the right to reside in European countries in which they were not born.[2] Second, the

---

[1] For some contrasting perspectives on similar questions, see David Miller, *Strangers in Our Midst: The Political Philosophy of Immigration* (Cambridge, MA: Harvard University Press, 2016) and Joseph Carens, *The Ethics of Immigration* (Oxford: Oxford University Press, 2013).

[2] Approximately 4 percent of the EU's birth population resides in a European country other than their birth country. See "Origins and Destinations of European Union Migrants within the EU," Pew Research Center, June 19, 2017, www.pewresearch.org/global/interactives/origins-destinations-of-european-union-migrants-within-the-eu/.

United States is home to a significant number of undocumented immigrants from Mexico and Central America.[3] Third, and perhaps most urgently, with the acceleration of the climate crisis, mass migration is on the horizon[4] – and likely to dwarf the highly disruptive mass migration that took place during the Syrian Refugee Crisis (and that fuelled support for the far right in many established liberal democracies). So, the question of how to treat non-citizens is not just important on its own right; it is also important for its implications on liberal democracy, bounded solidarity, the possibility of social inclusion, and role-based constitutional fellowship.

THE PROBLEM OF ENEMIES

Another line of inquiry concerns liberal democracy's enemies. Evidently, the threat of those who wish to destroy liberal democracy – not just of outright autocrats but also of so-called competitive authoritarians or "illiberal" democrats, including the contemporary far right – underlies my discussion of role-based constitutional fellowship. As I noted in Chapter 1, it is important for citizens who are committed to liberal democracy (or, less strongly stated, who can be considered members of the mainstream of society) to share in something like fellowship precisely because the absence of fellowship leaves liberal democracy more vulnerable to the growing influence of liberal democracy's enemies. When the differences and disagreements between liberal democrats and members of the mainstream "overheat," it becomes easier for liberal democracy's enemies to turn those liberal democrats and members of the mainstream against each other even more – and harder for liberal democrats and members of the mainstream to unite for the purpose of fending off those threats.

Yet how should liberal democrats consider and respond to liberal democracy's enemies more precisely? Clearly, confrontation is necessary at least some of the time. Further questions, however, follow. Should the proponents of liberal democracy, at some point, try to convert liberal democracy's enemies into fellow liberal democrats who can be treated as mere adversaries, or should the proponents of liberal democracy instead declare war – and foreclose the possibility of reconciliation permanently? Given the importance of bounded solidarity, does it matter whether liberal democracy's enemies also try to advance autocratic brands of bounded solidarity – brands of solidarity that,

---

[3] Approximately 25 percent of all immigrants in the United States are undocumented. See Abby Budiman, "Key Findings about U.S. Immigrants," Pew Research Center, August 20, 2020, www .pewresearch.org/fact-tank/2020/08/20/key-findings-about-u-s-immigrants/.

[4] See Abrahm Lustgarten, "The Great Climate Migration," *The New York Times Magazine*, July 23, 2020, www.nytimes.com/interactive/2020/07/23/magazine/climate-migration.html.

perhaps surprisingly, have some appeal to racial, ethnic, and cultural minorities?[5] Are all of liberal democracy's enemies made equal? Does the nature of the liberal democratic response to these threats change according to how many enemies are present, as well as according to how these enemies precisely threaten liberal democracy?[6] Moreover, even if responding to these enemies demands that liberal democrats do harm, must liberal democrats assume a sense of tragedy and responsibility to atone for these harms, or should liberal democrats not bother worrying about maintaining such a "tragic ethos" in the face of such existential threats?[7]

Answering these questions will demand another book. What is clear, however, is that regardless of what the answers to these questions are, in the effort to discern how the defenders of liberal democracy ought to respond to the enemies of liberal democracy, it is not enough to simply investigate how to safeguard liberal democracy's integrity as a legitimate regime type;[8] it is necessary to consider how liberal democracy can confront its enemies in manners that also safeguard the possibility of role-based constitutional fellowship. After all, fellowship is a vital part of the infrastructure of liberal democracy. If the effort to fend off liberal democracy's enemies undermines fellowship, then it becomes more difficult for fellowship to adequately sidestep the potential perils of difference and disagreement, in which case the legitimacy of liberal democracy too becomes endangered. We must care about how the effort to confront the problem of enemies affects role-based constitutional fellowship and the effort to sidestep the potential perils of difference and disagreement, and shape our approach to the problem of enemies accordingly. If we fail to do so, then in our effort to defend liberal democracy, we might put fellowship in jeopardy – and if fellowship is in jeopardy, then so too is the legitimacy and viability of liberal democracy.

---

[5] In the 2020 US Presidential Election, despite his racism, Trump increased his share of the minority vote, almost matching George W. Bush's showing among minorities in 2004. See Simone Esters, "Blunt's Wrong: Trump Did Not Get the Highest Minority Vote Percentage in 100 Years," Politifact, December 8, 2020, www.politifact.com/factchecks/2020/dec/08/roy-blunt/blunts-wrong-trump-did-not-get-highest-minority-vo/.

[6] Matt Sleat, *Liberal Realism: A Realist Theory of Liberal Politics* (Manchester: Manchester University Press, 2013) addresses some of these themes. According to many liberal democrats, albeit not all, populists figure prominently among these enemies of liberal democracy.

[7] Steven Johnston, *American Dionysia: Violence, Tragedy, and Democratic Politics* (Cambridge: Cambridge University Press, 2015).

[8] In response to the problem of political extremism and the problem of terrorism, respectively, both Alexander S. Kirshner, *A Theory of Militant Democracy: The Ethics of Combatting Political Extremism* (New Haven: Yale University Press, 2014) and Michael Ignatieff, *The Lesser Evil: Political Ethics in an Age of Terror* (New York: Penguin Books, 2006) are primarily concerned with how to preserve liberal democratic legitimacy.

Index

backlash against salutary hypocrisy, 145. *See also* shouting back
backsliding, liberal democratic, 8
Baker, James, 110
Baker, Peter, 110
Banting, Keith, 64, 70
Bejan, Teresa, 137
biases in civil society, 30–31
Biden, Joe, 103, 112–113
Bishop, Bill, 57
Black Lives Matter, 120
Blair, Tony, 144
Boroditsky, Lera, 118
bounded solidarity. *See also* liberal nationalism
    caution in inclusivity, 161–162
    constitutional patriotism as, 65–70
    definition of, 16, 64
    in political competition, 149
    promotion of, 158
    promotion of culture of trust, 157
    racial and economic injustices and, 158
    translucent (political) veils in, 158–161
bridging vs. bonding networks, 57
British Columbia Citizens Assembly (BCCA), 135
Brown, Gordon, 144
Brown, Michael, 120
Bush, George H.W., 109
Bush, George W., 109

campaigns, permanent, 165–167
Canada. *See also* English Canada
    Federal Election (2015) in, 149–150
    immigration in, 73–74, 161–162
    multiculturalism in, 160–161
    national symbols of, 79–80
    nationalism in, 79–82
    Syrian refugee crisis (2015), 180
cancel culture, 127
Capitol (U.S.), storming of, 112, 132–133
Carens, Joseph, 93
Catholic Church in Ireland, 3
centrism, Mouffe on, 43
chain of equivalence, Mouffe on, 40
Cheney, Liz, 113
China, Maoist ideology, 71
Chirac, Jacques, 108
Christian Democratic Union (CDU), 68
Christian Social Union (CSU), 68
Çidam, Çigdem, 41
citizens at large
    as distinct from formal political sphere, 88–89
    hypocrisy of, 154

importance of associations, 168
as moral strangers, 34
representative cynicism problem, 12–13
social domination problem, 12
as teams of partisans in U.S., 143
treating with equal standing, 97
trust among, 86–87, 90–92, 115, 150
trust between formal political sphere and, 87–88, 92–93, 141–142
trust in electoral systems, 162–164
civic aggression, 4–8
civic disruption, 123–124
civic education
    of children, 167–168
    national identity and, 71–72
    under liberal nationalism, 82
civic friendship. *See* political friendship
civic-national identity
    caution in inclusivity, 161–162
    Declaration of Independence in, 159–160
    difference and disagreement in, 82–83
    in English Canada, 160–161
civil disobedience, 31–33
Civil Rights Act (1964), 125
Civil Rights Movement
    allies in, 118
    civic disruption in, 120–121, 123
    racial inequalities despite, 5, 38
    success via resistance, 4
civil society
    biases in, 30–31
    Habermas on, 27–34
    inclusivity in, 30–31
    reasonableness in, 31
    voluntary associations in, 169–171
civilian service, 167
civility, 136–140. *See also* good manners (civility)
classroom councils, 167–168
climate crisis, mass migration and, 181
Clinton, Bill, 5, 144
Clinton, Hillary, 5, 143–144, 147–149
Coates, Ta-Nehisi, 125
collective assemblage, 37
Collins, Timothy, 143
common advantage, Aristotle on, 52–54
common currency of discussion, 25–26
commonality, 42, 44–45
communicative action, 28–29
competitive authoritarianism, 111
complicit oppressors, 121. *See also* harder complicit oppressors; softer complicit oppressors

CPSIA information can be obtained
at www.ICGtesting.com
Printed in the USA
LVHW080847130922
728238LV00006B/379